THE WORLD'S BEST

SAILBOATS

A SURVEY

To

Dad

keep Dreaming

Love Pete

Christmas 1989

THE WORLD'S BEST
SAILBOATS

A SURVEY

FERENC MATÉ

ALBATROSS PUBLISHING HOUSE

OTHER BOOKS BY FERENC MATÉ
From a Bare Hull
The Finely Fitted Yacht
Waterhouses
Behind the Waterfall—a novel
Best Boats
Shipshape
The Seven Seas Calendars

Published by Albatross Publishing House
Printings: 1986, 1987, 1987, 1988
ISBN 0-920256-11-2

Design originator and consultant: B. Martin Pedersen
Design: Candace Maté and Ferenc Maté
Production: Gloria Klatt, Keith Ragone, Walter Sipser
Typesetting: Haddon Craftsmen
            Trufont Typographers, Inc.
Printed in Japan by Dai Nippon Printing Co.

DISTRIBUTED IN THE UNITED STATES
BY W. W. NORTON, 500 FIFTH AVE., NEW YORK

CONTENTS

INTRODUCTION

This was a good book to research. Scrutinizing boat shows from Long Beach to Paris cannot be considered a hardship, and touring boat factories from California to Finland, from Maine to Milan, can't be called having a *bad* time.

You will naturally ask how the boats were chosen, and I'll tell you that no sales figures, race results, or opinion surveys were consulted, although some of the world's fastest production boats are included here—I simply picked the most beautiful and best-built boats I could find. The homely ones I cast off right away, even if they were built like fine Swiss watches. If you wonder what constitutes my concept of beauty, just flip the pages and you will quickly see. I then did a close inspection of the boats and left many by the wayside because of poor engineering, poor construction, or both.

I tried to limit the book to twenty builders in order to avoid repetition. (One builder went into receivership near the book's completion so we ended up with nineteen.) I left out a couple of Swan clones, even though they were pretty and well-built, to make room for more varied and more original designs. Had I expanded the list, I would have included boats like the Dutch Trintellas, the U.S. built Sabers, and the Italian Grand Soleils, but I had to draw the line somewhere.

Other important criteria were integrity and reputation. The youngest boatyard in this book is seven years old (not counting David Walters who owned Shannon Yachts before he started building his Cambrias) because I wanted proven consistency.

I also wanted range. I wanted the best of the more affordable production boats like Bénéteaus and Pacific Seacrafts to be included among the well-known luxury semi-custom Swans and Hinckleys, because a good walking shoe is at least as valuable as a silver slipper.

So I think we have a good mix. I'm sure there are many who will resent my excluding their favorites, but to them I say that these are just *my* choices, not an addendum to the Ten Commandments.

And a final, most important note. This book is not intended to be a shopping list. I wrote it to point out examples of good design and construction, so that when you look at *any* boat, you'll have some facts and ideas to guide you.

Ferenc Maté

ABLE
MARINE

C rozer Fox's boatyard sits among the trees of Southwest Harbor, Maine—a simple yard with a big new shed for building, a little one for casting lead, a clearing that holds boats needing a little care, and a pile of split rock maple to fire the stoves through the long, cold winters. And from this yard of no pretensions come some of the best-built and best-finished sailboats in the world.

Cro is as affable a boatbuilder as you'll find anywhere. He seems like someone who can't help but have a good time, who would never let bad craftsmanship pop up and ruin his day. He is forty-four years old, with the voice and energy of a much younger man as he bounds through his shops or cluttered attic office that overlooks the bay. He began building boats at a late age as those things go, started working twelve years back with Jarvis Newman across the bay and learned all about fiberglass there. He started his own boatyard here eight years ago with a little pocket cruiser whose molds he bought, which was named the Able 20 by someone before him, and even though the little cruiser is now history, the name Able somehow stuck with Cro and it fits him and his crew of twenty builders like a glove.

In a short time their reputation became such that the International One Design committee chose them as exclusive builders for all of North America, but I chose them for the *Whistlers* they build from Chuck Paine's designs. Chuck Paine has become known for boats with modern underwater lines but, with good looks above as individual as you could ask for. His lines are so clean and pure that you have to look twice to make sure nothing's missing. There are no curlicue trim pieces or early baroque taffrails; just very handsome fine lines with a personality all their own. No one will ever mistake a Chuck Paine boat for any other. It's almost as if he has somehow combined the clean lean looks of Swans with a traditional elegance, and that's some combination.

His boats are moderate in every way. There are no distorted bulges or stretched lines anywhere; the basic guideline appears to be proportionate beauty; somehow all the rest seems to fall into place. He indulges himself only slightly in graceful overhangs while keeping the hulls fine of entry and moderately full of power aft. The underbodies are fast, with rounded wide bottomed sections, fullness aft for power, and very fine thin keels, or Scheel keels or centerboards.

The displacement-to-length ratios are close to three hundred, just right for decent cruisers that will ride comfortably and carry a goodly load. The sail-area-to-displacement ratios are around 16.5 which will give you very decent light air performance without making you dive for the reeflines if a breeze pops up.

The lines of his deck houses are pretty indeed and he doesn't push or distort them in any way just to gain a few inches of volume down below. His side decks are always spacious and his cockpits truly comfortable, for he is one of the few designers who realize that much time on a sailboat is spent working and relaxing in the cockpit.

Cro builds the Whistler 32 and the new Whistler 48 in a way that complements Chuck's designs in quality and care. The interior of both are completely flexible, and in the case of the *48* so is the deck. Chuck has worked up deck plans for pilot house, traditional long house and center cockpit versions and Cro will be happy to build whichever you want. The first *48* was built as a low profile pilot house and I must say she was one of the most beautiful boats last fall at the Annapolis Boat Show. It's common knowledge that pilot houses are tricky things to make pretty, but with Chuck's clean lines and Cro's perfect trimming the boat came out a true queen.

Cro Fox has built himself a reputation for immaculate construction over the years—simple clean work of excellent quality—and after spending some time in the yard it was easy to see why. I was there late one winter evening making notes and taking pictures, thinking I had the place to myself, when a good two hours after quitting time I heard voices in one end of the shop. I went over to see what it was and found half the crew sitting around the stove, heatedly discussing how to build a perfect bulkhead. Now *that* is what I call service beyond duty. If people like boats that much, they can't help but build good ones.

Cro's dedication and perseverance isn't any less.

"We started building boats eight years ago in my garage down there " he said pointing out the window down toward his house, "That thing was so small that once I got the hull of an Able 20 in it, there wasn't even room to lay down a sheet of plywood, so I put it on top of the boat and cut it there. For my table saw and planer I built little trap doors in the side of the garage and fed the lumber through the holes.

"Then a partner came along and we built the big shop. We built that for the Able 20 and got production into high gear with *four guys.* Actually had four little hulls lined up here once and four little decks, and we went and built these little 20 foot long jewels, true yachts, that unfortunately not too many people could rationalize paying for. It was a funny little boat, kind of homely, but it grew on some people. It had four bunks and a galley with wonderful woodwork everywhere, a real good sailer too.

"We built some commercial fishboats too until we delivered two boats to guys who hadn't paid in full, who launched their boats, took on 800 gallons of fuel and motored right out of the harbor. I haven't seen another nickel from either of them since. That convinced me right then that I was finished building fishboats.

"My first love was always sailboats, so I decided we better have a nice one designed for ourselves. We chose Chuck Paine. He didn't have a big name then but his designs were beautiful and practical and our philosophies of what a good cruising boat should be were pretty close. So we fussed back and forth for nearly a year before we finally got everything so we were all happy, and that was the Whistler 32 cat ketch. I was just in love with that rig. It was easy to handle and a joy to sail. The mast was carbon fiber and so light that one man could lift it up and carry it like a flyrod. Had a 3-foot whip in it at the top. Weighed 120 pounds that's all.

"But the sails are hard to reef and a lot of work to put to bed at night; takes a man a good half hour. I mean hard labor. Because of that many of our Whistlers went out of here rigged as regular cutters. Such is life. But to *sail* that cat rig was a dream. Chuck designed her so well, you just set the sails and walk away; not even put the break on the wheel. That boat is *fast.* Convenient too with the centerboard, she only draws 3½ feet board up. Now the danger here is that people will be snaking into nooks and crannies where they have no business and they'll go aground once in a while and end up spending the night dry on the beach. So we built a boat with enough structural integrity in the keel and bottom that it can easily take that sort of thing resting on her bilge. I don't mean she can withstand lying on rocks in the surf; I mean she can happily lie on her side and wait 'til the tide changes.

"The *48* started, as a lot of boats do nowadays, by someone coming to me and saying that they wanted a certain boat. Actually the man was looking to get a Cherubini 48—boy those are beautiful boats! Anyway, he wanted that hull and asked Chuck to design a pilot-house-type deck, new layout, etcetera and wanted me to finish building the boat for him. But somehow he just couldn't fit everything he wanted in there. So we all agreed the best thing to do was to start from scratch. Once we'd done that, another guy came and saw the plans and said, 'Just what I've been looking for,' and that was that. So now we have a mold for a *48*.

"It takes us about 9,000 hours to finish out a *48* once the hull and deck are finished. We only charge $20 an hour, which is pretty cheap by industry standards, but then we don't have the overhead; you're staring at the whole operation.

"What do we do exceptionally well? To start with, we bond everything. The interior is completely honeycombed. All the furniture, and I mean every piece, every knee is bonded directly to the hull and will therefore stay in the hull just like it's supposed to.

"We do a pretty good job on everything, but then so do most of the good builders. I think our particular claim to fame is detail. People say we do great work on detail. That brings people in. Others come because we can give them exactly what they want. Our owners are fussy people. They seem to end up here after they've gone to most other yards and were simply not accommodated one way or another. Our ultimate aim is to build for the owner the yacht he always wanted, down to the last detail.

"Oddly enough a lot of our *32* owners are people coming down from bigger quality boats, because they are getting older and don't want a crew for sailing or a crew for maintenance. The *32* is a nice classy little yacht for a couple for cruising. Even extended cruising. But by the time they reach this stage they know exactly what they want, no question about it. And they just can't find it in the open, strict production marketplace. We can change decks; we even lengthened the stern of one *32* because the owner wanted more of an overhang. Anyway, they get exactly what they want."

"We are still in business," Crow said adamantly, "because we build basically custom boats except for the shape of the hull. That's why I don't want to build a mold for the deck of the *48*. If I build a mold I'm going to end up trying to sell people something they don't want just because I happen to have it. I'd rather give them what they want—pilot house, no pilot house; it's up to them. And we'll build to either a fixed contract price *or* time and materials, whichever the customer prefers. With our computers and our production manager who came from Tillotson-Pearson bringing some first-class procurement and planning know-how, we have become very efficient with our work and accurate with our

estimates. Another nice thing is that being a medium-sized yard, we have enough expertise to plan and install things like refrigeration systems, electronics and the like, instead of having to rely on outside help."

We walked down into the main shop, stopped under the hull of a *48* and Cro pointed to the big perfectly ground Scheel keel, saying, "We do pretty nice work at every step. We fit the keel as perfectly as possible so there are no voids, no chance for movement, no chance for leaks. First we fair and clean the lead, then pattern and shape it to fit tight to the bottom. Then we lay in two mats and a nice thick smearing of chopped strand, then lower the boat down on the keel and crank the eleven 1-inch silicon bronze bolts tight. As for the Scheel keel itself, the nice advantage it has because of its shoalness is that if you ground hard, you do not have this great deep lever arm trying to tear the bottom out of your boat like you do with a deep fin keel, which on a boat this size would be near 8 feet."

Behind the long Scheel keel, which gives the boat a draft of only 5 feet 10 inches, is a beautifully designed and built skeg with an aperture for the propeller.

"Inside, the skeg is solid." Cro says. "No fillers, no foam, no putty. Just strands and strands of unidirectional roving layed in. It's such a graceful design that we have to build it strong. For the hulls themselves we use biaxial roving with a ¾-inch core in the *48* and no core in the *32.*"

One big advantage you have with Cro is that Chuck Paine lives in nearby Camden and will happily work on revised plans for you. He is a very knowledgeable designer, very much involved in the lofting and building of his boats. He insists on the use of isophthalic resins which are more water resistant, and he also insists that his laminates be squeegeed to remove all excess resin.

For added strength, the hull of the *48* is reinforced with four big keel-area stiffeners. In the *32,* the internal ballast is bonded over with such heavy laminates that a second bottom —indeed a box beam—is created, giving the boat much stiffness.

The hull and deck joint is the standard flange, through-bolted every 6 inches and set in Henry and Frick hull and deck putty. That stuff holds so well that it had to be jackhammered out of a Cambria 44.

The rest of the boat is built with equal care. The chainplates attach to heavy solid fiberglass knees about ¾-inch thick and are backed up, not by washers but by another identical plate. The bonding of the cabinetry into the hull is done with beautiful quality laminations, the last of which is ground nicely so that there are no burrs, needles or rough spots inside your lockers. I'll tell you more about the boats in the captions, but be sure to look closely at the photos because it's hard to notice things like the perfect joints and good finishes that make these yachts excel.

I asked Cro about his future plans and he replied happily with, "We have a Whistler 40 on the boards right now, which we'll start building later in the year, and we're expanding our service yard with our new 25-ton hauler. Apart from that we'll keep building our Whistlers just like we have been."

And that has been very good.

On these pages are photos of Able Marine's Whistlers; the pretty little *32* below, and the graceful *48* above. Both are from the design-board of Chuck Paine, and both show his clean lines, controlled detailing, and—dare I say it—good taste. The unmistakable character of the boats comes from Chuck's good eye for classic lines; *not* from tacked-on nautica, as is too often the case with modern fiberglass boats in search of an identity. The *48* comes with—literally—the deck of your choice. There is no deck mold, so you can have Chuck design the deck you've always dreamed of —imitation *Santa Marias* not included —and Cro Fox will be happy to build it of wood with fiberglass over, or fiberglass with wood over, or fiberglass with fiberglass over; or you can just leave the damned thing off and have

yourself the world's biggest dinghy. The version shown has the pilot house with a fine interior steering station, which makes sailing in cold, wet weather an enjoyable adventure instead of a nightmare. The *32* is shown with the two available rigs: the cutter, and the cat-ketch which sports two unstayed

carbon-fiber masts weighing just over a hundred pounds each. The Cat-Ketch is an absolute dream to sail, but does require a good half-hour to put to bed. Anyway, the choice is yours. Under water, any trace of the classic boat vanishes. As you can see from the lines drawing adjacent, the boats

have modern, canoe-shaped underbodies and powerful sections aft. What the drawing doesn't show is the shoal but windward-efficient patented keel designed by Henry Scheel that has, in the last few years, become the rage with cruisers. You'll see a photo of it three pages further on.

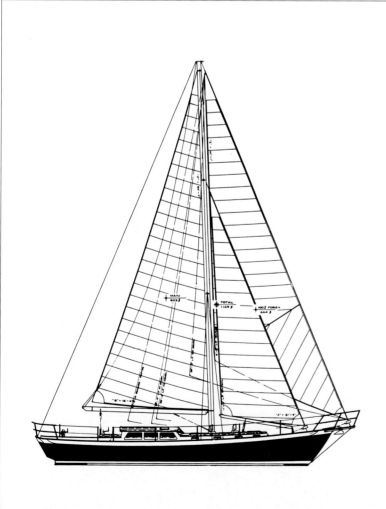

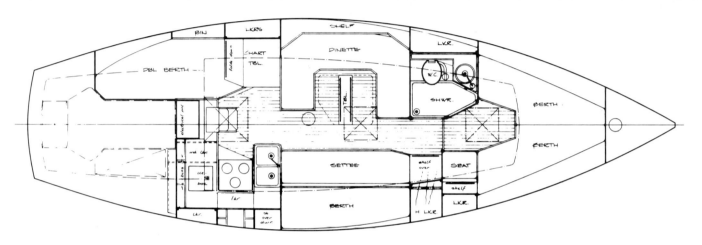

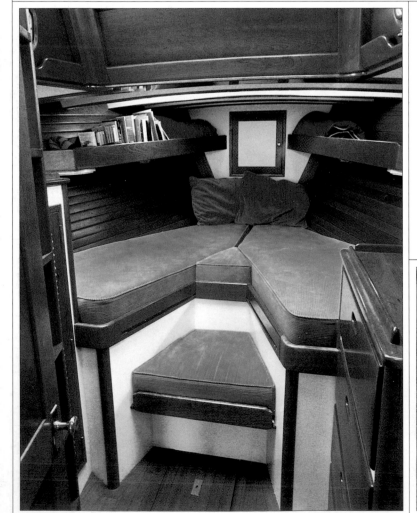

The interiors of the *32,* above, and the *48,* below, both show the elegant trim-work of Cro Fox. The color of the wood looks unusual because it *is* unusual; it's cherry wood—lighter than teak and harder than hell, and glows with beautiful golden color. The cabin sole is unvarnished teak which provides the best non-skid you can ask for. Both interiors have some well-thought-out touches. The *32* 's chart table has first-class drawers for charts; the bookshelves are among the best, for not only are they

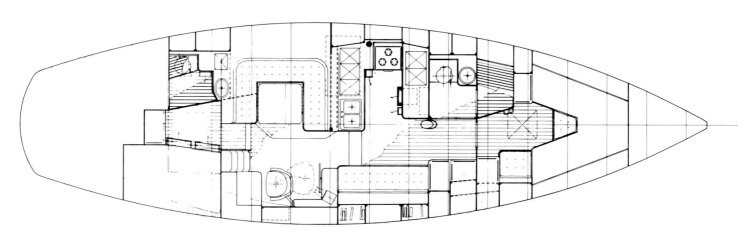

placed athwartships so they won't fly out when the boat heels or rolls, but they're also nicely recessed into the bulkhead. Bravo! The cabin heater is also recessed so the head gets heat as well. The *48* has a most intelligent chair that bends and twists and rises to serve either the helmsman or the navigator, and the dining area is raised to allow you to view the countryside while dining. If you look closely, you can see some of the very fine finish of the wood, but unfortunately you won't see any details of the tables, both of which, with their inlays and dropboards, are near masterpieces.

A boat is but a thousand details hidden in a giant shell, and that sure is true of the Whistlers. Start from the upper left-hand corner of this double page, with the portlight that doesn't hold water, giving you an unexpected shower when you open it. Continue downward where many long hours of work go into the grinding and fairing of the ballast of the Scheel keel. Below that is the beautifully sculpted aperture in the skeg. The skeg itself is faired to perfection, not only on its leading edge,

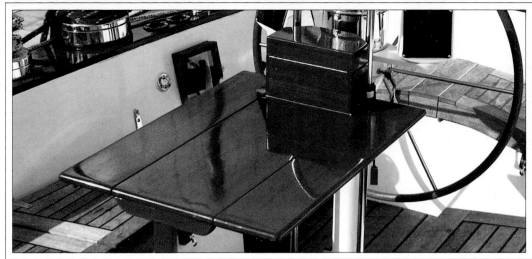

but also around the aperture, to keep turbulence and drag to a minimum. The photo beside it (God and the printer willing) is the rear view of the Scheel keel. Many people have been calling it a "clipped wing-keel" since the *Australia II* show. And what a dream a keel like that is when you want to set the boat

aground for painting or repair in distant harbors. In the photo adjoining, note the subdued trimwork of a Whistler 32. Inside the white molding behind the companionway steps is the tube that leads the centerboard cable to a winch in the cockpit. Not only is this good because it leaves the cabin

unviolated, but it also makes the raising mechanism handy to the helm, preventing grounding of the board due to laziness. This is too often the case when the winch is down below where no one ever bothers to go to raise the board. Oh yes. That's Cro Fox himself smiling up there in the corner.

Cro Fox is a good man to choose as a builder of your boat if it's an elegant, fast yacht you want built to your own needs. If you really know what it is you want built into your next boat—things you've thought out but could find nowhere else—and if you want personal attention from both builder and designer—something that you need for a good semi-custom boat—then Cro's yard in Southwest Harbor is as good a place as you will find. The fact that your boat will be crafted as well as an old-time violin will just be an added bonus.

ALDEN YACHTS

B ack in the first decades of this century when yachts were sleek and long, elegant and graceful, John Alden was designing some of the most beautiful of them all. From his legendary *Malabar* schooners to his small coastwise cruisers, each boat was a perfect homage to the sea. His company of designers still lives on in Boston, and looking at the sleek new Aldens drawn up there, you'd think somehow that old John was still standing at their sides. □ And Alden Yachts down in Melville, in Rhode Island, builds the boats with a reverence that would make John G. proud.

One of the best parts of writing this book was travelling the world, meeting people who love boats, and seeing all the factories. The other was actually crawling through the boats, and I have to say that because of all the amazing little hidden details in the Aldens, crawling through them was some of the best fun of all.

Aldens are certainly *the yachts* to be looked up to, simply for the old fashioned belief that permeates the whole yard, that nothing but nothing is too good for an Alden. So the boats are planned and built and detailed with superhuman care, each completely styled to each new owner, and each finished to such a degree that you almost hate to take the damned things out to sea. I suspect that much of this attitude trickles down the ranks from David MacFarlane, Alden's general manager, one of the most easygoing and enjoyable guides you ever want to spend a couple of days with.

"My father was captain," David begins reminiscing, "on George E. Roosevelt's *Mistress* for twenty-two years, until Roosevelt died. He had been aboard *Ticonderoga* as crew, the day she rolled down the ways on her maiden launch. I spent a lot of time on boats like *Windigo, Bolero* and *Niña*, and I guess I just developed a sense of what a yacht is like. Once you spend time on boats like that, it gets into your blood and you get this notion that a yacht has to have the best of everything. You don't even question it, that's just the way you think."

And when you think that way, it's only natural that you mock up an entire full scale interior out of 3/16-inch plywood for your future owner, to make sure the changes he suggests or wants will actually turn out the way he envisions them. Drawings on paper just aren't good enough. And you think nothing of picking out a few complete *sets* of bulkhead-destined plywoods and have the owners come in and tell you which they like. I don't mean the kind of *wood,* for that had been decided well in advance; I mean the kind of *grain.*

David just smiles and says, "We're happier this way and the owner is happier." When your boats start at a quarter of a million dollars, you can afford to do things like that.

"We are very particular about everything. We hand pick all our own wood for the boats. We reject so much wood that we were actually threatened with a suit for sending back $62,000 worth of wood in a few months. So now instead of them shipping to us and us shipping it back, I go down to the lumber place and hand pick the wood. When you're only building five or six boats a year you can take the time to do that. Then once the wood is in, we invite the owners to come in and choose the panels that they like best. You know, some people like a lot of grain, a lot of definition, others not so much. So we set out a few panels and let them pick the ones they like.

"We like to think up new and better ways of doing things. We had one owner—who had to do a lot of paperwork aboard at the large desk-like chart table—ask us to figure out a way to hide his electronics and toys so he would not end up spending all his working time playing with them. So we designed a little James Bondian now-you-see-it-now-you-don't panel which turns the chart table area into a peaceful study. It also helps to cut down on theft, for those glancing in through portlights won't see a vast array of expensive, inviting electronics.

"I think our whole attitude is that we are building *a* boat for a *specific* person, not the general public, so why shouldn't we go to whatever extent we can to make the boat suit the man?"

That *extent* includes having owners send in the glasses and dishes they wish to use aboard, and Alden fabricating the dish and glass racks to match, to eliminate any movement and abrasion. I have to admit that this is a might nicer than the great array of stuffed gloves and socks many boats rely on. And that *extent* also includes putting a duct for the heater into the foul weather locker to help dry out the gear. (That is the official story but I suspect the duct is there to warm up your booties so your feeties won't be cold when you go out into the big bad rain.) And the silverware drawers are lined with green baize—the only place I've seen the stuff before was on pool tables in pool halls—and they'll match the color to the interior you have chosen. (And if you're *really* nice, they'll match the formica in the head to the color of your eyes.)

But lest all this might tempt you to think that these boats are just frivolous, let me tell you that they are really built like tanks. If you get an Alden and think of chartering it, forget the Caribbean; lease it to the Canadian Navy as an icebreaker. I saw an Alden 44 that had hit a piece of underwater concrete slab at full speed, an impact that put a 2-inch deep dent, an actual shredding, flaring out to 2 inches on either side of the lead ballast, yet the ballast to keel seam barely showed a crack.

The hulls are built by Tillotson-Pearson, Alden's parent company, who are without doubt the most advanced in fiberglass research and technology in North American boat building today. For a complete story on the hulls and why they are built the way they are, read the chapter on Tillotson-Pearson. Until then here's some stuff in shorthand. The gelcoat is of Vinylester resin and that is twice as water-resistant and blister-resistant as isophthalic resin. And three times as expensive. Natch. But that's not quite enough for Alden. Just to be sure, they also cover the bottom with four coats of epoxy before the boat is launched.

The fiberglass in the hulls is unidirectional. The coring is vacuum bagged balsa. To see why they use balsa, read the Tillotson-Pearson chapter.

Great foam cored glass stringers run bow to stern for stiffening. Wires are run in a molded-in chaser so they are perfectly protected from flying objects and abrasion and they allow for future wires to be belatedly fed.

The main bulkhead on the big boats is 2¼ inches thick—don't blink, you read it right—a composite of five laminates of glass, balsa, glass, balsa, etc. The outboard edges of the layers of ½-inch balsa are faired down so that the last 2 feet outboard, in the area of the chainplates, the bulkhead is 2¼ inches of solid glass. Cannonball proof. The bulkheads are vacuum bag molded so the resin is sucked deep into the balsa to prevent delamination. Bonds of the bulkhead run a good 7 inches onto the hull.

Up forward is a very large *watertight* bulkhead built using the same composite system, the idea being that you can virtually destroy the bow in a collision, and the watertight bulkhead will keep the rest of the boat safe and dry. The Alden is the only production boat on which I have seen a watertight bulkhead of such strength.

For safety, all through-hulls are bonded together with straps of copper and then the whole grounding system is *glassed over* to keep tanks etc. from being layed over them, setting up little homemade batteries. The holes for the through-hulls are made in the hull during molding. That is to say, the location of the through hulls is defined early—which Alden can manage because of the extensive pre-construction mockup—and then the holes are blocked out in the mold so you get a solid gelcoated, finished laminate when the hull is layed up around the hole, instead of having to hole saw the hull, as is customary, leaving exposed and unprotected fiberglass laminate ends.

They use aluminum inserts in the molds to define location of portlights and hatches, so you end up with the most beautifully finished ports and windows possible, ones that do not have hunks of exterior trim on them. Using the aluminum blockouts for hatches, combined with the constant camber in the cabin top, allows Alden to move the hatches almost anywhere your heart desires, as well as allowing them to put in as many hatches as you like. And they'll all end up with finished and raised edges just like the real thing, because they *are* the real thing.

All these bits of engineering development, as well as more complex ones like hydraulic vangs and hydraulic centerboards, are an affordable luxury in a company that builds only five or six boats a year because they have the backing of their parent Tillotson-Pearson. And the way the Aldens turn out, one can only say that it's a wonderful arrangement.

"I think we have the best of both worlds," David says, "We operate a small independent company that builds the Aldens with small crews, meticulous traditional methods, on an almost entirely custom basis, but we also have a large technical facility, the laboratory, advanced research on resins and laminates, and yes, even the money if and when we need to make large investments for new models, etc.

"We can stay ahead of small builders by researching things first instead of advancing by trial and error. If Alden were an independent company, it could never afford to do all this testing. And we also learn from all the tests we run on Freedoms and J boats and the other products like those great rotors they build for wind generators. We can afford to grow at our own pace. We started nine years ago with the *44* and we're on hull #32. Not too fast but high on quality. *Practical Sailor,* the only truly non-biased magazine that accepts no advertising and no fees, last year said, 'The Aldens are now the benchmark in quality.' " It's not hard to see why.

The tanks are all certified, pressure-tested aluminum. The fiberglass work is immaculate. The joinerwork, although simple and elegant, reflects risks and indulgences like no other builders. The grabrail, which runs beneath the portlights, is a piece about 13 feet long cut from a mammoth piece, of which about 65 percent is scrap. To make it even more astonishing, both ends of this mammoth thing fit *perfectly* against the bulkheads. As a further touch of practical—though invisible—advancement, the *inside* of the rail has been shaped concave to give you a genuine handhold.

The seating cleats for drop lids are not assembled out of four bits of plywood as is customary, but rather cut out in one continuous piece from one large hunk of plywood. And the seating cleats as well as the drop boards themselves are beautifully bullnosed and varnished. The bottom of almost every locker is finished out in wood with further drop boards inside the locker bottoms to give access to the bilge. Even a space between the sink and the outboard cabinetry which one could, in a generous mood, call 9 inches, even that is utilized with a little flap door. And seemingly hopeless triangular spaces have been made utile, at no small expense, to provide other ideal small storage spaces.

The drawers in the Aldens run not just on earthly slides which sometimes jam with humidity and age only to come flying into your stomach with your final desperate tug; instead they have rollers that, judging by the their smoothness, must use graphite bearings. The drawer sides are solid wood. A solid teak face covers a mahogany box that is dovetailed together. Now *that's* a drawer. The searails are screwed from *underneath* so you don't even have plugs showing. That's class. The insides of all lockers are varnished and sealed to cut moisture absorption, and thus mildew, to a minimum. There are blind hinges and felt-lined jewelry drawers; all those little things that make life worth living.

The cutting board is attached to the bottom of a lid so it can be flipped over and into the hole and will be perfectly usable without sliding around on a heel. All hidden areas are totally finished out and that is really the sign of a true yacht.

"Inside," David says, "the whole boat gets at least six coats of varnish. After that, they just keep varnishing until I go through the boat and finally say, 'Okay.' So you can get anywhere from six coats up. This tabletop, Ferenc, believe it or not, has twenty coats on it. The trim next to you has ten.

"And just as other people use our ideas, we try to keep up with any new ones others may have. We give our guys tickets to the boat shows and ask them to go aboard all the best boats; if they see anything that the competition is doing better, something that is more intelligently or beautifully done than ours, then by George, we improve that aspect of our boat in the very next hull. We try.

"We have a great fiberglass pan that holds three batteries and contains spills. We have gauges on the fridges so you don't have to open the door and lose cold air while you check the interior temperature. The standard stove is a Luke, probably the best and most expensive you can buy. Our drawers are compartmentalized. In the galley even the interiors and shelves of cabinets are formica-lined for easy maintenance."

Then there is an amazing corner piece that is cut from solid stock with so many slopes and bevels and curves that neither a photograph nor words will do it service; you'll just have to go and see for yourself. There is beautiful finishing work where three bulkheads come together at odd angles. The piece that joins them is a genuine Y with *six sides to it plus three grooves;* a triumph of workmanship.

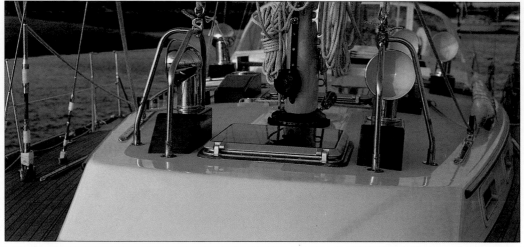

Most of these photos are of the Alden 44, for the simple reason that no one had gotten around to taking any sailing shots of the newer boats, and I sure wasn't about to volunteer in the middle of December up in Rhode Island. But I did manage to defrost the camera long enough to snap the shot directly above, showing the forest of beautifully beveled and dove-tailed dorade boxes, and the absolutely second-to-none fiberglass work on an Alden 54. The cabintops of the Aldens don't have any set hatches per se; they can be

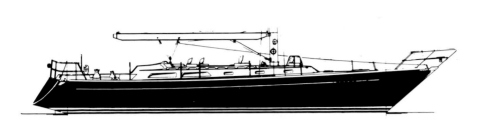

located wherever, and with as great a density, as you like. The holes for the hatches are then blocked out in the mold, giving you perfectly finished edges. Now for the *44*. Starting in the upper left hand corner of this double page and working— God knows why— counterclockwise, we first see the pretty, tucked—up

stern (smaller and more graceful than most of the new ones) and the wide open side decks. In the photo below, where the bow is about to land right in your lap, the tumblehome of the hull becomes apparent. I have no idea why a hull with tumblehome looks so much prettier than one without, but the *44* has just enough

of it to make this hull one of my all-time favorites. The two photos below show the *44* performing downwind and to windward, nearly jumping out of the water under spinnaker and settling in nicely with a mule and staysail working close to shore. Her graceful sheer shows in the small photo above.

Down below, the Aldens are as outstanding as they are above. They cater to the owners' wishes down to the last detail, from the complete alteration of parts of the interior—the drawing shows just one of many—to the color of the baize in the drawers for the silverware. The interior wood you choose yourself (one interior here is teak and the other is ash) and you can even specify the type of panels you want in your doors; canes or solids or louvers. As you can see, many of the ideas are excellent. The galley, below, is the ideal fore and aft one that doubles as a passageway to the aft cabin; the other galley has nicely rounded corners to maximize space and eliminate dangerous pointed corners. The chart table has a curved seat and a large surface, and is deep enough to store a good number of charts. The trim is simple and elegant.

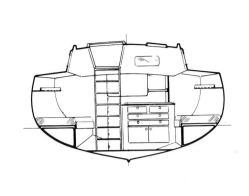

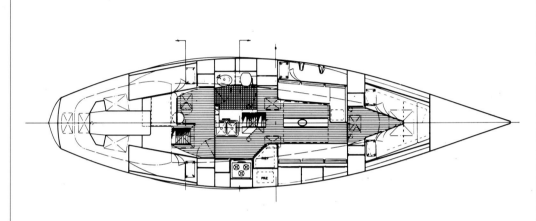

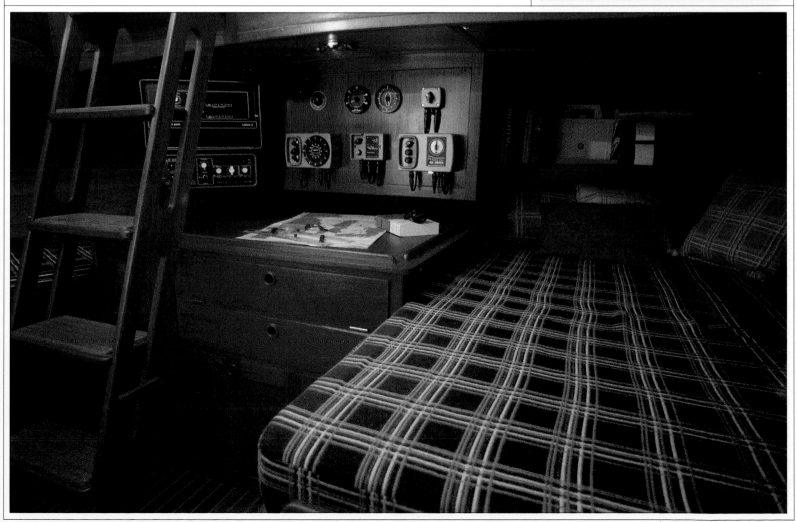

Some of the true-yacht details of the Aldens. To the left, note piano quality dorade-cum-stowage box with extra set of grabrails amidships, which is where you need them when you're on the lee deck with the boat heeled; the ones on the cabin's edge are hard to find when they are down around your ankles. Photo to right shows the carpet lined and —Good Lord— teak-soled and teak-trimmed sail locker with huge sliding hatch. I swear a place like that could fetch a thousand a month in the middle of Manhattan.

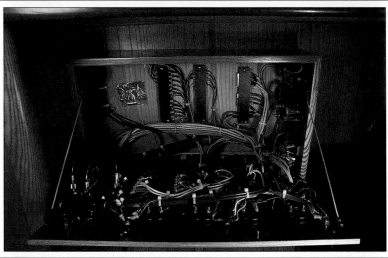

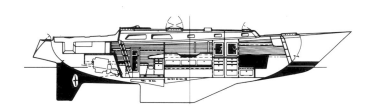

The electrical panel hinges down for easy inspection and repair; the gauges for the fridge and freezer are located *outside* the unit so you don't defrost the thing while checking if it's cold enough; above the galley stove the overhead is lined with stainless steel for easy cleaning and fewer fires; and best of all, they'll mock up a whole interior for you, incorporating your ideas, so that you will understand *why* you can't fit the pool table *and* small garage where the wet locker used to be.

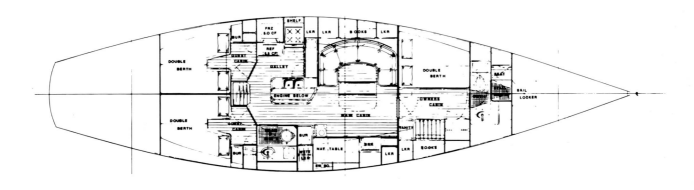

Perhaps Paul Petronello, who is in sales at Alden, gave the most meaningful clue of all as to why so much care and attention go into the boats. □ ''You know, we take about eight months to build a boat. They are each here so long—almost the gestation period of a baby—and I get so close to them, that sometimes I walk through here in the evening and catch myself talking to one. Maybe it sounds foolish but you really become kind of emotionally attached to these things.''

BALTIC YACHTS

There are remote little pockets in the world where the building of modern sailboats has reached the level of true art, where small groups of creative men have gathered the native talents of a region to build the very finest sailboats in the world. □ The little town of Pietarsaari, Finland, is one of these, where a few miles up the road of Seven Bridges, Baltic Yachts, whose five founders were mutineers from nearby Nautor twelve years ago, build their version of the very best.

Compared to the silent countryside that surrounds it, the Baltic boatyard looks like a science fiction movie. The first thing you notice is that the cement floors of the shops are just like polished glass and the whole place is as clean as if it had been scrubbed down for surgery. And when you are told why, you start to smile because you realize that Baltic really is the boatyard of the future.

A special sealant is used to make the floors as smooth as ice, because that is what you need when the cradles your boats sit in move on cushions of air. And you stare in sheer amazement when you see a man move a 6,000 pound lead keel with one hand because the cradle the keel is in hovers on air too. And when you see the Olympic-pool-sized testing tank, and the building for the heating system that's bigger than most boatyards, and computer programs that can calculate the hull construction, mast construction and the size and shape of a new rudder within minutes, then you realize that the folks at Baltic have a lot to teach you.

We were lucky to have as our teacher for most of one weekend P.G. Johansson, whom everyone calls PG. He was one of the original mutineers from Nautor, and is one of the most well-spoken and knowledgeable men we encountered on our travels, who knew not only a lot about building sailboats but also about many little mysteries of life.

The plant was empty and silent on Saturday morning and we stopped with PG in the shiny-floored shop with the sun shining through the skylights, and we talked.

"You can build a boat in so many different ways," he began. "You can solve the technical problems in so many different ways and a lot of them are good acceptable solutions. But whether you choose one acceptable solution or the other, you can still end up building a good boat or a bad one, depending on how well you apply the method. Like sandwich materials, corings or what type of roving you use; the main thing is that you understand how these materials all work, otherwise you end up with things working against each other instead of strengthening each other.

"People think that a material or a method that has become 'in,' as you say, is the thing to go for; like some new salvation. It's not. It has to be used properly. A boat is a lot of small, individual, technical solutions, which, if *all* done the right way, will result in something good. For example, with our custom yachts we use a lot of Kevlar and carbon fiber. Those and E-glass and S-glass are all good for some applications and bad for others. So you have to know the strengths and the weaknesses of each material and how to combine them. It takes a lot of time and experimenting before you learn all this. Things just don't come overnight.

"My philosophy is that when you are born into this world you know nothing. When you leave this world, by far the biggest percentage of what you have learned will have come from others. Your parents teach you things and your teachers teach you things and your friends teach you things; so you have to be open to what other people know, what other people think. So we look at other builders to see what they are doing, then we think about it to see if we can adapt it to our production, even improve it maybe.

"So what you learn from others is vital, but then you have to combine that with what is even more vital—your own creativeness. Because however small a part creativeness is of your total, when you leave this earth, *that* is the thing that counts. Without creativeness, I think you will end up a copier who hasn't added much to the world.

"It's a funny thing, because at the other extreme the truly creative people reject the works of others because it's against their nature, and go completely on their own. I think it's very difficult to combine the two things—to be an observant copier who is truly creative. In a company you have the possibility of doing that by mixing the right sort of people. You can have someone who looks very coldly and analytically at things—he might be a great copier. That's one very good type to have. Then you have the creative one who never looks at anyone else's work and even hates to do the same thing twice. These two kinds of people seem to balance one another. I think we are lucky to have that kind of balance here at Baltic.

"When the five of us left Nautor we were very aware that we were different personalities; we had a good cross section of knowledge and attitudes to form a good company. That was so not by accident. We loved to work at Nautor. We learned a lot. But in a big company it's very difficult to make changes. Sometimes you come up with a suggestion that you think is just beautiful and you end up getting no response. And at that time Swan was pretty much alone in building top quality racer-cruisers so they really had no incentive to change.

"But aside from that, I think every human being would like to go it alone at least once in his life. You have to give your capabilities a try, otherwise at the end of your life you might not be too happy with yourself. Sometimes it works out like you thought, other times it doesn't. But both ways you learn."

"Has it worked out like you thought it would?"

"No, no " he laughed. "To a great extent yes, but what a tremendous part of my life it took. One thing that changed our plans a lot was that three months after we started, the world had its first oil crisis. That made us do a little thinking and changing of plans. The world doesn't always co-operate.

"Our basic idea from the beginning was that we didn't want to go head to head with anybody on the market at that time. Although our philosophy might be close to other people's out there, I think it's vital that every company find its own niche. You have to consider pretty hard what it is you're looking for; what you are trying to achieve.

"We wanted to create a top quality, comfortable, cruising boat, but one that was lighter than most, not only to increase performance but also to make life easier, more enjoyable. I always found smaller sails easier to handle and feel comfortable with, and in close quarters and harbors the light boat responds much more quickly, is much more manageable. A heavy boat is harder to slow down, harder to turn. And if you have good designers design fast hulls for you, then it's foolish to destroy performance by building the boats too heavy. The closer you get the boat to its designed displacement, the better for both performance and, I think, cruising.

"There is little doubt that the modern hulls with flat bottoms and light displacement are the fastest, but even forgetting racing, I find that many of our clients who don't even do club racing just don't want to be overtaken by another boat. It's against their nature.

"And the other thing. I have been out in our boats in really heavy conditions, both with boats that were relatively free of gear and boats heavily loaded with spare anchors, great lengths of chain, and the like, and the unloaded boat just flew happily along, dry and fast, whereas the loaded-down boat was beginning to pitch and struggle and was wet. Ninety-nine percent of the time most people will be coastal or weekend cruising, and even when they go long distances there is no real need to carry five years of supplies; you can get most things in most places now, so a lighter displacement boat will not be a disadvantage.

"To keep developing, the custom boats are very important, *because* to keep developing, sometimes you have to take calculated risks. If you do something experimental in a production boat, by the time you find that your new idea wasn't so great after all, you might have built a dozen boats and have a dozen problems. But if you do it on a custom boat and the owner has been made aware of what you are trying to do, if it was honestly explained to him—and on most of the big custom racing machines certain risks are taken that you would never take on a production boat—then if you make a mistake, you have only one boat to correct. You can test methods and materials and equipment on a custom boat that you just can't on a production boat. Without our custom boats, development would be a lot slower for us.

When I commented on how almost inhumanly thorough the construction of the boats was, PG frowned and said, "You know, too often people do things in the boat business for marketing reasons. I can't object to that because that is their philosophy, but I think *we* are guilty at the other end. We do all these little things because we think they are important, but then we forget to tell our clients about them. We are a strange people here: We are very proud of what we do but we hate in one sense to advertise . . . I mean . . . Ah!" He said, for the first time frustrated with himself. "It's silly. We have to do that. We should inform people what goes into our boats just so they understand and are able to make intelligent comparisons. I'm not saying we should try to convince everyone to sail in Baltics. There are thousands of sailors who don't want or need anything like a Baltic, and that's wonderful; honestly, I'm happy for their sakes, but for the others who are looking for something else, maybe of higher quality or performance, then for those people I think we really ought to explain why it is that they can look at a boat the same size as ours, same engine, same winches, same number of berths etc., and for the life of them they are unable to tell why that boat costs only half as much as ours does. Maybe they can see that our quality of finish is a little better but, good heavens, that can't be worth twice as much. And of course they are right. I think it's our duty to explain to people just how our boats are put together. And you can't blame people for not knowing or not seeing right away, because you have to start from one end and go through all the details, and by the time you get to the other end you have a good list of why this is a good boat.

"For example, when we put a teak deck on a boat, that owner should not be punished in performance just because he wants to have a beautiful deck. So we calculate exactly how much structural support that teak deck set in epoxy produces, and then we can cut back on the materials in the deck to try to make up for the extra weight. I'm not saying you can take as much weight out as the teak deck puts in, but you can make an effort to compensate.

"The good thing with epoxying on a teak deck is that if after a few years the deck wears down a little and a few plugs pop out—which will always happen in any deck—then you can just remove the screw and replug the hole. The epoxy will hold the deck very ably without those few screws. The screws are just clamps anyway; theoretically you could take them all out once the epoxy sets. We have used epoxy ever since we started, and we have found better results with it than we expected. We also do other nice things on the decks, like rounding the ends of planks where they fit into the covering boards.

"In the floor grid we use unidirectional fibers. With them you can stretch the material to a high strength so the fibers act as the steel rods do in reinforced concrete. Now if you were to bend the steel rods, put all sorts of waves into them, then under stress the rod would just straighten out and the concrete would crumble. You can roughly compare that to woven roving where the fibers go up and over each other in a million little bends.

"We did testing on panels with unidirectional and woven roving and the difference in strength was substantial. What is even more important to me than the actual failing is that when we loaded the test panels under stress, long before we could actually *see* the panel fail—because that takes a lot of load—we could *hear* through listening devices that we attached to the panels, the small fibers coming apart in the woven roving. That means that the longevity of woven roving just would not be as good.

"The nice thing with unidirectional is that you can orientate the fibers in the direction of the load. In a boat you always have concentrated loads in certain areas going in a certain direction. So we have a relatively complex lamination schedule. That is why we have a book for each boat we build, not just each model, but each and every boat, with a page for each layer of laminate. Then as the guy lays up the laminates, he signs off each page and the book goes into our files. We have to do that. If you overbuild anyway by a long shot you don't have to worry about a guy forgetting a layer; it wouldn't make that much difference, but when things are engineered, you have to keep tighter control. Plus you can go back and see how well specific things you did worked out.

"We like to use glass floor grids and longitudinals instead of wood or metal floors, because if you work the glass right, and you stagger the dimensions down the further you get from the load concentration, you get no critical point in your construction. All your materials are then of the same elasticity. If you use metal floors—and I speak from experience because we have used different materials on the custom side —you are going to have critical spots where one material will start behaving differently from another and you'll have problems.

"We have developed our own computer program for calculating almost everything on a boat. A few years ago we set one of our boats up with a computer and a great number of sensors that recorded loads. We went out many times in all kinds of conditions and we got thousands of readings that we then developed into computer programs that form a book this thick, for calculating rigging, rudder stock, laminates, everything.

"But the computer is just the first step. It's very easy to design programs that will spew out a lot of fancy and impressive, but sometimes unreliable, numbers; so you have to take a computer for what it is: just one of the many tools. The most important factor is still the people who build the boats. So often you work out something on the computer and in the design office and it seems absolutely perfect, but then you come out into the shop and start building the boat that way, and all of a sudden you take a few steps back and you say to yourself, 'That just doesn't *look* right.' You have to have the ability and experience to recognize that. There is a combination of mathematical, high level know-how and practical instinct and experience. And you need a balance, just like with the creative and the methodical people we talked about. You need that balance to be able to do the best.

"In the hull and deck joint we use a layer of flexible resin and mat, and then we bolt the toe-rail on. That gives us about ten times the strength we need.

"In the bottom of the boat we can build heavy beams for strength. Adding weight down there is no problem because the ballast is there for that very reason. You should have laterals to support the torque of the keel, and then heavy longitudinals to support the laterals.

"All our tanks are bonded in because that's the safest way to hold them in place. We also pour two-part foam between the tank and the bulkheads and the hull to make things more secure and to get away from the noise of water sloshing in the tanks. Besides, you won't have things falling in there, bouncing around and making noise.

"High strength aluminum is what we use on the rudder posts because we don't want extra weight out in the end of the boat. This specific aluminum has stronger properties than most stainless steel rudder posts, but it's much more difficult to handle. You can't weld it, for instance, or the weld will just break. You have to attach the rudder reinforcement plates mechanically to the rudderpost, which is a more expensive method, but it does save a lot of weight and with our philosophy it is worth doing. On custom boats we use titanium and carbon fiber—all sorts of things.

"The seacocks are bonded in with fiberglass material instead of using an outside flange because if you want to get an outside flange flush to the outer skin for performance, you have to weaken the hull by feathering it to make room for the flange.

"I'm not saying that building a boat in two halves is the only way to lay up a boat, but it does make it easier for the

men to do their work. I do think you end up with a better quality hull. Some people say that builders only do that to speed up production by having two crews working on one hull at once, but when you are putting out a total of forty boats a year of all models combined, then, believe me, speeding up lamination is the last of your worries.

"For us, setting the keel is a one-man job. That is nice because the man can take all the time he wants, check it, remove it, fit it again. He's not in anybody's way and no one is waiting for him as happens when a bunch of people are moving a hull and lowering it onto the keel. And when people are relaxed and enjoying themselves, they can do a much better job. Around the bolts we use an elastic sealant but between the keel and the hull we use chopped fiber and a form of resin that remains more elastic, thus less liable to crack than ordinary resin.

"We have had a number of boats grounding very hard and all sailed away. Most weren't even hauled until the end of the season. I'm not saying that we are building amphibian landing craft, but if you use a little caution when you're close to rocks and don't run aground at full speed, then a well-built boat should take that. But if you hit the ground so hard and stop so fast that you sheer the engine bolts and the engine flies into the salon, then you should expect some hull repair.

"I am not a believer in a small skeg. Many people think that it helps support the rudder but I think that's mostly myth. We built a custom boat with a deep narrow skeg, and believe me, we tried to make it as strong as we could; but when that boat came out of the mold I could move the skeg back and forth by hand. And that was a 60-foot boat. But once the rudder was put on, the skeg became very solid, so I really have to ask myself just who was supporting who. But then you do have to steer more carefully because a rudder without a skeg can stall if the rudder angle is increased too much. And you don't get as much warning when it's about to stall as you do with a skeg.

"The best directional steering is provided by a very long, narrow boat because it will be nearly symmetrical no matter what heel angle you have. But once you start building boats with great beams for their length, for reasons of racing or accommodation or whatever, then those boats will become asymmetrical once they heel, and the more asymmetrical a hull becomes, the less it tracks, no matter what kind of skeg you put on.

"Chainplates? Well. The more you can spread the chainplate load longitudinally, the stiffer the construction is. It's not just a question of a chainplate being strong enough so it won't break, its foundation also has to be solid enough so it won't move. If it gives and the plate moves, then your mast tuning will change dramatically and you might lose your mast.

"We always use rod rigging. It stretches less than wire so you have a safer mast, because whatever happens that changes the tuning of the mast—a chainplate moving or a wire stretching—the rig is more likely to fail.

"Our computers help a lot. They can tell us what we need in a mast—cross-section, wall thickness, spreaders, rigging, everything. We can imput an outside laminate requirement and the computer will calculate weights and layers and direction of weave. It also gives us total weight, weight per square meter, and required stiffness. We do that for side shell and bottom shell laminates, or bulkhead laminates if we want to make up bulkheads out of balsa and fiberglass. Of course we have to consider whether the panel is curved or straight, because a curved panel will have additional strengths compared to a straight panel.

"We can feed in size of boat and displacement and the size of rudder and it will then give us the amount of reinforcement necessary, the size of rudder shaft, and wall thickness. We check all the designers' figures and calculations. If something happens, the yard is responsible, not the designer. We have a program for calculating keel shape, vertical and horizontal center of gravity, etc. We like to do all those things ourselves because then we can be sure of what is going on and why. Then we can understand, and if we understand we can go on learning. That is one of the best parts."

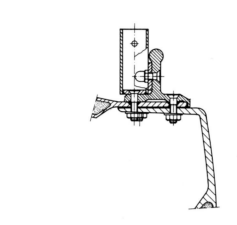

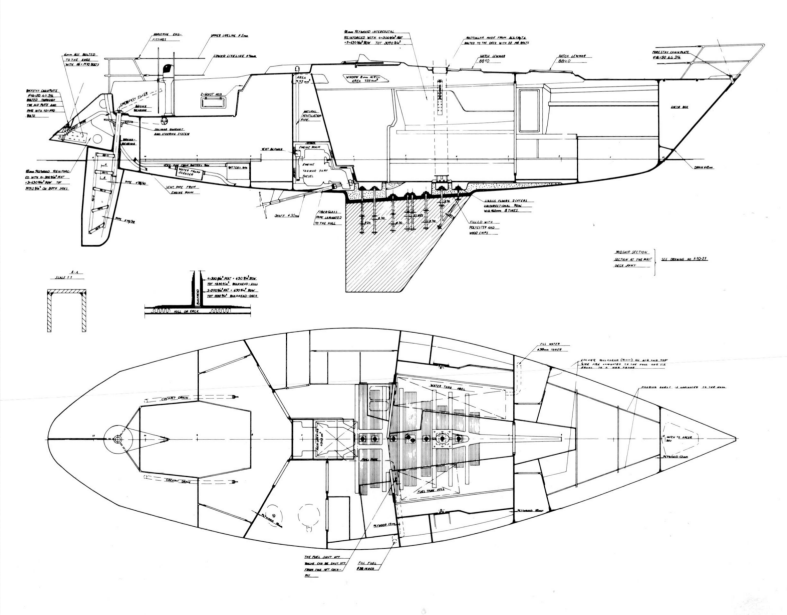

A dozen years ago five ambitious men of varied talents left Nautor Yachts in Finland to start their own boatyard a few miles down the road. Within a few years designer Tor Hinders, PG Johanson and the others, made themselves a worldwide reputation for building fast light racer-cruisers of extremely high quality and distinctive good looks. The hulls were designed at first by the C&C design group, later by Doug Peterson, and most recently by World Cup-winning designer Judel-Vrolijk, but the

unmistakable decks and distinctive interiors were conceived by the designers of Baltic Yachts, led by Tor Hinders. The grace of the hulls is best seen in the two photos of the Doug Peterson-designed Baltic 55, above, while the unique crisp angles of the deck and house show best in the small, aerial photo to the left. It is of the new Judel-Vroljik-designed Baltic 35. The angles serve not only as a stylistic trademark, but also aid in maximizing the space belowdecks while maintaining the grace of the hull and the house. With the main hatch and companionway well forward, a very comfortable aft cabin is created quite a feat on a sleek looking 35-foot boat. She is an excellent light air sailer, displacing only 9,877 pounds on a waterline of almost 29 feet. For complete specifications and drawings, see the section in the back of the book. For now, feast your eyes on the Baltic sterns, which are as pretty as you'll find anywhere.

"Maybe one last thing. So many things are machine-made today. I'm not saying that is bad, because I enjoy having a lot of the things that machines make, but I am very happy to be involved in the building of something that is still done by hand. There is a special sort of feeling there. □ "I know what our people put into these boats, I know what they feel. I mean sometimes it hurts when you deliver a boat. In one sense you are happy because your client is happy—you feel happy because you've achieved what he was looking for—but on the other hand you feel sad that you have to part with something that you have put your whole heart into.''

BÉNÉTEAU

Once upon a time a hundred years ago, on the southwest coast of France in a little town called Croix-de-Vie, Benjamin Bénéteau slid the first fishing trawler of his own handiwork down into the sea. For the next eighty years the Bénéteau family built fine wooden fishing boats, at first powered by wind and later on by engines, sturdy boats of many sizes that plied the Bay of Biscay in search of sardines and mullet, seabass and tuna.

Not much really changed until 1964 when Annette Bénéteau—by then married to a Monsieur Roux—came into the little company and saw that what was going on wasn't going to last. The boatyard was down to only seventeen men, many of them just putting in time, the market for fishing boats had nearly vanished and the eighty-year-old family business was threatened with the end. Madame Roux had to choose between change and oblivion.

She chose well.

Chantiers Bénéteau changed from boats of work to boats of pleasure and from traditional wood to polyester resin. The firm recovered. They built thousands of little sports fishers and day fishers, and less than ten years later they went back to what they had done best, building boats that moved under the power of the wind.

And then the miracle decade began.

From a small yard, they blossomed into seven different plants, from a work force of near one hundred they grew to eleven hundred strong, from an income of just twenty million francs they went to five hundred million by 1985, and along the way they won a Boat of the Year award and an Admiral's Cup as the top-scoring boat, and the name of Bénéteau, which was in '75 only barely known, had by the end of '85 taken both Europe and America by storm.

All this was achieved by a tightly organized group of forward-thinking people led by Madame Roux. At first glance, with her quick mysterious smile full of a charm that's almost shy, she does not look like the lady in charge of the world's largest builder of sailboats, but the efficiency of her thinking has built a company of amazing scope, alacrity and strength.

The first thing that strikes you about Bénéteau's offices as you come in from the sleepy autumn countryside is the efficiency and speed with which the people here work—it makes some Madison Avenue agencies look like homes for the retired. The shops and yards are clean and organized, layed out by engineers; the production lines are spacious and airy and highly efficient; the production methods thought out in every detail, and the boats that come out at the end are good and fast and able and certainly deserving of the popularity they've gained.

I am not suggesting that the boats are Swans or Hinckleys. If they were, at their current prices, I would have written this book on Bénéteau alone, forgetting all the rest, but they are —without doubt—some of the very best boats for the money you'll find anywhere today. (As I write this, the dollar is bouncing like a ping pong ball so Lord knows what will happen, but as of April of '86 the above statement is true.) And whereas many builders seem to be building boats for people who also own a bank, I am happy to say that Bénéteau builds boats for those of us whose interests are more varied than counting piles of money, then counting them again.

The Bénéteau line begins with the *Wizz,* a glorified windsurfer that you sit on like a boat, then it goes in small increments from a lightning-fast little 22-foot racer up to 51 feet in length. And in between there are twenty-five—honest—twenty-five different models of every shape and size, from the quick little class racers to full-blown hefty cruisers; and as homage to the great French sailors who, in their multihulls, have broken every record ever dreamed up for sailboats, there is even a very livable 34-foot catamaran.

Bénéteau, at last, has brought the fun back into sailing. And they did it with boats that are pretty to look at; with their well thought-out engineering, a true joy to sail; and because of their integrity of construction, reassuring to take to sea.

I have written much about Bénéteaus in the second edition of *From Bare Hull,* where I used many of Bénéteau's ideas as good examples to follow, so I won't go into great detail here, but I will say that in general the boats are layed out with extreme care and inovation.

The designs come from such famous names as Jean Berret and German Frers who seem to be in competition for drawing the prettiest and fastest hulls around. With three separate lines of boats—the *Class* racers, *Idyll* cruisers and, my favorites, the ocean going *Firsts*—the keels vary from the deepest finest fins to twin bilge keels for sitting on the mud, to shoal draft keels and even centerboards.

It's hard to generalize about decks with all the different models, so I won't even try, but I will say that a genuine effort is made to keep them clean and uncluttered. Once size allows —over 25 feet—they become very comfortable to use and over 35 feet, downright vast.

The one thing that does seem invariably consistent is the comfort and spaciousness of the cockpits. The engineering is thorough, with curved backrests, good bracing and good winch layouts and small vital details like recessed cleats which let you keep your ribs in one piece like the good Lord meant for them to be, and best of all—and why every boat in the world doesn't have these I'll never know—teak slats on the seats. These are not merely decoration, but one of the most important safety features on a boat, for fiberglass cockpit seats make untenably slippery footing when wet. The non-skid patterns built into them are almost never coarse enough—if they were, they would rasp off half of your behind—so with any rain or spray or suntan oil they become truly first class icerinks. And the worst part is that you'll go flying when you unsuspectingly leap onto them after having done fancy footwork on the deck. Teak slats are a must. End of lecture.

Let's go belowdecks where I'm sure most of you are by now dying to be. My initial reaction when I went below my first 42 foot Bénéteau some years ago was, "How the hell do they afford all this wood at such a price?" And it's not just wood slapped in there and forgotten, but well finished, well designed and pleasing to the eye, like the rounded doors in bulkheads beautifully trimmed, and complex curved moldings well fitted around chart tables, galleys and all cabinet doors. Only after much scrutiny and explanation by my hostess, Madame Fontanet, did I understand that all these curved moldings are not only prettier than trim that's fit together out of many bits and pieces, but, through the use of well planned jigs, much less time consuming to fabricate and fit.

Upon very close inspection the differences between Bénéteaus and the more expensive boats do begin to show. The difference is not in quality—which as I mentioned is just fine—but rather in quantity and complexity. There are no small bits of cabinetry as found in expensive yachts, or costly bits of trim in hand-holes and table corners, or complex and hard to fit wood cabinside liners. But there is a teak cabinsole and many opening ports and grabrails where you need them and a very nicely made, solid looking overhead.

As for layout, the French have always been accused of cramming too many berths into a small boat at the cost of necessary space for other functions. In the Bénéteaus this simply is not true. Although there are certainly enough bunks here for the average army, they were not installed at the expense of something vital, for even on a little 26 footer there is a proper sit-down chart table and that, to me, is the best measure of a builder's priorities. The galleys are on the average more modest in size than what you might be used to, but this stems from the fact that the French don't believe in large iceboxes or storage of much food because they like to eat things fresh—not limp and dry and tasteless—a marvelous habit of the highest order. But even the 30-footer has a stove with oven and a double sink and elbow room to work and good storage for galley gear. For specifics look at the many photos.

The construction of the boats is sound from the foundation. The hulls are all hand laminated from high quality roving and the conditions in the layup shop are as good as I have seen. This I bring up because a man *blotto* on resin fumes and blinded by ground glass will simply not put heart and mind—what's left of them—into his work, because he's just too busy trying to survive.

At Bénéteau the laminating shops are as fresh and clean and orderly as if set up for a visit from *Better Homes and Gardens.* The material for each boat comes precut and folded and numbered on a trolley, so there are no loose pieces of trimmed-off sticky bits lying everywhere. The roving is wetted out evenly with a gun and then rolled by hand to assure removal of any excess resin. Don't forget they're building some very competitive racers so they're conscious of the weights.

All boats over 35 feet are approved for world navigation by the French Merchant Marine. They use different criteria from Lloyds of London but ultimately what they expect from a boat will be the same thing.

Much stiffness is added to the hulls by the well engineered liners, which are on the minimal side in size for production boats. For example, on the 42 footer, the liner is only 2 feet high, adding great rigidity in the keel area and the bilges, but most of even that is cut away—leaving large accessible areas everywhere. Then *all* the edges of the liner around *all* the openings are hand bonded to the hull. Any solid liner panels that remain are generously covered with a thick layer of resin armored glue; then the panels are set in place and held down by great weights until the glue hardens. Don't forget that all this is done in the laminating shop while the hulls are still green, to assure ideal bonding.

For further hull strength the major bulkheads are all double bonded to the hull as are some secondary bulkheads, others of which are bolted to the liner.

Joel Jarrijon, who was my most gracious host on my third visit to Croix-de-Vie, summed up the question of liners this way: "Basically what we want to do with Bénéteau is to build a high quality boat in a regulated production system at a competitive price. We invest more in moldings and liners because the boats can be built more efficiently, and with the rigidity that the liner provides, we can build very light boats that will perform well. Our production philosophy is based on the belief that volume not only brings prices down but also creates experience in both building and engineering, which in turn enables us to improve our boats in performance and in quality. If we were to make comparisons with the automobile industry, I would say ours is closest to the Toyota philosophy.

"Take a *42* for example. She's almost half the price of the top of the line competition, yet she has beautiful woodwork, good laminating, good hatches, good reinforcement, top quality deck fittings. We do have good quality and exceptionally good quality control. Every Monday morning we have a meeting to discuss any complaints that come in, and of course we keep track so that within a couple of weeks we can establish whether it is a design problem or a fluke or whatever. And accordingly we can correct it so we do not get a great rash of problems because we catch them in time." And that from a man who seems as open and honest as they come.

How then, you ask, do they save the money? Well the partial liners are one way, streamlined production with no owner-initiated changes is another, no extra cabinetry and simple trimwork another still, and last but not least proper engineering. Everything is planned meticulously in advance, so there are no costly hold-ups and changes once the boat has been started. In the cockpits, for example, things like locker lid handles, drains, and small compartments are all taken care of in the tooling of the molds, not "added on" later. On the cabin top the bases for the handrails are also in the mold, instead of relying on the more expensive—albeit prettier—traditional rails. Some of the ideas used are extremely advanced and save much time and money; for example, the hull and deck are through-bolted in a standard fashion but the bolts used by Bénéteau are a special, self-bracing kind which wedge themselves in the hole while the nut is being tightened from below. This not only eliminates the need for the second man above deck—who would normally hold the head of each bolt with a screwdriver while the other tightens below amid much yelling of instructions—but it also prevents the nicks and gouges which slipped screwdrivers cause, which have to be touched up at some cost. I could go on, but these few things should give you the idea.

And yet there are some extraordinary things that Bénéteau does that most production builders shy away from, like covering all hulls below the waterline with a triple layer of epoxy to prevent osmosis; like the construction of solid molded fiberglass pipes for draining the cockpits, pipes that are jointless from cockpit to the hull instead of the more vulnerable soft rubber hoses that rely on hose clamps; and last, like the complete and thorough tank-testing and spray-testing of each boat before it leaves the yard.

Aside from that, seacocks, tanks and tank fittings are among the very best, as are the mast, boom and rigging which are as advanced as any.

"As for service in North America," Joel Jarrijon continues, "We have twenty-five dealers for whom our subsidiary, Bénéteau USA, is directly responsible. We provide as solid a service as most American builders; sometimes better. And we're a good solid company, everyone pulling in the same direction, so we will be able to back up what we build for a long time. We don't want people to say, 'Well, yes, Bénéteau builds a good boat but what will happen when I need parts, and what will happen ten years from now?' We do love boats, but we handle this as a very serious business and that allows us to remain solid and survive. I think we'll be around a long time because we are a tightly knit family company."

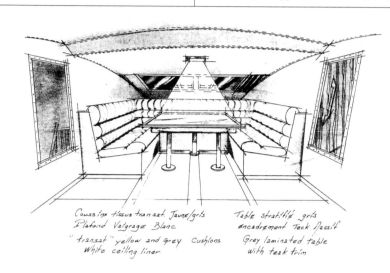

Coussins tissus transat Jaune/gris
Plafond Vaigrage Blanc
"transat" yellow and grey Cushions
White ceiling liner

Table stratifié gris
encadrement Teck Massif
Grey laminated table
with teak trim

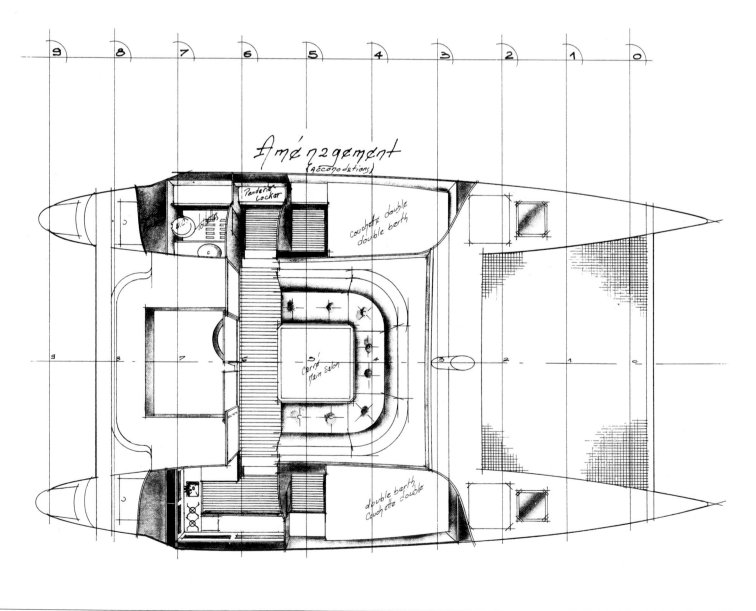

Aménagement
(accomodations)

Penderie Locker

couchette double
double berth

Carré
Main salon

double berth
Couchette double

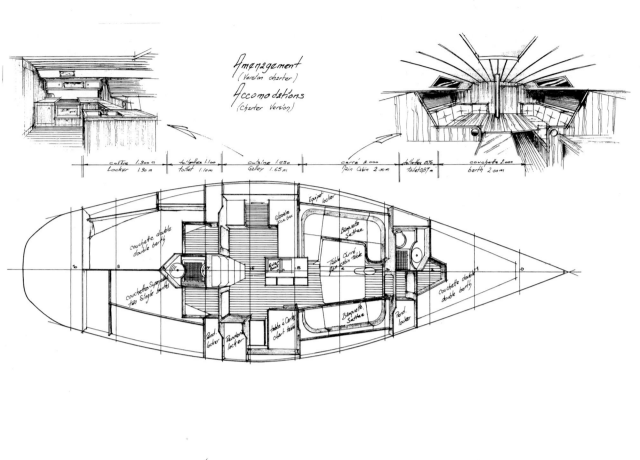

Aménagement
(Version charter)
Accomodations
(Charter Version)

| Coffre 1.30 m | toilettes 1.10 | cuisine 1.650 | carré 2.000 | toilettes 0.70 | couchette 2.000 |
| Locker 1.30 m | toilet 1.10m | Galley 1.65 m | Main Cabin 2.00m | toilet 0.87m | berth 2.00m |

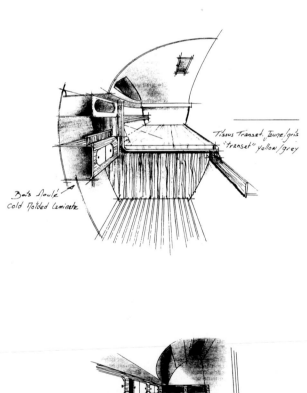

Tissus Transat. Jaune/gris
"transat" yellow/grey

Bois Moulé
Cold Molded Laminate

Bois Moulé Stratifié
Cold Molded Laminated wood

Blue II

Silhouette

47

And now we have a couple of pages of the greatest range of sailboats generated by a single manufacturer: the miraculously varied boats of Bénéteau. They start about as small as you can get with the windsurfer, (I'm amazed they don't build the rubber raft beside it) and work all the way up to 50 footers. In between there are *twenty-five* models of racers, cruisers, racer-cruisers, cruiser-racers; everything but Noah's Ark. They also build fishing boats. The large boat in the picture with the windsurfer is of the Idylle line of spacious cruisers (some have pilot houses), while the one with the large numbers on it is the First 456 designed by German Frers, who consistently draws some of the most beautiful boats in the world. As further proof, look at the sensuously curved stern of the *456* in the quarter shot of her under

sail. If you look closely in that photo —maybe with a magnifying glass— you'll find some nice features like the high toerails which provide secure support; the simple solid rungs on the stern for getting lost crew back on board; and a bridge-deck which juts into the house, creating not only additional space belowdecks, but also a secure passage between the cockpit and the companionway. I do prefer this to the hole-in-the-cabin-top companionway, which necessitates not only an amazingly long vertical hike, but also makes communication between the helmsman and people belowdecks infinitely more awkward.

A commendable family company indeed. And with their pretty boats that are great fun to sail and affordable as well, they have made a lot of other families very happy. ☐ Bénéteau is truly a credit to sailing, and with their inventiveness and good intentions they're most certainly a credit to boatbuilding. And just in case I'm not in town when the next birthday rolls around, to Joel Jarrijon and the Fontanets and of course Madame Roux, ''I wish you a Happy Two Hundredth Anniversary.''

CAMPER & NICHOLSONS

W hen you stand outside the vast brick shed where some of the greatest yachts of this century were built and look across Portsmouth Harbour, you see the raked masts of Nelson's *Victory* reaching toward the heavens. And as you work in the yard day after day and glance up now and then, you can't help but be reminded of the Golden Age of Sail when ships were built of fine woods by fine craftsmen in this place. Perhaps it's the long shadow the *Victory* casts over them, or maybe it's the ghosts of yachts that haunt the shed at night that have kept the spirit of fine craftsmanship alive at Camper and Nicholsons Yacht Builders, in Gosport.

Mr. Tony Taylor, the director and part owner of Camper and Nicholsons, is a gentleman of impressive humor, intelligence and girth, one of those few men who is completely enjoyable company, who will happily digress to anecdotes about Rolls Royces and royalty or whatever else may be tangential to his thoughts. He seems to find an endless joy in life—in his work, in his boats, and in being with the men out in the yard who not only respect him but enjoy his presence. He was a surveyor with Lloyds of London before he came to work at "Campers," as he calls it, and has stayed for twenty years. His knowledge and understanding of boatbuilding can be mildly put as "complete" and he was my host at Nicholsons for two bright autumn days.

"You know," he began, resting his hands on his ample middle, "our company was already twenty years old when *Victory* fought her last battle at Trafalgar. Of course a lot of things were different when we started—for one thing, I sure wasn't here in 1782—and things changed for better and for worse and back again as they are wont to do, but I guess you'd have to say the brightest flames at "Campers" burned between the wars.

"Then a sad chapter came just a few years ago, during the big recession when, to make a long story short, a large company simply gobbled us up. They didn't have the damndest notion of what a yacht was all about, so the quality of our boats began to suffer. Those people, lacking boatbuilding instincts, began to follow some strange statistics and market trends, trying to find a new place for Campers. It was mad. People who traditionally came to Nicholsons were sailors of experience with a very high demand for quality. Let's be truthful, Camper and Nicholsons was known for building luxury yachts. We had built some of the finest in the history of yachting, and all of a sudden here we were trying to capture the eye of the man new to sailing with a perfectly average little 27 footer. I mean who wants to buy a tiny boat that costs a fortune and looks like every other boat?

"Anyway, one day I became totally disheartened, got together a group and said, 'Come on chaps, let's buy the ruddy thing.' We did what is called a "management buyout." That was four years ago.

"Well the first thing we decided right in the middle of a recession—and don't forget even though we now have one hundred twenty people here, we were a tiny new company —we decided by rather simple and unhappy logic that during a recession the rich get richer and the poor get poorer. I mean that is what happens. So we decided to take a hell of a risk and build a 58 footer, and the boat—thank heavens—did fill some sort of a gap in the market. We have contracted for eleven of those in just three years so we are very happy indeed. We are fortunate that we and Nautor are going after a rather different market, they after the racers and we after the cruisers, so that we don't end up stepping on each other's toes.

"When the *58* was well established we decided to introduce a new *46*. Now why, you may ask, did we do that? I guess really because although during a recession you can always sell to the really wealthy, you have to think just how many people are there who can afford to buy a 58 footer at seven hundred thousand dollars? So I decided we should do the 46 footer. That was just launched and we have six on order already.

"We also have the little *31* which everyone loves because it's a jewel, the *35* which was probably our best known boat and the *39* aft and center cockpit.

"The first production Nick *32* in 1962 was, I think, the first production GRP. That sold about 400. We would like to bring out a new 36 footer because the *35* is getting a little long in the tooth. I think we need a little more beamy hull with a new hull shape, but still a very beautiful boat. My philosophy in yacht design, first and foremost, is that a yacht has to be like a woman—beautiful to look at. We would like all our boats to be around for a long time, and in fifty years we would like people to look at them with as much admiration and respect as we now look at a beautiful Nicholson built back in the thirties. That is my personal philosophy.

"I'm afraid the large classic yachts have drifted away from us but we are slowly getting back to them with quotes out on yachts up to 40 meters—both power and sail—in steel, aluminum and GRP. We certainly have the talent.

"We do have quite a tradition here to honor. I think we have a name that is the most famous in the world—I mean it has to be; it started back in 1782—and I feel very strongly that we must live up to that name *and* reputation. By that I don't just mean how we build the boats; I mean the total integrity of all the people who work here. About 85 percent of our boats go to America, and I think that we have to prove to people a few thousand miles away that they can indeed trust us and will enjoy working with us. I feel that with every boat you have to sell a little bit of yourself. My wife always asks me, 'just how many can you afford to sell?' and I answer that 'I'm fairly large, so a few more yet.'

"When prospective owners come here—I mean it's not a grandiose office, it used to be our mast house —one of the things that I find important and most satisfying is that as you sit and talk here for a while, you begin to see them relax and grow to trust you. That to me is extremely rewarding, and I must say even flattering. When people, the husband and wife or husband and mistress, look at each other and then say to you—and it's happened a lot of times although the words are always a little different—'Tony, we have a very good feeling about this. We feel happy.' Then *I* feel very good because I feel that somehow I have conveyed to them the integrity of Camper and Nicholsons, an integrity that has been built up over two hundred years. I know that may sound a bit idealistic, but that is how I feel about this company."

We walked from the old mast house and crossed Quay Lane, and across the harbor the setting sun lit up the rigging on *Victory*.

In small buildings beside the great brick shed where C.E. Nicholson greeted his clients long ago are a maze of old shops and lofts and stairs and attics, neat but well lived in, like a good place out of Dickens. Everywhere we walked the men greeted Tony, men like "Stumpy" Mugford, who has spent forty years as a rigger at Campers and to whom rope makers now come to learn how to work a splice with their new ropes. And men like Mr. Weighell who has been here thirty-five years, doing every kind of master woodworking imaginable. We stopped inside the great brick shed with the late autumn sun pouring through the skylights, the great shed where *Creole* was built in 1929. The shed is vast, nearly 30 feet in height, but *Creole's* builders had to duck their heads beneath the beams as they walked her deck, and the shed is a hundred and fifty feet in length and she still stuck out the end by nearly forty. But now in *Creole's* place the Nicholson hulls gleamed. The quality of fiberglass work is one of the finest in the world.

"We now use isophthalic gelcoats," Tony explains, "as well as isophthalic resin in the veil layer as a preventative measure against osmosis. As a further precaution, we use only powderbound mats and rovings, for in the past we found that the emulsion holding the fibers together was not totally dissolved by the resins. Now when that occurred, the resin was unable to penetrate between the fibers, leaving tiny microscopic voids between the fibers and the resin. Through these voids the water was osmosed, causing what we call here 'the pox.'

"The *58* has a balsa cored topside which ends 8 inches above the waterline so you get the positive aspects of coring —stiffness without weight, and good insulation—without its negative one, which is potential water absorbency below the water. We don't like the idea of having a balsa core below the waterline, where you may just get seepage or some sort of water penetration in time, through a rather thin skin. If you weigh some cored boats five years after you build them, you will find the boats have gained sometimes as much as 20 percent of the original hull weight. It's quite colossal. Hence we use core structure only above the waterline. But even here it has disadvantages, for the thin outer layer is not as impact resistant or as abrasion-resistant as a thicker, uncored laminate. So to compensate we put Kevlar into the outer laminate in way of the topside core and in the forward half of the bottom."

When I said in amazement that C.N. is almost unique in an industry which uses Kevlar mostly on one-off racing boats, Tony smiled and said, "We don't use it in the same way as those people or for the same reason. If we were using the Kevlar for tensile strength, we would put it on the inside, but we use it for abrasion resistance and impact resistance, so we put it on the outside. This seems to make the hulls bulletproof. One of our owners was a little skeptical, so we made up a small panel for him, identical to the hull, and he took it out behind his house in Palm Beach, stood it up against a fence post and from 40 feet opened up on the poor thing with five handguns. Not one bullet passed through the laminate. That Kevlar is jolly good stuff.

"And we use balsa instead of the closed cell foams because since balsa is absorbent, it will pick up a lot of the resin from the wet mat it's layed into, so that we are assured that there won't be any delamination between skin and core."

The more I find out about coring materials, the more I find out that balsa still seems to be the best.

Below the water, the hull is further stiffened by fiberglass floor beams which reinforce the hull against the torquing of the keel. The engineering of these beams is perhaps the best in the industry. They are hollow units with their walls built of unidirectional roving which is fairly common, but what is excellent about them is that they are cleverly tapered upward and are faired *into* the hull so you won't get a hard spot anywhere—a common occurrence if you have a heavily built stiff beam meeting a more flexible hull skin. There are also longitudinal beams down here to give the hull more stiffness.

One of the best things about Nicholsons is their bulkhead installation. To preserve the hull shape and make sure that the bonds adhere perfectly to the hull, they put the bulkheads in while the hulls are still in the mold which is fairly common with the best of the best, but what is nearly unique is that the structural bulkheads are marine plywood which will later be *covered* with a layer of teak ply. Now the good thing about this is that the bulkhead can be ground mercilessly back on a broad bevel as far as 8 inches (most people do 2 or 3 inches), exposing the beveled ends of the plywood layers. This means that the fiberglass will not be bonding to only a *single* outer layer of veneer, but rather to *every* layer. You might say that's a pretty small thing, but then it's the many small things that make the difference between a yacht and a floating nightmare. And there is a nice aesthetic advantage to this as well. Since the bonding and the bulkhead will be covered with teak, there is no need for large flat pieces of trim which have a definite look of unsubstantiality about them.

To create an extremely solid hull-to-deck joint, the hull has an enormous 8-inch-wide flange upon which the deck sits. As a nice touch, the flange is abraded or roughened up to aid adhesion to the wet mat that is layed over it. The deck flange molding turns up to create a bulwark, and the ensuing void is flooded with a thickened resin mixture to give additional strength. As if that weren't enough, the stanchions are through-bolted to further hold the hull and deck together.

All construction is well in excess of Lloyds standards. In a *46* that was half complete, I could see the monstrous fiberglass floorbeams, an average of 10 to 20 inches in depth, tapered upward and faired where they come up the sides of the hull. The longitudinals running along the waterline average 4 inches in depth and are completely interlocked with the transverse beams, creating great unified rigidity in the keel area. The beams are all limbered for absolute drainage.

The stainless steel fuel and water tanks in the Nicholsons are all 316 stainless. The tanks are set onto foam pads so there is no hard edge or corner sitting on the laminate. Then two-part foam is poured around the tank to avoid any movement, and then the tank is bonded to the hull much the same way as a bulkhead. Tony insists on this method because, apart from solidly holding the tanks, (which are later held in place by wood floor pieces or furniture) it prevents anything —a tool, rubbish, anything—from falling between the tank and the hull and staying there for good. He calls it "just good housekeeping," but in truth this method also prevents potential electrolysis between the tank and whatever metal object may have fallen next to it.

Now, even though they use 316 stainless which will not

Camper and Nicholsons have improved steadily since the inception of the company over two hundred years ago. In the first half of this century they became the world's foremost builders of luxury yachts in wood and steel, and today they build some of the very best fiberglass boats, ranging from their much-respected *31* and *35* to the new *58*, which you see in the photos on these two pages. From their long experience, Nicholsons has well established criteria as to what makes a boat beautiful, and thus uses classically modest lines, avoiding all extremes; lines which bespeak a yacht at first glance. The underbodies of the new boats are very modern, canoe-shaped, with fin keels and skeg rudders and big powerful rigs to move them along at a good clip. The construction methods are as modern as the designs, using balsa core to provide stiffness and light weight; isophthalic resins to guard against what they here call "the pox"; and even such exotic materials as Kevlar to guard against abrasion. With their state-of-the-art construction, classic lines and meticulously crafted interiors, Nicholsons are exactly what fine yachts should be.

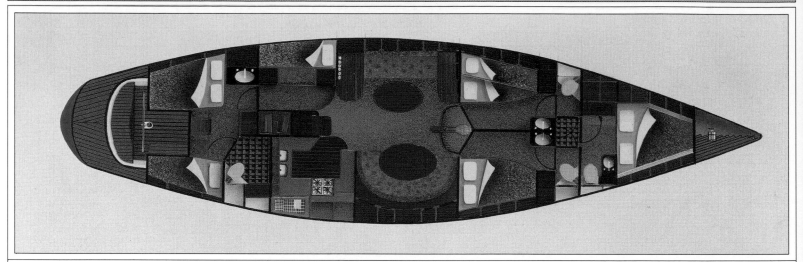

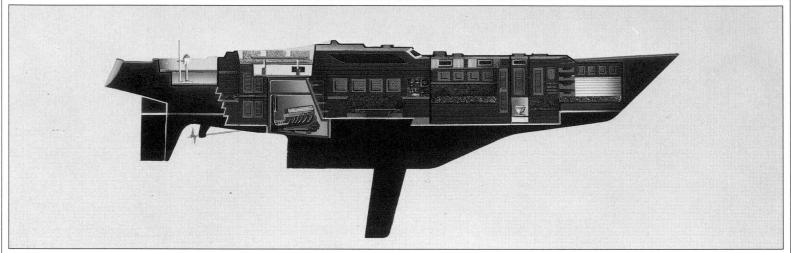

The interiors of the big Nicholsons show an attitude carried over from great yachts of the past. The key word belowdecks seems to be comfort. The double berths are well proportioned and beautiful to boot.

The salons are spacious and filled with light through the many hatches and long but low profiled windows. The 58 comes with a number of interiors, one of which is perfect for long distance cruising with a vast sail locker and a good number of excellent sea berths, while another is a charter captain's dream, having four private double-cabins, and a fifth one for himself. The latter interior comes equipped with four heads, each with its own sink, so that the toilet needs of the crew need not take up most of each day. The styling is very clean and the workmanship precise, befitting the Nicholsons tradition.

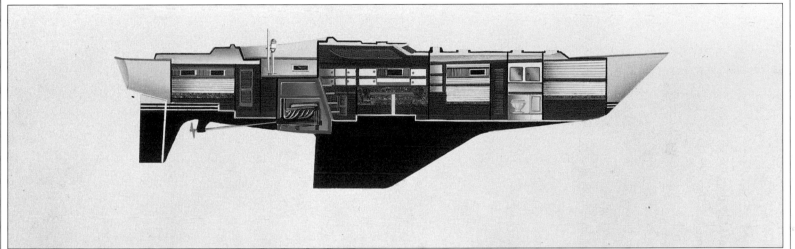

A boatyard is only as good as the craftsmen who work it, and Camper and Nicholsons has some of the very best. On the red page you can see Mr. "Stumpy" Mugford, the master of all rigging, be it wire, hemp or dacron, a man who can splice anything to anything given a little time. He has been head rigger at Nicholsons for four decades now and has added his share of good cheer to the place. A real character in the best sense. Heading the blue page is Mr. Weighell, who has been at Nicholsons for thirty-five years

and is their senior master woodworker, is shown here fitting removable table fiddles with brass dye-makers' plugs and sleeve so the holes will never become loose, not in a thousand years. Most boatyards would cherish the delicate hand tools he uses as museum pieces, but with them Mr. Weighell and the other craftsmen execute some of the finest yacht cabinet work in the world today. The rest of the blue-clad Nicholsons crew turn out excellent work in all departments: perfectly pre-fit teak decks; massively bonded bulkheads aided by broadly beveled bulkhead-edges and equally broad laminates; louvered door pieces cut to the intricacy of a Chinese puzzle; and installations that could generally withstand the inspection of the Queen, never mind old Lloyds of London. They even put brass labels on all their petcocks so you always know exactly what you're turning off or on. Oh, the thoughtful little luxuries of life.

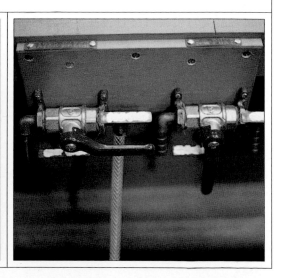

oxidize or pit like 304 stainless sometimes does, they worry about the entrapment of carbon in the welds which *will* corrode. To avoid this, they wire brush the welded seams and coat them with epoxy and then paint the entire tank. Let me tell you that is a lot more than just good housekeeping.

And now for a few more tidbits to show you all the care they take. The wood floorbeams which support the cabinsole are nicely installed with the first stainless steel joist hangers I have ever seen.

Conduits are glassed into the hull from stern to bow so all wiring is safely concealed and sheathed.

The cockpit drain systems is the very best. Molded fiberglass tubing gelcoated inside is laminated directly to the cockpit sole and the hull so the chance of leakage or damage is virtually nil. It's not even worth comparing these to the traditional drain-fitting-and-rubber-hose mess, whose hose can be cut or collapsed and whose clamp joints can cut through the hose or sometimes loosen off.

Tony pointed to the engine room with pride. "We have managed to mount and install our generators in good fashion. We actually had an owner and his skipper come aboard once, and the skipper asked the owner if he'd like him to flash up the generator to see what it sounded like. The owner was just coming down the companionway and he said, 'Yes please Dave, flash it up.' So David smiled at him and said, 'It's already running.' "

Of course this kind of craftsmanship takes time. A 58 requires 17,500 man hours to complete *after* the hull and deck are molded.

"We learn from long experience," Tony went on. "We like to do a lot of maintenance and repair work, because we feel it's an excellent way of keeping track of ourselves, keeping track of just how well we built the boats. Seeing our boats year after year, we can learn what, if anything, should be changed, and also it makes our chaps think during building, 'I might have to repair the bloody thing in two years time, so I should think of just how to get at it!' "

The cabinet work on the Campers is excellent. The cabinet shop is full of craftsmen who make the finest fits with the most traditional of hand tools. Their work is well shown in the photos so I'll just relate one anecdote here.

"Some years ago," Tony begins with a smile, "some blokes from the Chris Craft Corporation came over here—they wanted us to build their sailboats for them—and they passed through the wood shop and saw our chaps at their benches working with bevel squares and small handplanes and whatnot, and one of their supervisors walks up to our shipwright and says, 'Gee. You actually know how to use them things?' Our poor chap didn't know whether to laugh or cry."

P.S. Since the above was written—three printings ago— Mr. Taylor has retired and Mr. Jim McEwan—whose years of shipbuilding experience includes supervision of a refitting of the QE2—is now Managing Director at Campers. With his arrival the line has once again grown to include a just-launched 83 foot sailboat and motoryachts to 115 feet. The quality remains unchanged.

And so the fine craftsmanship—a sadly rare sight today—still goes on in the great brick shed at ''Campers'' as it has now for two hundred years. And so it should. In these times of great impermanence and change, it somehow feels good that the nation that once ruled the waves still builds some of the finest yachts in all the world.

CHERUBINI

T his chapter on the Cherubinis was the toughest in this book to write. The winter sun was low and there was snow in Central Park and an icy wind shook the naked branches. Strewn around the floor were pictures of Cherubinis—ketches and great schooners, with fine clipper bows and beautiful long sheers and varnished house sides glowing, and as I stared at them I could almost hear the warm blue water rushing by, and I kept saying to myself, "What the hell are you doing here when you should be on that schooner sailing in the South Seas."

The boats of Frit and his son Lee Cherubini are certainly the stuff of dreams. As you can tell at first glance, you are looking at a proud descendant of the great *Ticonderoga* of L. Francis Herreshoff, and that is no coincidence, for both Frit and his brother John, who drew up the lines, had a lifelong love affair with the works of Francis Herreshoff.

Now there have been designs based on legends that have turned out to be nightmares, but in this case one would have to think that the perfect lines of the Cherubinis would make L. Francis proud. As you know, the smaller the boat the greater the designer's challenge, for the more difficult it is to keep lines graceful and proportionate and balanced, especially if it's a long-distance cruiser you are after, one that has to sail well and carry with it a goodly load of gear. And even if the designer does succeed, as John Cherubini did, in bringing out the best in a design, his efforts will have been wasted unless he finds himself a builder who can do his good plans justice, not only by building a boat that's nice and shiny, but by building her with integrity, to take the ravages of the sea.

Lucky for John Cherubini that his brother Frit is a boatbuilder whose mania is perfection, and lucky for Frit that his brother John had a perfect eye for beauty. If you think those are superlatives, you ain't heard nothin' yet.

I have known Frit and his son Lee for going on five years now, and the one thing that strikes me each time that I see them is that their enthusiasm for the the boats they build not only doesn't fade with time but actually blooms. To say that they are obsessed with their boats would be like saying that the universe is big. They live boats and breathe boats and even name their kids after designers of boats. Nathaniel Cherubini is five years old and there are two things he likes to do: shoot a mean game of pool and mess around in his dad's and granddad's boatyard. When you ask him what he'll be when he grows up, he looks at you kind of puzzled as if to say, "Well isn't it obvious?" but just to be sure he says, "Boatbuilder." I mean, is the Pope Catholic?

Then there are Scott and Nora-Louise the teenage Cherubinis who work in the shop on Saturdays, and cousin Joe who, along with Ed Durphy, is crew leader and boat carpenter extraordinaire. And in the background holding things together is Mark Kramer, who has been with them from the start and now looks after production; and Bruce, who does procurement as well as all the drafting. Then of course there are the Cherubini ladies without whom the whole thing would have been just a dream, and I don't mean maybe.

The Cherubinis are now in a pretty little boatshop they just built for themselves on the shores of the Delaware River, with their own docks and a marina next door whose hoist can wander right into the yard to launch or haul the boats. Now when I say "boatshop" you have to realize that this is a family type affair that can hold a total of four boats at a time if they snuggle.

But let's talk about the boats. First there is a Cherubini 44 ketch whose design is perfect, then there is a Cherubini 48 schooner whose design is perfect, and the construction of both boats is perfect too, so the only question still remaining is how to get my hands on one and run away to sea.

For those among you who are sticklers for detail and can tear your eyes away from the pictures for a moment, I'll mention a few odds and ends. The *44* has a regal, lively sheer, just enough tumblehome to give her a look of strength, and an absolutely graceful deckhouse that comes as one piece, or for the more traditionally-minded, split in two at the main mast. I'm getting the split one.

The keel is very long, yet the fore foot is well cut back for ease of coming about and ease of handling in tight quarters and the draft has been kept to only 4 feet 10 inches by the use of Henry Scheel's miraculous patented keel. The Cherubinis have used this keel for nearly a decade now, and perhaps it took an aeronautical engineer like John and a constant tinkerer like Frit to appreciate its fine qualities that so many have, until now, ignored. I say "until now" because there are four builders in this book now regularly using the Scheel keel, including one of the most respected and most conservative, Nautor, who builds the Swans.

The theory behind this stout wing keel is that, (a) it gets the bulk of the weight down low where it's needed, and (b) it "cups" the water as it claws to weather, thereby having a better grip than a simple fin would have. If you squint a bit when you look at the lines dead on, you'll notice the keel bears a resemblance to the wings of *Australia II.* Nuff said.

Now look at the profile drawing of the *44.* What will strike you if you look closely is her enormous waterline length. She is 40 feet on the waterline, and what that means is that she'll hit 9 knots on a reach and surf happily at 11. Her displacement-to-waterline-length ratio of under 200 and her sail-area-to-displacement of almost 20 means that she is going to go like a bat out of hell, and will certainly accelerate very well in light airs. To validate that, she took first place overall in the seventh annual 160 mile Fort Lauderdale to Key West race, beating boats like *The Dealer, Running Tide,* and *Stars and Stripes* on corrected time. No mean feat that.

Of course the boat is powered by 1,133 square feet of sail meaning you'll have your work cut out hoisting and dousing, but then all that will keep you young and strong. And she is a staysail ketch, meaning that your headsails can be kept moderate of size.

The deck layout of the *44* is an absolute marvel, and I don't just mean the broad comfortable side decks and the perfect visibility for the helmsman; I mean also the beautifully-shaped twin cockpits, with the elliptical one for the helmsman and the square one for the rabble; the well-placed jib winches which can be worked comfortably from either cockpit; and as mentioned before, the harmonious blending of house, coaming and hull.

The 48-foot Cherubini schooner might just be every romantic yachtsman's dream. I'm not sure what it is about those damned schooners but there is a certain nobility and serenity about them, and maybe even a sense of eternity.

Everything I said about the *44* goes for the schooner as well: the grace, the balance, the speed and the beauty, with the added feature of more room down below, and, in spite of what you may think, the relative ease of handling of the rig. Before you start objecting, remember that the *48* has only 80 square feet more sail than the *44,* and a schooner, by virtue of the smaller foremast, will carry smaller headsails which are normally the things that call for hand-to-hand combat anyway. You can, if you wish, equip her with furling gear, but then you deprive yourself of the sight of a great headsail billowing down to the sun-warmed deck, and since you chose this damned boat for her beauty in the first place, you might as well go all the way and enjoy every quirk.

Oh yes, before I forget. If you look at the entry of both hulls you will see that they are very fine indeed, and flair broadly near the sheer. The fine entry means you'll go windward like a banshee but the flair will take over when you begin to plough deep, and will stop the boat from burying her bow. Bow burying not only impedes your progress but it also increases your chances of pitchpoling when you run from a typhoon. But more commonly, the flair makes the Cherubinis dry and comfortable to sail.

Then there are the smaller thoughtful details which make the Cherubinis a joy to be aboard. The openings in the deckhouses, namely the hatches and the skylights, show the Cherubinis' creative tinkering genius. The hatch boards, instead of following the verticality of the end of the house, are actually framed to slope *out* away from the house end. This means that you can leave your hatch closed but the boards *out* in bad weather, allowing you to go below quickly and safely without having to do hurdles, and enabling the boat to remain well ventilated in the tropics in the rain. There is nothing worse than having a nice refreshing downpour in the tropics only to be forced to batten down the boat as if she were a submarine.

The portlights are designed to serve in the same manner. Look closely at the illustration and after you stop laughing, try to comprehend that these are the best portlights in existence, the only ones that can be left open in the rain. The casting is one piece, meaning that the sleeve is an integral part of the inner piece, in turn meaning that any water that falls within it will be stopped by the returns and drain directly out. The piece of edge-ground tempered glass sits in the trough loose. When shut, it is held against the rubber gasket firmly by the wooden wedges. In the rain it can be leaned back against the returns, stopping the rain from slanting in but allowing the air to circulate freely above it.

Now for belowdecks. The Cherubinis build their boats on a semi-custom basis which, in essence, means they'll listen to your wishes. Most things work well in their suggested layouts, but, as I say, you can do what you like. But if you know what's good for you don't touch the aft cabin on the schooner. It's vast and airy, and as comfortable as most houses and as livable as most great cabins of old, but I'd raise the chart table to stand-at height. The story related by Lee of how that layout was arrived at is a perfect example of lucid reasoning.

"We kicked around that layout for months. Pulling our hair out moving everything around in every position at least ten times. Then we came in one Saturday morning, Dad and I, after celebrating a launching the night before, both quiet as church mice, barely alive, and we started erasing lines. This and that; a bit here a bit there, and I tell you within a

half hour we had that layout finished. It was as if we had to be in a stupor to do it."

Now if you have thought the designs to be impressive, listen to how the boats are built because that's really the best part. Only the hulls of the Cherubinis are made of fiberglass —and very well layed up as you will read later—but the rest of the boat is built entirely of wood and then epoxied over. The very vital exception to this is the cockpit which, with its many joints and corners, is traditionally the most rot vulnerable part of a wood deck structure. So Frit and Lee have built the cockpit as a one-piece fiberglass unit that incorporates the entire aft section of the boat. Bravo.

Anway, as I said, the house and sidedecks are all wood, and here is how that's done. First look at the drawing to get an idea of what's doing, then read on. The flange you see coming off the hull is layed up as an integral portion. There are two layers of biaxial roving that form the flange, then— and I don't think anyone else does this—two more layers of biaxial come down from the top to support and reinforce the whole flange from above. Next, 1⅜-inch by 2⅜-inch mahogany beams are layed in on 12-inch centers and bolted to the shelf. A double layer of ⅜ inch prefinished marine ply decking is epoxied and screwed to the beams, then through-bolted to the sheerclamp on 4-inch centers. Next a ⅞-inch plank is epoxied to the inner side of the bulwark to lock the deck mechanically to the sheer clamp.

The sides of the cabin are 1⅜-inch solid mahogany, vertically through-bolted to the deck with twenty-two pieces of stainless steel all-thread plus 4½-inch stainless steel screws on 4 inch centers. Ought to hold.

The cabin top is cold-molded on a jig, out of three layers of ¼" marine ply with each layer drenched in epoxy to assure good adhesion. Then the preformed top is screwed onto the house sides. Now comes an exceptional part. Traditionally the second most vulnerable part of such construction is the cabin-side-to-deck joint, for here cracks could develop because of the extreme angle. To avoid this, the Cherubinis lay a cove of epoxy putty all around the base of the house as well as the base of the bulwark, so that when the cloth and epoxy come over all this to enbalm the whole structure, the cloth won't have to make a sharp bend, but makes a gentle curve instead. In ten years of building, these joints have never leaked, and I saw hull Number Two sitting there as good as new.

The sides of the house can be painted out or, if you wish, overlayed with teak. (Mom, send some money. Quick!) This kind of construction not only looks beautiful on the outside and saves about 1,500 pounds, but it also creates a beautifully-finished underdeck with varnished beams and painted wood in between instead of the Naugahide or astroturf or fake dog hair that you often see on production boats.

Then there are the hulls. First of all they carry a *lifetime* warranty to the original owner because they are so well done. All the fibers used are unidirectional or biaxial—no more resin-heavy woven roving—and they go something like this: Gelcoat, mat, mat, cloth, two layers of 9-ounce unidirectional running diagonally, then two more layers of 9-ounce unidirectional running diagonally at 90 degrees to the first two layers. Then layers of the same stuff run fore and aft, then two layers athwartships. Then some coremat to deaden sound and offer some heat insulation as well, then two layers of 24-10 biaxial roving to finish off the inside. Whew. And that's just in the topsides; there is lots more in the turns and even more down the keel.

Each layer of laminate is not just rolled to get the excess resin out but also hand squeegeed. Lee calculates that by using the new unidirectional fibers instead of the woven roving, and hand squeegeeing instead of just rolling, they can save almost two barrels of resin per hull. Not only does this save money and excess weight, but it also makes for more fiber-dense, thus stronger, laminates.

I very much like the way the ballast is layed in. Lead pigs are set into a a shallow pool of epoxy to bond this first row to the bottom of the keel, then the spaces between the lead are filled up by bits of lead you get from wheel-balancing shops. Next a little molten lead is poured over the whole show to fill what voids are left, melt the pigs together to form the base for the next layer of lead pigs. So what you end up with is a perfectly solid unbudgeable mass that is then bonded over.

The bulkheads are all set onto fillets of foam so they don't sit hard against the hull and are bonded all the way around with massive layers of bonding.

The chainplates—really Navtec U-bolts through the deck —are reinforced by a webbing of unidirectional roving that runs athwartships from gunwale to gunwale. This webbing is 5 feet wide. It's made of two layers of 34-ounce triaxial (equal to six layers of unidirectional) which creates the preform, then they hang three layers of 27-ounce unidirectional on that, then they reinforce *that* with a strip of ¼-inch stainless 2 inches wide that runs the full 5 feet of the web.

The tanks are aluminum—the best material for diesel with the exception of monel—and to prevent any exterior corro-sion the tanks are epoxy coated. They are designed to be easily removed for cleaning.

If you can afford the cost, they will build you traditional raised panels over the bulkhead, and if you can't afford the boat, at least get a couple of these panels and stick them in your front room. They are beautiful!

Now I had better shut up soon or you'll fall asleep before you get to see the pictures, so here are some more goodies in a nutshell:

The *44* takes about 10,000 man hours to complete.

The drawers are solid wood—not plywood.

The floors are plywood bulkheads, stiffened with 1-inch by 3-inch solid wood on either side.

There is a magnificent piece of molded corner about 8 inches in radius that is made up of twelve beveled pieces of solid mahogany. If you wondered before where the 10,000 man hours went, now you can begin to know.

The cockpits hold the least amount of water on any large boat I have seen, for they are kept reasonably shallow with the seats high, which gives you very good views forward.

There are beautiful bronze castings for the main track. The stanchions are solid stainless—not hollow tubing—machined out of ⅞-inch stock.

The main skylight is an enormous 36 by 30 inches and traditional and beautiful.

All the hatches and the turtle hatches have the wood strips that they're made of splined. That means a third strip of wood is let into each of two adjoining pieces to eliminate any cracking, warping or movement.

The propane tank is just outside the main hatch in an isolated box in the bridgedeck, eliminating a lot of lengthy tubing and gives you direct access to a shut-off valve on the tank very close to the galley. With his valve *off* when the stove is not in use, the chance of being blown halfway to China is virtually eliminated.

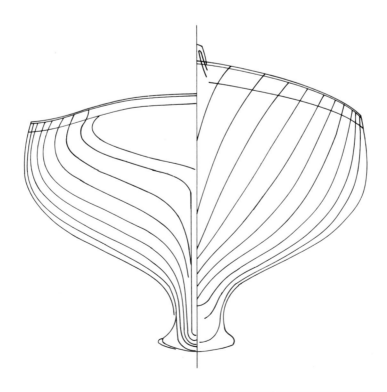

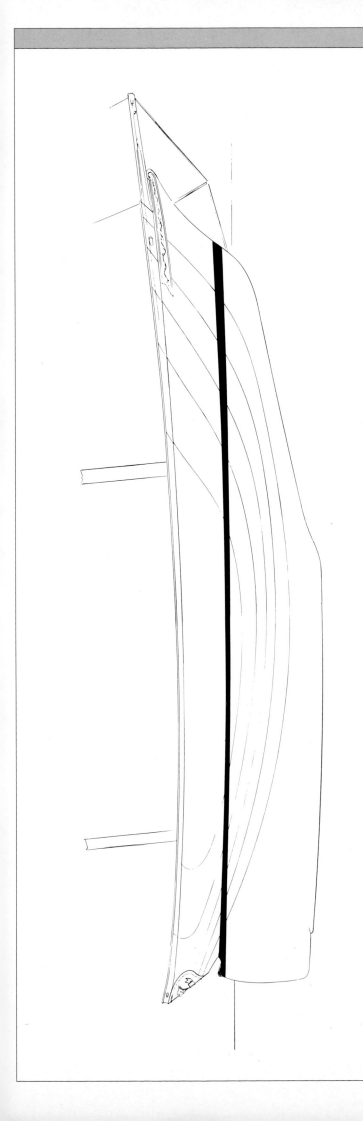

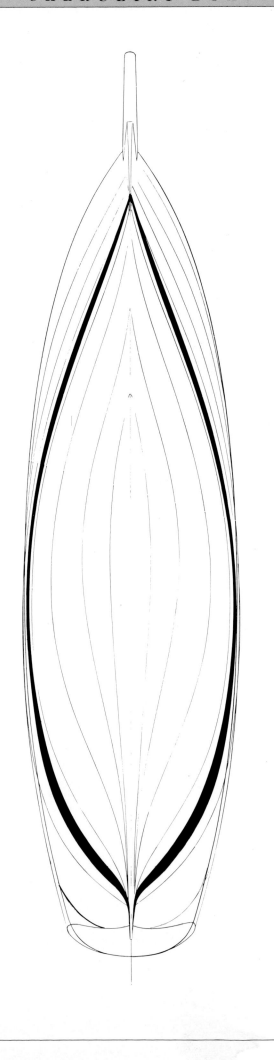

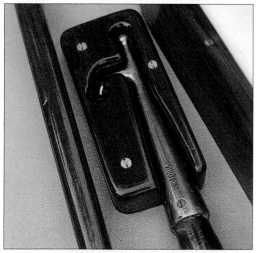

How can you say enough about these boats? The pictures are much more eloquent than I can be with words, and the handiwork of the Cherubinis speaks well enough on its own, so I'll just be a tour guide and point out a few odds and ends. The photo on the title page is of Frit Cherubini himself, founder of the yard now presided over by his son Lee, who is just as maniacal about perfection as his dad. The next double page shows the queen of the Cherubini yard, the beautiful 48-foot schooner designed—as was the *42*—by Frit's brother, John.

The lines and grace of both are those of a perfect yacht. And the boats sail extremely well; a thing that's often lacking in boats of such great character and beauty. The exterior photos depict the world's most beautifully designed cockpit, with an elliptical helmsman's area, similarly beautiful elliptical grates, and a teak-lined helmsman's seat whose elegantly swirled scarfs align perfectly with the joint of the lazarette cover to the covering board. Now that's perfection. In the photo with the skylight, you can see a deck storage box that is truly a masterpiece. It smoothly incorporates dorade boxes and an airhorn, and even a pair of Lexan pieces to provide more light belowdecks. The solid teak hatch cover behind it has its pieces splined together for longevity and beauty. Unique details like the varnished teak holder for the boathook upon whose end is engraved the boat's name seem to be the norm at Cherubini.

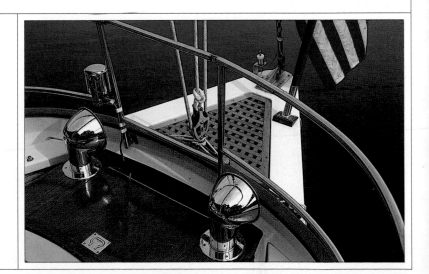

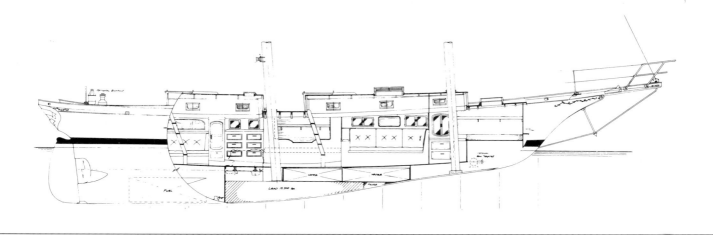

The interiors of the Cherubinis are so beautiful that you might end up just sitting below staring, and not once leave the harbor. The most striking thing belowdecks is the relief in the bulkheads, a classic touch which you will rarely find on any yacht. The cane doors are as beautifully made as an antique violin, with all curves perfect and the seams aligned. The portlights—a Cherubini invention—are guaranteed to keep the water out even if left open in a rainstorm. A great advantage offered by the Cherubinis, shared only by a handful of yachts in this book, is that if you are not very rich, and you take pride in working with your hands, then Lee Cherubini will be happy to sell you a boat finished to whatever stage you like.

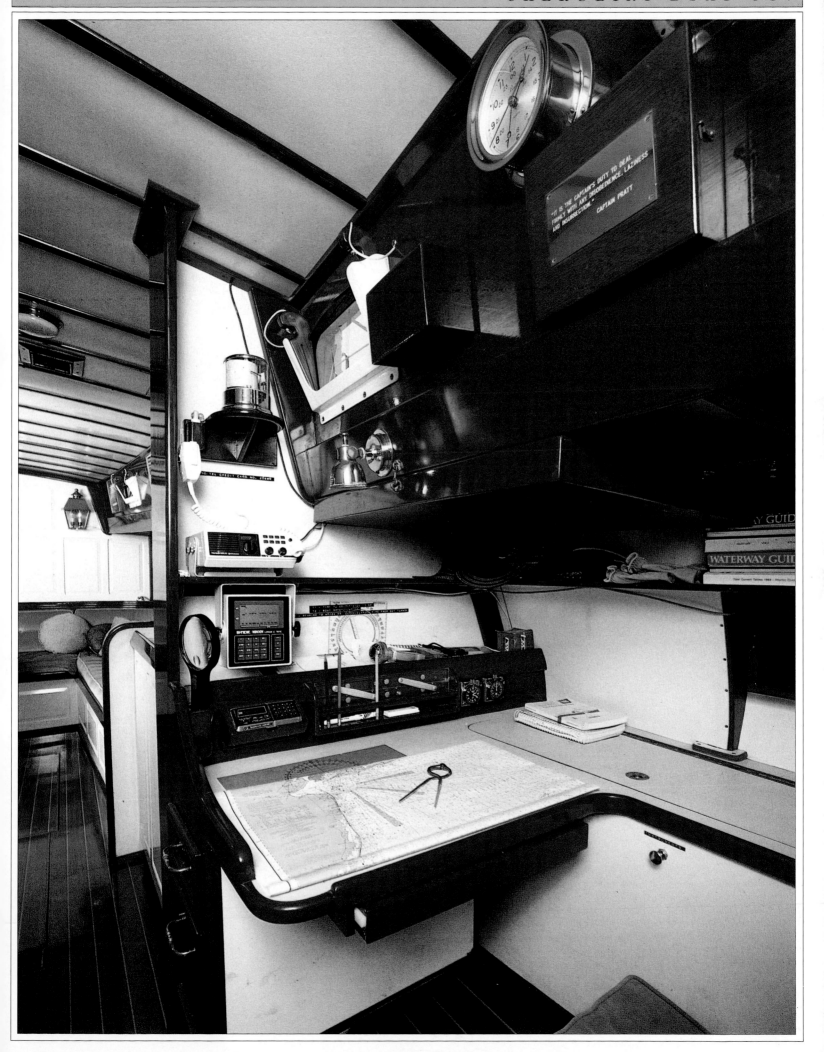

"IT IS THE CAPTAIN'S DUTY TO DEAL
FIRMLY WITH ANY DISOBEDIENCE, LAZINESS
AND INSUBORDECTION." CAPTAIN PRATT

WATERWAY GUIDE

John Cherubini once said, "A yacht should be graceful enough to be worthy of the sea." The ones he designed certainly are. And to that can be added that a yacht should be built well enough to show the sea respect. The ones that Frit and Lee and little Nathan build are certainly among them. □ We owe much to the sea. Not only for what she gives us in sustenance and beauty, but also for all the horrors that we have committed upon her. We should thank the Cherubinis for starting to pay our debts.

CAMBRIA

I n boatbuilding of days gone by, it was commonplace to find the *complete builder* on our shores, the builder who could also design fine lines for a yacht, then in his own shops give them life with good craftsmanship and care, and at the end set on the sea a craft of complete vision. There were men like Bill Luders and Bill Atkin and Herreshoff himself, whose convictions and beliefs seeped into the boats at every step, whose honesty and hard-earned knowledge created yachts of truly fine quality and beauty. Few such men remain today, but David Walters up in Newport keeps the tradition alive.

David Walters didn't just start building good boats overnight. He was building himself rowboats when he was a kid, then he learned to sail and soon sailed well enough to become national champion in his Bluejay. He began working with big boats at Allied, where the first fiberglass boat to complete a circumnavigation was built, then in his twenties he ran his own boatyard, providing service and repairs, and finally in '75 his big dream came true when he and Walter Shulz began the company called Shannon, which in a few short years became one of the world's finest builders. But one day he decided he had done all he could at Shannon, sold his half to Walter and went off to create a new boat all his own, one that would have modern lines to compete with the world's finest.

But his experience with sailboats didn't become landlocked with his Bluejay days, he kept going back to sea to learn what she demanded of a boat. He sailed in races of all kinds, from Block Island to SORC; from Fastnet to Bermuda, so when he sat down to design his boat he knew what kind of craft it took to sail fast across the seas in comfort and security.

He didn't rush. He never does. He spent six months doing research before developing his design. Weeks went into perfecting the sheer—the biggest single item that decides a vessel's looks—until he achieved one that nicely blended the classic and the modern. Then he spent months on the lines, followed by computer testing with one of the best prediction programs to achieve the ideal in all-round performance. Then he gathered a small expert crew and began to loft the hull. And he did it in his own tenacious way that doesn't stop until he gets things perfect, then he takes a little breather and does a little more—just in case.

So it was with the plugs for the molds. When the plugs were fair, smooth as a baby's bottom, the crew went back and faired some more, to the point where glasswork on David Walter's boats is truly second to none. And it's not only the hull that's fair but the entire deck mold, every cranny every nook as beautifully smooth as you could ask for. The best proof is found when you sight along the long curved edge of the fine-radiused cabin top—a radius so fine that most builders avoid it, especially in such length because it tends to show up all the flaws. The cabin top edge of David's boat is perfect. And this is true of every aspect of his boat for as he points out as selflessly as possible, his small proud crew of thirty seems to care about their work just as much as he does.

"I named the boats *Cambria,*" David explains slowly, "because the name stood for a lot of things that I believe in. *Cambria* is a Welsh name. My grandparents came from Wales so I named the boat after the mountains there, or rather the people in them—a simple, hardworking lot who enjoy their families. We have a lot of that type working here so I thought it would be a good name for the boat."

Now coming from a lot of people a statement like that would sound sentimental, but David Walters is so honest about his feelings and convictions that you can't help but be touched.

But back to the boats.

The *Cambria's* lines may just become classics. The sheer is elegant but speaks of speed, the long flat trunk is perfectly sized—barely 5 inches at its forward end—the bow is fine and nicely angled, the stern is powerful but kept visually pleasing, and if you prefer the traditional transom they will build that too. In short, David achieved a yacht with its own unique good looks without going to extremes or even calling on colored striping or varnished wood for help. The boat just works.

And with its long waterline and the full lines aft, she will be a fine sailer indeed, moved by a modern rig that carries 1,000 feet of sail with the head sails split for easier sail handling. For a keel, you have as broad a choice as possible: deep fin or shoal fin or a centerboard. On deck the Cambria is exceedingly pleasing with broad, clear sidedecks and double cockpit and double companionway which allow for a complete division of the boat into two large private areas of excellent proportions. This arrangement will not please those who prefer spacious cockpits where the whole crew can lounge and where you can stretch out to sun or sleep under the stars, but then to achieve that arrangement you would either have to raise the stern and create unpleasant lines or give up the perfectly sized aft cabin. You just can't have everything on a 44-foot boat.

The aft cabin should not be touched, for it's the best I've seen on a boat under 50 feet. Floorspace and headroom are excellent, the double berth is large and accessible and airy, the chart table is enormous—and what can be more fun than to work your charts in your own private stateroom—and the aft head is so vast that there is a true sit-down shower stall next to the head compartment.

The fore-and-aft galley is ideal, for the engine room bulkhead will give good support in any seas without your being strapped in. The salon is perfect and the forward cabin is just that—a true cabin—with its own head, vast lockers and a big berth that *at last* has good space for four human feet.

What will strike you, aside from the the layout, is what ad people call a "quiet elegance" of detailing. All cabinetwork is well thought out, proportionate and practical—like the kick-space below the galley counters so you can do your work without stubbing your toes. The execution of joints and cornerposts and trim pieces is among the very best. This in part is due to David's good taste, but also to a large degree to Phil Galgarneau, who runs the woodshop, and pattern specialist Kenny Wright who did woodwork at Rolls Royce for years, back when most of the car was still built of wood.

Phil selects Cambria's teak and goes to great lengths to find the best color and grain and then to match the grain in every cabin. Hundreds of sheets are inspected at warehouses throughout New England to choose the few that meet the color standard for the bulkheads. The solid woods and veneers for molded pieces are all hand picked by either Phil or David.

Ron Levesque is general supervisor and directs the wood finishing in the boats as well. He pre-plans and pre-fits every piece of trim, and checks for looks as well as fit, then takes it out and radiuses the edges before placing it for a final time. On the rare occasion the thing isn't perfect, it gets redone.

The exterior detailing is also masterful. The top 3 inches of the cockpit coaming is drastically sloped so it won't dig into your back; the cleats in the coaming are recessed for the same reason; a beautiful stainless bow fitting equipped with anchor roller extends 7 inches past the bow to allow for anchor stowage and to guard the gelcoat; the portlights (even the opening ones) are set directly into the fiberglass without trim rings, a job extremely time consuming, but boy are the results easy on the eyes. You begin to wonder how anyone can care so much about a boat.

"You know," David said, "I first thought of building the type of boat I'm building now when I was fourteen years old, sailing my Bluejay. Then when I saw my first Swan I thought, 'What a completely well-thought-out boat. Great lines, fine deck layout, built like a rock.' Since then I wanted to build a fast-cruising boat that was exceptionally strong. I was in the Fastnet race with Dick Carter in '67 that was pretty rough, and in '72 I was in the Bermuda race in which nine boats lost spars—the one that was compared to the Fastnet disaster race in strength. I tell you, when you see 10-foot high foaming white water coming behind you—I think we had about 60 to 70 knots of wind—you start to respect the notion that boats should be made well.

"It scares me that people know so little about the boat they spend so much money on. They just don't know what represents sound design and construction. They don't take enough time to learn about this object that they want to take offshore and risk their lives in.

"The one question I'm often asked is, 'Why does your boat cost so much more than a production boat?' Where do I start to answer?"

Well let's try the beginning. Let's start with the plug.

"It took six of us four months to build the plug and mold," David explains out in the shop. "We began with fairing paints after the wood plug was finished and glassed over, and went on longboarding for five weeks using long, two-man boards most of the time to get the truest fairing. We finished up with 1200 grit sandpaper which isn't much rougher than my sweater.

"The next important point is laminating. Tony Pavao and his two sons do our hulls and decks. Tony faired our molds, so you know what a perfectionist he is. A lot of companies start with two mats right against the gelcoat, which could be a potential problem because you can't see how flat you're rolling. We start with one layer of 1 ounce and roll it nice and tight. The result is a good bond to the gelcoat without the risk of trapped air from too thick a layup."

"Once the first layer cools, we grind the seams. We grind between every layer to remove any high spots over which the next layer would tent and create a pocket of weak resin or air. After additional layers of mat, we use layers of unidirectional roving because with unidirectional you get a stronger laminate than with woven roving whose fibers have to bend over each other. And with the uni, the fibers lie flatter so you can squeegee out more resin and end up with a better fiber-to-resin ratio. After we finish the outer skin, we bed Airex core into 1½-ounce wet mat. To get full penetration of the resin between the blocks, we first lay the Airex over a convex shape

to get the blocks to open up and let the resin in between. We don't vacuum bag because I feel that that's a blind operation.

"We carry all topside laminates up to the sheer to form the integral hull flange to which we bolt the deck. We carry all our laminates across the centerline so in the keel we have 1½ inches of solid glass. And what is really important, we hand squeegee all our laminates to remove excess resin. You know we put in over one thousand hours of fiberglass work alone into each 44, which is what most production companies put into building a complete 30-footer."

Tony Pavao is an affable man with a big friendly smile who seems to enjoy working more than most people enjoy playing.

"We have a lot of pride in our work," he says seriously, "It takes us two hours to grind the hull between layers. It's a messy job but it's the best way to build a boat, so we do it. And we don't do multi-layers in a day; that's very important. We bring the coring into the bilge, while many people stop the core at the waterline. Our engineers say that this way we have uniform strength in the hull so that the loading on the keel grid is carried more evenly."

"For our hull and deck joint," David starts again, "we use 5200 bedding compound which has 4,000 psi holding power, then we through-bolt every 4 inches.

"Our bulkheads are precut from patterns then we hand scribe them to the hull to insure that an even ¼-inch is left for a foam edging. The foam prevents hardspots on the topsides which could result when the bonding shrinks as it cures and pulls the bulkhead in against the hull. I almost forgot, we also put deep grooves in the bulkheads before we bond them to the hull so the bonds can get a better grip. Another thing I know you will like, we drill ¾-inch holes on 8-inch centers in the bulkheads all along the bonding section; then we run bundles of glass through the holes and bond them against the hull, on either side, so the bulkheads can't pop loose."

He was right; I like that.

"And we bond the bulkheads to hull, deck and cabintop with unidirectional, double bias roving—not woven roving—because this stuff is much stronger."

In one end of a long shop, Mike Cyr was down on his hands and knees on a new lofting floor he built to such perfection that over its length of 42 feet it is level to within a sixteenth of an inch. It's this kind of care right from the start that makes the boats so good.

Signs of thought and care are evident everywhere and I'll mention but a few to give you the gist. The teak decks are a full ½-inch thick so you'll have plenty of wood over the screwheads when you plug. The decks are layed into an adhesive that has a holding power of 200 pounds per square inch, which means if you want to take the teak deck off, you'll have to use a crowbar. The chainplates get bolted to a solid glass knee 1 inch thick, made of up of twelve layers of mat and roving. I counted them. The stainless steel plates themselves are ¾-inch for the backstay and ⅝-inch for the uppers, and they don't use washers, but duplicate chainplates 3/16-inch thick as backup plates, then washers, then locknuts. Ought to hold.

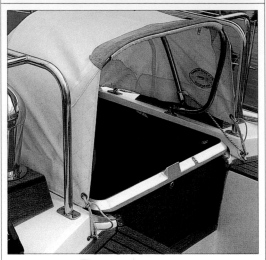

You have to admit at first glance that David Walters' Cambrias are classy-looking yachts. David—seen on the title page—in his dinghy in a picture taken some decades ago —has incorporated all the elegance and grace of yachts of old into his boats, with an added feature—a daring simplicity. This is noticeable only after studying the boats carefully, for it is only then that you notice that there are no colored stripes to embellish the boats, or much varnished wood to seduce you; there are only the well drawn lines that work so well on their own. The photos on these two pages depict only the *44* because the first *40* is just out of the mold, but as you can see in the beautiful drawings by Steve Davis if you flip the page, the proportions of the *40* are, if anything, even more pleasing. This

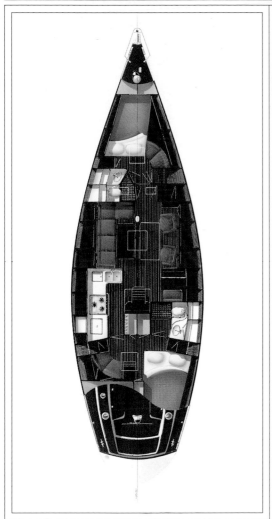

boat may just become a classic. The reverse transom in the photos seems to suit the design better, but as the drawing shows, a traditional stern is available for those who can't live without it. And you can have your choice of varnished teak or aluminum toerail to match. As you can see, the fore-triangle is split into jib and staysail, which is an excellent idea, for two small sails are infinitely easier to handle than one big one. Having always been a great fan of cutters, I can assure you that when the wind really pipes up, it's most satisfying just to reef the main and drop the jib and sail on.

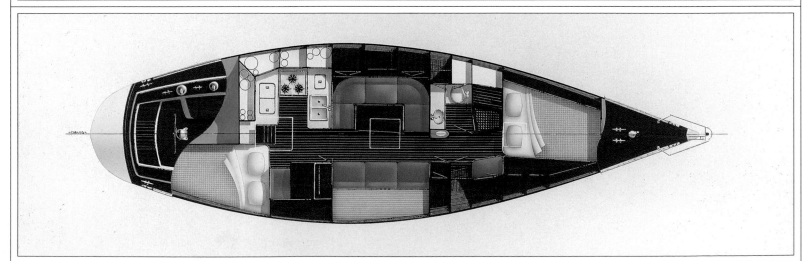

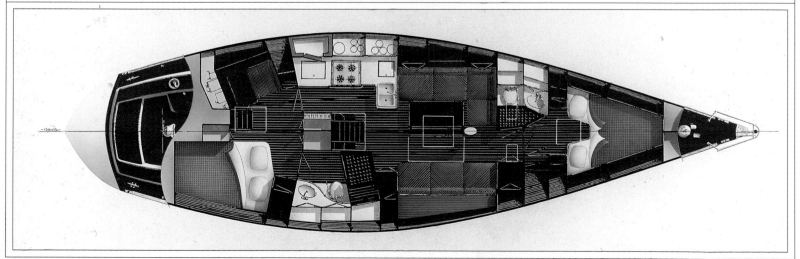

The layout of the boats is extremely good. I'll talk here mostly about the *44* because the photos are all from it. First of all go back a page, look at the layout drawings. Notice that the aft companionway comes into the vast owner's cabin. This does not only have good head and floor space, a very comfortable berth (see photo above) and a large private head with separate shower stall, but best of all, it has an enormous chart table with room for all sorts of electronics around it. The galley is perfect and the salon is intelligently proportioned, nice and cozy and full of small, useful, elegant cabinetry. But it's the small details that make the boats excellent, like the louvers in all the doors to keep the lockers vented; the shelves above the berths in both cabins for all the things you

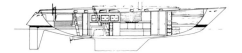

need close at hand; the nightlights—there are many throughout the boat—which will let you roam at night without waking up everybody else and, even more important, without destroying your night vision; the big piano hinges and large hand holes in the sail-bin lids; the recessed foot space under the galley counters; the insides of lockers stripped with teak; a canvas laundry bin hanging on snap pins in the aft head; cabinets varnished even on the inside, and flawless cabinet work everywhere. The best description of a Cambria would be *the complete yacht*.

When you have a boat built by David Walters, you will be delivered a yacht of excellent design, engineering and—dare I say it—good taste. His boats may not be inexpensive, but then the Cambria quality is among the world's very best. □ And you get more than just quality. □ You get many years of experience and a lot of knowledge, and you get all the heart and soul that David, Mike and Tony and the others have to give. When you're out at sea with your life depending on their handiwork, *that* can make an awful lot of difference.

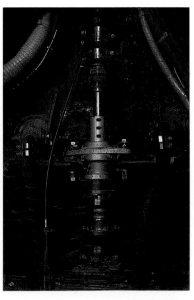

Some good construction: Left, a solid fiberglass back-up plate behind a bronze seacock, and right, a constant velocity joint that greatly reduces vibration in the hull. Builder-designer David Walters can be very proud of his achievement.

DICKERSON

Not far from Chesapeake Bay, among tall pines and corn-fields and dark meandering creeks, on the edge of woods and marshes, is a small quiet backwater with wild geese and wild swans and the modest wharves and buildings of Dickerson Boatbuilders. □ It was near here, forty years ago, that Bill Dickerson went out in his back yard, dug a hole in the ground beside the small vegetable garden, melted down some lead and poured a keel, and with that he got himself started building sailboats, setting a standard and philosophy that Dickerson Boatbuilders has followed ever since. It was best said by the name of a bugeye ketch of which he built four dozen back in the 1950's. Her name was *Simplissima*.

Simplicity was deeply rooted in the Chesapeake, in the crabmen and the oystermen who work in simple, well built craft through winter blows and summer squalls, who need their boats not as fancy yachts but good sturdy craft that won't sink beneath their feet. The Dickerson boats, like the workboats around them, were designed and built simply and well and, because of that combination, have gathered a following almost religiously devout, second on this continent only to the zealots of Henry Hinckley. One of the most fervent I happened to encounter while I lay on an operating table getting stitches in my head to close up the gash of a falling pipe wrench. He was the the surgeon doing the sewing. When he found out that I was working on this book, he immediately plunged into accolades about a Dickerson 35 he once owned, and talked nearly non-stop for an hour, during which he inserted a total of three stitches. My Granny, may she rest in peace, could have needleworked up a whole table cloth in less time, but of course the sweet dear hadn't owned a Dickerson.

Anyway, the ruggedness of Dickerson boats became so well known and respected that the US Navy hired Bill to build them some patrol boats. He still continued building fine wood sailing craft at very reasonable cost, and his boats, from the early *26* and *32* to the later *35,* gathered a great Chesapeake Bay and Long Island Sound following, whose devout members still meet in associations and regattas every sailing season.

Bill Dickerson retired almost twenty years ago, yet the tradition goes on, and in a much improved fashion. Don Griffin, who is tall and slow spoken and laughs a good gravely laugh and who's as good a story teller as you could ask for to pass a foggy winter evening with, has owned various Dickersons for twenty-three years now, and has been part owner of the company for some time, tells the best stories of Bill Dickerson, whom everyone, even his wife, called "Dick."

"Dick used to live down there at Church Creek outside of Cambridge, and a guy named Ted Graves, a retired naval architect from Boston, lived across the way from him, as did Howard Chapelle, who wrote *the* book on boatbuilding and was curator of the watercraft section of the Smithsonian. Ernie Tucker, who was a retired designer, lived nearby too. So there were all these geezers who knew more about boatbuilding than most people have a right to. Well, Ted Graves and Ernie Tucker ended up doing the designs, and Chapelle did the kibitzing and Dick built all the boats.

"Dick was always practical, a simple guy. You know those big samson posts of his with that pin through it, well in the old days he would finish off these boats good and sturdy, but he just couldn't bring himself to spend good money on the pin that went through the damned post. He'd just walk around the yard until he found a piece of something—an old rod or a piece of bolt—and wham, in she went and that sir, would be the finishing touch.

"Then when he retired, he built himself this beautiful wood sailboat, just for him and his wife to sail, all varnished —the transom, the house, masts, everything, all brightwork.

It was gorgeous. Well, he took it across to the Bahamas, and he told me, 'One day I was out there doing the bright work, sanding her all down getting ready to varnish, and I look up and there were all these guys sitting in their cockpits drinking gin and tonic. Well, I said, the hell with this. I threw down the sandpaper and went out and bought two gallons of white paint and I painted that sonofabitch from the masthead to the waterline. Wham! That goddam boat turned white just like she hit a blizzard.'

"I just wandered into his yard one day, I didn't even know it was there. A friend of mine took me, and we found the place, which wasn't easy cause there weren't any signs, down a back road somewhere, and I just stood there all day fascinated, watching these guys strip plank a hull. Well Dick came up and he says to me, 'What kind of a layout do you want? What kind of headroom? We'll build it for you.'

"So, back in '63 I bought a brand new 35-foot ketch from Dick for $10,500. I thought that was a hell of a buy. Even in those days, don't forget, a boat used to cost about a thousand dollars a foot, and here I was with a 35 footer for eleven thousand, with sails, the works. I mean they were simple, simple boats, the interior all plywood. Solid, but simple. Now, they did vary a lot because Dick would come out one morning and say to himself, 'What the hell is that cabinet doing there?' and that would be the end of that piece, plus he had a bunch of pretty good old carpenters there who'd pretty much do what the customer wanted, so you'd never get two boats that actually looked the same.

"And you know. There are still a lot of guys building boats around here, crab boats and oyster boats; the backyard boat business is flourishing. A lot of the good workboats are still built out of wood."

Dickerson switched to fiberglass boats in the early seventies but the real "new" era of Dickerson began with a 37 footer designed by George Hazen, a Princeton and MIT whiz kid, who helped develop the use of computers to analyze flow patterns around a hull. He grew up sailing on his father's Dickerson 35 on the Chesapeake, so who else could possibly have been a better choice?

George designed the 37 footer with a very modern underbody, but the classically pretty sheer, the overhangs, and all around deck and house purity remained. Overall the boat is so cleanly designed that there isn't a single hump or line or ridge anywhere that could be removed. She still looks completely clean and pure just like Bill Dickerson would have wanted it.

The first *37* was launched in '81 after three years in development, followed in '82 by the new 50 footer, and strangely enough a Bruce Farr-designed 37-foot SORC racer which proceeded to win nearly every race she entered in her first season, including the Annapolis-Newport race, as well as taking 1st, 2nd, and 3rd in the Annapolis Yacht Club's summer regatta.

Dickerson Boatbuilders was doing well.

Then came the slowdown of '84, the strong dollar which made European boats a good deal in this country, and some high expenditures for dredging out the basin and building new piers, and Dickerson skidded onto hard times. But now

Dennis Blaeuer, a solid business thinker with a background of good Swiss business sense and hard work, and a great respect for tradition and good boats, has become the major owner of the company, and has begun the slow and cautious process of modernizing Dickersons, which was among the last on this continent still doing "stick" building. Now, like most others—Hinckley and Alden among them—they are assembling sections of the cabinetry outside the boat and then fitting and bonding them into place as separate units. Cabinet assembly outside the hull is infinitely more comfortable because there is more space, air and light, resulting in a better and more economical job.

So the company seems in fine hands indeed, and with the management they now have and craftsmen so abundant all around the Chesapeake, Dickerson should go on building good strong simple boats another forty years.

But back to the cruiser for which Dickerson is famous. The draft of the new 37 has been intelligently kept to a moderate 4 foot 6 inches, a shoalness mandatory in the Chesapeake and certainly much needed on the East Coast where the best and most beautiful places have shoal waters, forbidden to 6- and 7-foot deep fin keels. The skeg was kept for steering and tracking stability while the wetted surface was kept to a low sail area/wetted surface ratio of 2.73. The displacement was made a moderate 15,950 pounds, resulting in a sail area/displacement ratio of 17.1, and that means she'll be a very decent light air sailer.

The rig is available in a multitude of choices from sloop to cutter to ketch, although the single mast rig with its 2½-foot taller mast (hence longer leading edge on the headsail) will certainly outperform the ketch going to windward and in light air.

Great service was done by George when he developed a computer-aided program to predict the boat's performance in various conditions. Without going into great detail, let me say that his Technical Performance Studies, which are available to owners, will tell them exactly how well their boat performs at different wind angles and different wind velocities. This will leave out much of the guesswork that most of us mortals spend years indulging in, trying to figure out how to sail our boats most efficiently. In other words you can have your boat sailing to its maximum potential after a few long outings.

The construction of the 37 is as straightforward as her design. The hull is balsa cored (which after all is said and done will prove to be the best and most long-lasting core material), or Airex cored, if the owner wishes. The deck is cored as well, and attached by the usual flange-and-through-bolt system using 5200 bedding compound. With a Dickerson you actually get a double seal, for the cap and rubrail form a second bedded barrier against leaks.

The bulkheads are stripped of surface veneer and bonded to both hull and deck, and that's as good as you can get. Extra rigidity is gained by bonding all berth tops and cabinetry, including the knees, to the hull, making for a strong, solid, single unit.

The seacocks are the normal high-quality bronze, with the coring material removed around the through-hull and re-placed by fiberglass.

The mast was traditionally stepped on deck but has recently been moved down to the keel.

The deck on the 37 comes in two versions: center or aft cockpit, and although I would always choose the latter, I must admit that the center cockpit creates a first rate aft cabin. Besides, Dickerson has kept the cockpit very wisely deck level making the boat look very handsome, instead of building it up to create more room below.

The decks of the aft cockpit version are extremely broad and clean. The shrouds are inboard for sheeting the genny tight, thus improving windward performance.

All the epoxy-coated aluminum portlights open—a wonderful thing during sultry East Coast summers—and there are a couple of good-sized dorade vents to help out.

Oh, before I forget—the 37 has a fine 4-inch by 4-inch samson post rooted in the bow which not only looks great with the molding that it fits through, but also works much better than cleats, which tend to work loose eventually and leak.

Belowdecks, the boat looks like a true old wood boat with white bulkheads and cabinetry and varnished teak trim. Physically the layout is very simple yet remarkably well thought out. The large double quarter berth is a good 2 feet farther forward than in most boats, so it's very airy and very easy to get into. One of the nicest touches in Dickersons and one of the most intelligent ones in any boat I have seen, is found here. As I have moaned about in the past, most quarterberths are unventilated tombs in which the air becomes unbreathable within minutes. On a hot summer evening, the thing is a sauna. Dickerson has solved the problem by having the foot of the berth extend into the opening of a cockpit locker so that you can leave the locker lid slightly ajar even in a rainstorm, and the berth will still be perfectly ventilated. To keep out mosquitoes and other biting critters, a nicely framed mosquito screen fits into the opening. You other builders read and heed.

The Formica-covered cabinsides look clean and airy and are easy to maintain.

The large fiberglass engine pan is well bonded down and the engine has good-sized bedlogs. The plumbing is good, with solid brass joints and elbows instead of hoses bent to the verge of cracking or collapsing, something one sees far too often in poorly constructed boats. The engine is very well insulated from both the cabin and the cockpit so you won't go deaf when running under power.

One interesting aspect of the engine is that it is reversed with a V drive. This is a bit more complicated than normal but allows you good access to the most critical part of the engine, namely the linkage to the transmission. The linkage is most likely to fail because of neglect, which is normally caused by inaccessibility. I use the word "critical" without exaggeration, for the linkage usually fails going from reverse to forward or vice versa, a thing you normally do in a cluttered harbor to keep from smashing into things. A well-serviced linkage will keep you from becoming your marina's demolition-derby champion.

Before I talk about the boats, I have to tell you that I took the title page photo of the Dickerson 37 from the Dickerson docks in Trappe, Maryland, with the setting sun aglow behind it. Can you imagine working in a place where most days end in such a blaze of glory? The daytime photos were taken in their backyard as well, so you can see that Dickerson is worth a visit for the scenery alone. Anyway, on these two pages we have photos of the *37*, above, and the *50*, below. As you can see from the small drawings, the underbodies of both

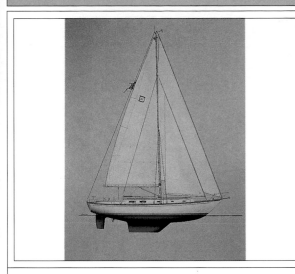

boats have moderate draft fin keels with deep skegs, and they both have nicely proportioned hulls with elegant overhangs. The rigs are tall and modern and inboard. The cockpits on both boats are kept slightly forward, making room for a small aft deck and an enormous lazarette below it. The cockpits are perfect for coastal cruising with high, comfortable backrests, and the side decks are kept good and wide without squeezing the accommodations below. The house of the *50* is beautifully low, and has a plethora of opening ports and hatches for light and air. For the ingenious ventilation of the quarterberth in the *37,* read the text. In the top left corner, you can see the Dickerson charter fleet at the Dickerson yard, which is a good kickoff point for cruising the Chesapeake. You had better allow yourself a lot of time, because there are literally hundreds of picturesque nooks and crannies to discover.

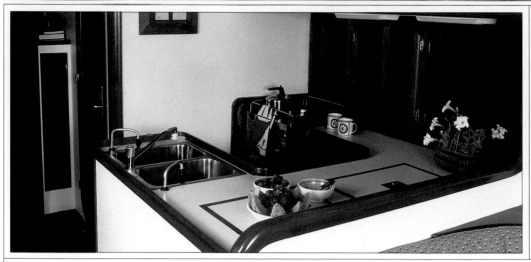 

Т he photos above and below are of the *50,* and the three tucked up in the right hand corner are of the *37.* Note the classically simple interior of the *50* with the white bulkheads creating a sense of airiness. I like the big oval doors and the rounded corners of the small louvered doors, and the shaping of the sea rails around the counters, giving you a good grip. How they fabricate and fit the inside and outside corners of those, I couldn't tell you if you tortured me. The galley is wisely layed out fore and aft, making it easy to use on a heel; the chart table is vast; the salon table with its base is one of the nicest I have seen; and the pilot berth is a perfect bear's lair. The layout drawing and the little drawing above it are of the spacious aft-cabin version of the *37.*

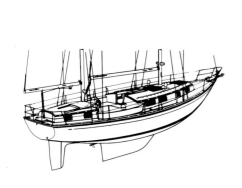

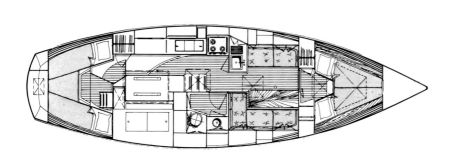

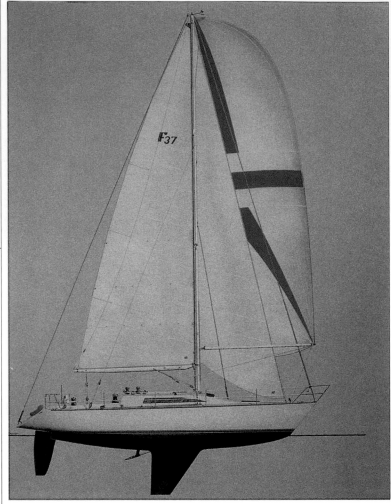

The drawing above is a profile of the Bruce Farr-designed IOR racer built by Dickerson. She is 37.5 feet overall, with a 29.1-foot waterline, 12.2-foot beam, and 12,200-pound displacement. Her IOR rating is 28.4. Farr designs some of the world's fastest racers. The *37* put on a show in its first season, winning the Annapolis-Newport race and coming in second and fourth in the Block Island Race Week. She is well priced for a production racer, and adds interesting depth to the Dickerson line.

The rest of these two pages is a potpourri of Dickerson shots. The one in the top left-hand corner is one of my favorites; the off-center companionway to the aft cabin of the Dickerson 37. Below it is the mosquito screen and vent I mentioned before for the quarterberth; read the text for details. An interesting thing to note in the shot in which the deck is being lowered is that the cradle the hull sits in has a full female bottom (you know what I mean) so the hull is completely and evenly supported, eliminating the chance of deformation during construction. The shot above shows some of the very nice trim around the cockpit of the *37,* while the shots below show the exactness of the work even in the floors. The little drawing to the right is of the 34-foot bugeye ketch of the ''Simplissima'' class.

So in all, the Dickersons are very good indeed, with many important touches, like the pair of long grabrails that run the length of the salon to keep you from being tossed about helplessly in a seaway. You won't find a lot of bits and pieces to look at, but what is there is beautifully done. ☐ If you love to cruise the shallow southeast coast and the Bahamas, in a good coastal cruiser that is fine and simple with lines that warm your heart, then you can do no better than to amble down to the boatyard on the creek, and see if the folks down there would build you a good sailboat, just like old Dick used to.

FREEDOM

W hen so much credit nowadays goes to the Europeans for building things that are well engineered, tested, and researched, it will probably shock most of you to hear that behind Freedom Yachts stands one of the most sophisticated builders of fiberglass products in the world today. That company is Tillotson-Pearson and the man behind it all is Everett Pearson, 52, considered to be the father of fiberglass boatbuilding in the U.S. As a kid fresh out of college he started Pearson Yachts, back when Annette Funicello was still singing M-I-C, K-E-Y.

Now at first glance you may question why seemingly innocuous boats like the Freedoms are in this book. It is true that the boats do not have the yachty elegance of Aldens or Hinckleys, nor do they have the romantic appeal of Cherubinis or the Bristol Channel Cutters, but they do have three very positive factors going for them which made their exclusion from this book almost unthinkable.

The first is innovation. Certainly no other line of boats has taken the chances in rigging development as have the Freedoms with their unstayed, unsupported carbon fiber masts and self-tending sails; to tack, you just turn the wheel and finish your sandwich as you watch the sail come over. This rig has brought more ease and fun back into sailing than nearly any other achievement to date.

The second plus for Freedoms is their new designer, Gary Mull. Now I do respect Gary Hoyt who started Freedom Yachts, for he made his boats perform near miracles, like John Carson's winning of both legs of the Bermuda One-Two race, setting a new record in the process. But even the most benevolent among us will have to admit that some of his designs were just downright homely. Mercy to heaven those days are over. Since Tillotson-Pearson bought Freedom Yachts, they have very wisely brought in Mr. Mull, who has designed two new boats for them, one 36 feet, the other 30.

Now Gary Mull knows about high performance—he's designing a contender for the next America's cup—and both his new Freedoms sport modern powerful hulls with highly advanced concepts, such as elliptical rudder blades, meaning that the boats should perform even better than the old Freedoms. But apart from that, he has a good eye as well, disguising literally vast interiors behind simple, understated lines. In short, his two new boats have the perfect look of an ideal family cruiser. The fact that they go like stink is just icing on the cake.

The third reason I included Freedoms—and I must tell you I left the best for last—is Everett Pearson himself and his almost prodigious knowledge of the working of fiberglass. Now I know that many among us, myself included, would rather forget that our nice wood interiors are guarded by fiberglass shells, but one of the main reasons for this book is to make us aware of how a boat is built, and to explain why a Hinckley costs more than a rubber duck. And since most fiberglass boats are built mostly of fiberglass, there is simply no better man to enlighten us on the subject than Everett Pearson, who has built almost everything out of the stuff, from giant tanks for dangerous chemicals to lamp posts nearly one hundred feet high, and even monster-sized propellor blades for great wind generators that fly at 250 mph and flex like Junior's fishing pole.

With this last point in mind, I will refrain from talking too much about the boats themselves, I'll do that in the captions, and I'll concentrate on the experience of Tillotson-Pearson which has led to their building the most sophisticated fiberglass products imaginable.

To start with, I'll tell you that they have a full-time laboratory on the premises, testing everything from panel-strength to the erosion of stainless steel, so when in the following paragraphs you read Everett's explanations, you know the man is not just grabbing numbers out of the air. He *knows*.

Everett Pearson has bright enthusiastic eyes and a seemingly limitless joy in talking about his products, explaining everything with great care as if for the first time.

"I had my first sailboat when I was six years old on the Kickemuit River," he began. "I sailed on the river and met my wife there when she was thirteen and I was fourteen. That was thirty-seven years ago. I took economics in college then did two years in the Navy, and when I got out of the Navy I started Pearson yachts with my cousin Clint. We were by no means the first though. Even before the war, Herreshoff Manufacturing had made some fiberglass dinghies, well not exactly fiberglass, but using a resin to impregnate some material.

"We first started building boats using the system of a Professor Musket, which involved drawing resin up between a male and a female mold with a vacuum system. You had a male mold and you put glass over that and you had another female mold over the top. Then you had this trough around the bottom into which you poured the resin and you had a vacuum pipe at the top so the resin crept up, was sucked up through the glass. You hoped. Then you opened it up and there was your hull. That's how we started making our first dinghies and after maybe thirty hulls that had great big holes in the bottoms where the resin didn't quite fill, we turned to the hand-layup process.

"That was in '53. We had the same materials then as we had up to a few years ago. Cloth, mat and roving. Same weaves, same weights. Not much change came until four or five years ago when people finally started to produce unidirectional fibers with some accuracy and control.

"When I left Pearson I signed a noncompete contract for three years so I went into building fiberglass products for industrial use. Tanks, ducts, that sort of thing. Here weight wasn't important but we had to guarantee the *strength* of the tank. A lot of weaving technology has come along and I must say much of it came about from boats racing in SORC where the weight was critical and the strength was critical. By this time we had a great advantage, because we knew so much about weave strength and resins from our industrial background. We had ninety guys in the layup shop then, so you can imagine our involvement with research. We had to build perfect products or they would have been rejected, so we got good. When we went back into the boat business starting with the Etchell 22 and later the J 24, both of which were high performance one designs, we were already accustomed to weighing fibers and resins and building very high efficiency products.

"We do the same quality control on all our boats, which is good and bad. Bad because we are competing in a marketplace where very few builders bother with exact glass control, and it's very difficult to sell the general public on the fact that we spend so much time and money doing such a good fiberglass job. To most people a hull is a hull and that's it. What is in it and how, just doesn't interest them.

"One of the most critical things is the resin that is used.

Six months ago we changed all our resins to prevent blistering. We had started a study three years ago to see where all our warranty money went and found that bottom-blistering was by far our largest claim. As you know there wasn't anyone in the industry who escaped scot-free. Everybody had blistering at one time or another. So we started working on the problem in the lab, worked with different panels, started to boil some, things like that, to try and get a panel to blister. Then we'd try different resins and different laminates to try to eliminate it. What we finally came up with was vinylester resin, something we used back in our industrial days when we needed a resin that was excellent against all sorts of corrosion, caustics, things of that sort. So we tried vinylester on the laminates backing up the gelcoat. We made some panels and boiled them for twelve hundred hours and we could not make them blister. This is a denser resin with a shorter chain of molecules that really ties the thing together so that there can be no room for moisture to penetrate.

"I like fiberglass. And from what I know the stuff not only doesn't weaken with age but actually gets stronger. The Coast Guard cut some panels out of a boat that was molded in 1946, had been kept in the Gulf of Mexico, the panels had been tested when the boats were first laminated, and twenty-five years later Owens-Corning tested them again. The panels tested slightly stronger than they were when originally put in. No degradation at all. Now Owens-Corning is testing panels in their Ohio labs where they have achieved accelerated aging, and at the age of three hundred years the panels show no deterioration. Fiberglass is good stuff.

"Anyway, back to blistering. We found that some blistering problems were caused by the finish on the mat, the binders holding the fibers together. Some of the binders were reacting with the salt water, forming acetic acid which caused the blisters. So we found that if we used gun roving, that is, just loose strands of fiber side by side without any binders on them, then we didn't have this problem. That is what we use with the chopper gun which spits random short fibers between the hand-layed-up layers of roving. So we now put that right next to the gelcoat. We monitor the gelcoat to insure that it is properly cured so the next layers won't print through as they are likely to do if you don't wait long enough for the gelcoat to set up. Then we lay in the chopped fiber, then the unidirectional or biaxial roving or whatever is required.

"We average 53 or 54 percent glass content. With mat and roving the average boat comes out around 35 percent. With choppergun you get about 25; if you're good."

We walked out into the laminating shops where rows of Aldens and J Boats and Freedom Yachts are being molded, and Everett pointed to a man rolling a hard roller furiously over some dry-looking roving until the resin from below started seeping through.

"To make sure we don't get resin-rich hulls," Everett said above the din of the shop, "we measure out the amount of resin a hull is to have and the guys know that's all they'll be getting so they have to work the resin through the fibers by leaning on the rollers. They spray the resin very sparsely, then the pressure on the roller brings the resin through the next dry layer of roving. This guy's been rolling glass for me since 1957. In this layer you're looking at the fibers running 0–90, then the next layer will be unidirectional and with that we pick up the load right from one side at the chainplates, then we run it through the mast step to create a band to tie all the loading together.

"We make J Boat bulkheads of composite glass and balsa because a J 41 will have 28,000 psi compression on the spar. A J 30 bulkhead will have five layers of unidirectional roving built up solid in it in the areas where the loading from the shrouds comes through. These are the problems you don't have on the Freedoms because they don't have the rigging to try and pull the boat apart."

This composite system certainly seems the best way to build bulkheads, for you have solid glass laminates spreading broadly onto the hull where the loading is, and you have balsa in the other parts where you would normally have plywood with a lot of weight that's not really doing you any good. At the end they laminate a veneer over the bulkhead.

"One of the things that building all the industrial products has done for us, building all the wind blades, is that we now have engineers who understand laminates and how they work under enormous stresses. Those products have generated enough in-house knowledge so that now we have a computer system that allows us to mount twenty-four strain gauges onto a boat—gauges that record the stresses, with the aid of an onboard computer, ten times a second. Then we can go out and sail the boat and we record the activity of the strain gauges so when we hit a sea, we can tell what the loads are in the forward section, what the engine mounts are seeing, what the rudder shaft is feeling, what the bulkhead bonds are feeling, what the gooseneck is feeling, the chainplates, all the components. Then the engineers can come back and they get from the program the maximum loads any particular gauge saw and, simultaneously, what the load was on all the other gauges. They read that over and what we can then do is go back to the shop and put in more glass as, and where, and in what direction, it's needed, so that we know that we have uniform stresses in all the laminates throughout the boat. This kind of engineering needs sophisticated equipment. It's not something you can do by guessing, or trial and error. We can be sure we don't over-build, causing excessive weights and costs. We engineer the laminates to do the job.

"We did these strain gauge tests on our big blades mounted in a tower and we could read all the loads on the blades. Now of course those blades have been spinning for a few years so they have taught us a few lessons. One big thing was the coring. Don't forget that those blades really move; they get up to 250 mph out on the tips and they oscillate back and forth 7 or 8 inches. That's a hell of a lot of torquing action. We tried coring them with all kinds of foams, you name them, but the foams did not stand up for more than two weeks. They actually crumbled. Fell apart. The only core that maintained its stability was balsa. The foams just couldn't stand the vibration—the flexing in the blade.

"When the blades are spinning in the tower they actually spin at 72 rpm so you get some answers in a hurry. Now you have to do a bit of thinking to translate that into what that means to a boat, but the glass behavior won't be all that different. I mean if you ship a boat cross country at 60 mph it's going to move a lot and vibrate a lot. Now I'm not saying a part of the hull will deflect 7 inches from one end to the other but it does move constantly, and once it's in the water, it takes some pretty good kicks falling off waves and being slammed by waves. And you've been out in enough storms to know just how the whole hull vibrates once the wind starts screaming and the harmonics in the mast get going. Plus every time you have that engine running, the boat is usually doing some quivering. So we use only balsa as core material on our boats.

"We ship 126 blades a week. Each blade is 366 pounds, plus or minus 3 pounds. That's one percent of latitude we can have, otherwise the blades vibrate and beat themselves to death in a week so we have to be pretty careful building them. If the blade is outside that tolerance they don't go out of here. I'm just telling you all this stuff about the blades to show you how much depth we have in determining what is best where.

"When we use balsa as a core on the big boats, we vacuum bag it to make sure the resin is sucked in between the blocks and into the cells."

Vacuum bagging is a simple system using simple poly sheets with a string around the edge to allow the air to bleed off. On the system they use, they can get up to 25 psi. The perfect vaccum you can get is 30. Now don't try to rush out and build a cored hull with your vacuum cleaner because that poor thing won't suck more then about 7 psi. Conversely, you do have to take care not to use too much suction or you'll suck the resin right through the balsa and starve the other side and cause delamination. In a hull, Tillotson-Pearson pulls only about 14 or 15 psi.

"The balsa is so stiff," Everett went on, "that if you put a typical panel in the lab it will not deflect until about 1,800 psi. The same panel using an Airex core, (a high density rigid foam) will deflect at a much lower loading of about 400 psi. The Airex hull will also cold flow, which means that the laminate will deflect and stay deflected if enough of a load is put on it. When you tighten the upper shrouds and you look along the sheer, with an Airex core you can see where the hull starts to deflect and the bulkheads stop it. A hull should be engineered so that the glass takes all the load. You want the hull shape to be held as the designer drew it so it can go through the water at the maximum speed instead of breaking the lines through flexing and distorting. You don't want something that will vary and move under load. And the more the hull moves the more you begin to rely on the interior structure and the secondary bonds.

"Balsa gives us a hull whose shape will never change and yet we save a lot of glass, therefore a lot of weight. If you wanted this kind of stiffness from glass alone, you'd be up to a 1½-inch thick laminate and you can imagine what that would weigh. As a nice bonus, balsa is about half the cost of Airex.

"We sound the hull with a hammer after lamination to make sure there are no air pockets. Maybe we're overly cautious. I don't know. We start our scrutiny right at the doors. Every shipment of resin that's received is analyzed in the lab to make sure it will catalize properly. The storeroom temperatures are always kept at 80 degrees to keep the gelcoat warm so it goes on uniformly.

"For the J Boats, which we build for the Johnstone brothers, we send all hardware we receive through our own destruction tests before we use them. Sure the manufacturers test them but we like to be double sure. We don't just do this because we like to play with computers and things, but because we like to build the best product we can. We have built literally thousands of those carbon fiber blades and what we learned from them allows us to give *lifetime* guarantees with our carbon fiber masts on all our Freedoms. Lifetime."

Paul Petronello, the sales director of Freedom Yachts, told me a story that shows the strengths of these masts.

"We were out with one of the editors of *Yachting* on one of the new Freedoms and it was blowing about 25 and I said, 'Watch. I'm going to do an uncontrolled jibe.' And he yelled out, 'Hell, Paul you'll dismast us!' So I went and did a whole *series* of crash jibes. Bang, shudder, bang, shudder. He just hung on with his fingers welded to the coaming and kept saying, 'Aren't you afraid something is going to break?' I told him of all the tests the boat has been through which taught us how to build the boat to be nearly foolproof. We just want to be sure that if Mom and Pop get caught by surprise they don't get hurt."

"We pressure-mold our rudder stocks," Everett went on about his beloved fiberglass. "That means putting a bladder inside the rolled tube and then inflating it at high pressure to squeeze out the excess resin. This way we get about 72 percent glass content in them. And you know how important rudder stock strengths are. We are now looking into using glass-reinforced nylon through-hulls and seacocks. This is great because it eliminates problems of corrosion and electrolysis. We froze them solid in the lab, and when it was really cold, about 10 below zero, we finally managed to brake a handle but the seacock held together. So we'll see.

"Oh I didn't finish about our resins. We put each batch of resin that comes in into a heat bath to see at what temperatures they exotherm so the men in the shop can use the same amount of catalyst and get consistent results. If the resin is out of spec we reject it. We don't want to create confusion and inconsistency with the molding.

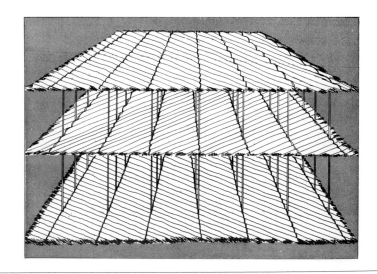

Don Street, certainly one of the great practical authorities on sailing, spent much time cruising and racing on a Freedom cat ketch and had this to say: ''Once the sails are up they are dead easy to handle. This is a real cruising man's rig. The boat is extremely fast. You set the sails and then there is nothing to do; just two sheets to trim and a boat to steer. To tack, one simply puts the helm down and the vessel is off on the other tack with nothing else to be done.'' Sounds like the ideal boat to do some enjoyable sightseeing with. These two pages have the oldest and

the newest of the Freedom line. In the top left-hand corner and bottom right-hand corner (that ought to keep your eyes busy) is the new Gary Mull-designed *36*, showing off its tapered carbon-fiber mast which (along with every Freedom mast) carries a lifetime guarantee. The pesky little *30* is in the drawing above and in the left-hand photo below. You would never guess that these moderate looking hulls are actually concealing very comfortable aft cabins, but more about them later. The big photo above is of the largest of the fleet —the Gary Hoyt— designed *44* which, with its high free-board, has vast amounts of space below and a football field for a deck above. I'll let Don Street tell you about how she tacks. "While all the other crews are killing themselves cranking genoas, the hardest work for the Freedom's crew is opening beer cans for the skipper." Amen to that, brother.

One day about twenty-five years ago, a young shipwright named Christoph Rassy pushed his old black bicycle off German soil onto the ferry bound for Sweden. He took a job on the island of Ellös on the rocky western coast and built other people's boats until the mid sixties, then he got his own place and kept building good boats out of wood.

Meanwhile a Mr. Hallberg, who had been building pretty folkboats out of wood since the war, was making himself a good reputation on both sides of the Atlantic, having charmed the American market with a pretty little boat called the P 28.

The Hallberg and the Rassy yards merged in '72. Mr. Hallberg retired soon after and Christoph Rassy now stood by himself. Within a dozen years the size of the yard doubled until now, at 250 boats a year, it is the largest sailboat yard in Sweden.

Christoph Rassy is a stocky, jovial man with boundless energy and a handshake like a vise. His dedication to his boats is unfailing and he constantly searches for better ways to build and improve them. Yet, in a sense, he's still running an old wood boatyard, for, in what seems a Swedish tradition, the hulls and decks are laminated by outside fiberglass specialists. The Swedes, in spite of their leadership in many modern things like engineering, are still a people of tradition and this island region has always built wooden boats. The expertise for fiberglass is in a region farther north, where every Hallberg-Rassy hull is built under the personal supervision of a Lloyds' surveyor to qualify for a Lloyds of London Certificate of Hull Construction. For the hulls of the smaller boats they use a unique method of chopper gun layup reinforced by a dense grid of fiberglass beams laminated to the hull. It's common knowledge that a 35 percent fiber-to-resin content is the best that can be achieved with chopped strand—compared to 50–55 percent with a hand-layup of biaxial or unidirectional roving and mat—so the grid system is put in place to compensate for the difference in strength. Besides checking the hull and deck, the surveyor also checks bulkhead installation, chainplate installation, rudder and fittings and engine foundations. That's a pretty good start.

The designs come from a combination of scientific and traditional methods. In the old days the first step used to be the carving of a half model of the boat. The owner could then say, "Yes. That's what I want," and they'd cut it into stations and do the lofting from them. Mr. Rassy still personally carves a half model, whittling it until he's happy. It is then discussed with different people at the yard, cut up, the calculations are made, and a set of lines taken off them. After the needed corrections, they build a prototype.

It seems to work, for they have never had a model that was not well received, but then don't forget that Mr. Rassy goes to every boat show to ask a million questions of customers. He actually begs people for criticism. He wants to know what he can change, how he can improve things, so he gets a pretty good feel for what makes people happy and what annoys them.

What seems to make them happy are the distinctive Hall-berg-Rassy lines. Even from a distance these cruisers stand out. They have been conceived to give maximum space below, but through finesse, the lines have been kept moderate. Part of this finesse is evident in the high freeboard with the portlights inbedded into the broad blue sheerstripe, yet the mistake of creating too high a hull by putting flush decks on relatively small boats was avoided and the headroom below was achieved by having a very low—half height—trunk cabin do the work.

This semi-flush deck may not strike you as a revolutionary concept, but just wait until we go down below. But before we do that let's consider the decks. With the high freeboard, good volume and vertical space is achieved in the forepeak without the need for a full-length high trunk cabin, hence the half-height cabin can terminate well back from a normal one —just 2 or 3 feet forward of the mast. The result is a beautiful, spacious foredeck which is a dream for handling headsails and ground tackle, and an absolutely wonderful place to lie in the sun or, on warm summer nights, unfurl your sleeping bag and sleep under the stars. This deck arrangement is unusual, and certainly the most successful of the roomy, high-cockpit genre of boats. As Mr. Rassy said, "We didn't invent the flush deck but we certainly have made some favourable modifications. We try very hard to design pretty boats."

The only one of the line—which starts at 29 feet and goes to 49—with a standard house arrangement is the little 29. All the rest have the tucked-up decks and half-height houses and vast spaces below.

All boats other than the two smallest have another thing in common, and that is the design of the cockpit. Now I'm not sure just what you would call these—the first inclination would be to call them "center-cockpit" types, but that would not be entirely true, for only on the two largest ones does the cockpit approach midships. Nonetheless, the cockpits are raised and slightly forward, providing amazing accommodations in the after cabins.

Now, you may say that lots of boats have aft cabins nowadays, and that's true, but not until you get into the mid 40 foot range do you get an aft cabin as airy and spacious as an HR 38, and the nice thing is that all this is achieved with hulls that retain pleasant lines.

But back to the cockpits. The slightly elevated cockpits are very safe and dry and made so by an amazing standard feature: a fixed windshield. As you may know from my previous books, I have never been a fan of shields and dodgers, but after spending a week in Sweden and watching it blow and howl and rain and spray day after day, I quickly remembered all the times I had been soaking wet and miserable and freezing at the helm, and all of a sudden these things seemed a godsend. I must emphasize that these are *fixed, rigid, tempered glass windshields* with extremely sturdy frames, not flimsy plastic windows which rattle in the wind and are visually useless in the rain, and get so badly scratched in a short time that half your life you think you're sailing blind.

The tempered glass stays clear and there is a windshield wiper for the rain. If you want the wind in your face, then just flip up the center portion and inhale, and if you want more sunshine, then fold down the little roof. In bad weather you can sit under the roof and have a nice warm lunch on one of two varnished tables and feel sorry for the wretches eating soggy sandwiches. As I said, these windshields are tough and sturdy; in the past dozen years they have lost only two in spite of a number of knockdowns.

"And we still get some people," Mr. Rassy says, "who come to look at the boat and ask if they can have one without the windshield because they don't like its looks. We don't say anything. We just take them out sailing, and once they see the windscreen drenched, they never say another word. It really gives a fine view and great protection. And it is strong."

Indeed it seems that most things on the boats are built after Mr. Rassy himself gives it personal testing. As I said, he has a grip of steel and his general build would make you think he moves the boats around the yard with his bare hands, so if something is strong enough for him, it ought to be strong enough. Period.

With this in mind, the hulls are reinforced with a gridwork for added stiffness. There are no liners in the hulls, everything is hand fit and bonded in. The hull and deck are joined by the best method possible—layers of laminates applied from below to create a single leakproof unit. The space in the bulwarks is then filled with a dense filler for extra strength.

The stanchions are installed using an ingenious and deceptively simple method. At first glance it appears that the stanchions sit atop the teak cap over the bulwark and are held in place by a meager little plate around the base. At a boat show, a lady brought this to Mr. Rassy's attention, saying that that piece of fluff wouldn't support a butterfly. At this point Mr. Rassy grabbed the stanchion and hung on it with his feet against the hull until finally the stanchion bent in half, but the base just stood there as if it had taken root. And it had.

What they actually do is drill a hole through the 1¾-inch thick caprail, *then* a further 4 inches down into the solid, compound-filled bulwark. Into this hole is fitted a *solid* stainless steel rod that is to be the stanchion stem—with the little round plate welded around its middle. The top of this stem sticks 6 inches above the caprail and the stanchion slips down over it and is held there by a set screw. All the little plate does at the base is hold the stanchion *down*. To tear that stanchion out of there you'd have to tear apart the deck, a task which will not be easy considering the hull to deck joint.

The rubrail is large, with a strip of brass over it for added protection. Again, massiveness, solidity and simplicity are the keynotes.

The hardware used is no less impressive. Just as an example I'll tell you that the mooring cleats on the *42* are 15 inches long, perfectly suitable for towing the *Queen Mary*. And not only are they big and sturdy but they are mounted very intelligently out of the way of toes, up on the caprail. The heavy 1¾-inch caprail is not just plopped down and fastened, but nicely routed out to a depth of ½-inch to *cover* the hull-to-deck joint with an additional watertight seal.

It's in comfort and touches of quality, however, that the Hallberg-Rassy boats really excel far beyond standard pro-

duction boats. All but the little *29* come with teak decks as standard. You may think that an unnecessary luxury, but they are still the best nonskid surface available. The cockpit sole, as well as the seats in the cockpit, are covered with teak, and this is one thing that is a virtual necessity on all fiberglass boats whose seats and sole on a rainy day become as slippery as an ice rink.

Down below, the first thing you notice, aside from the volume and light, is that every little corner is filled with small cabinets and shelves—bits of extremely useful storage which on many other boats, especially high under the decks, are left as wasted, empty space. A most necessary and outstanding storage idea is the long mahogany rack over the chart tables, for pens, pencils, dividers, etc.; objects which otherwise are forever on the missing-in-action list.

The overhead is filled with rigid panels instead of the droopy, obnoxious loose plastic. The teak cabin sole is protected by a layer of nicely fitted—and because they're in small pieces—easily removable carpeting which is nice to have to keep your feet warm on cold nights.

The problem of condensation under bunk cushions is relieved with a series of large holes drilled and nicely finished in the tops of the bunks.

One of the most civilized features is found in the head, where the sinks are not flimsy plastic or stainless but *solid* china that does not scratch easily and feels and looks first class.

To insure a problem-free boat, *all* boats are launched and tested in the bay at Ellös, even the ones that are being shipped out by truck. Each boat is taken for a run and everything conceivable is checked.

The list could go on indefinitely, from the full length grabrails overhead to the stainless-and-rubber non-skid steps on the companionway ladder rungs that make for first class footing for wet soles. But that is not the purpose of this book. The purpose is to show you through a few examples the care and thought put into these boats, so that when you go to make a choice, you'll know what to look for.

These many good ideas don't just get dreamed up in isolation. As I said, Mr. Rassy is constantly at boat shows looking for and soliciting new ideas and comments.

"Since I came on my bicycle from Germany," he says in his thick, friendly accent, "I have learned that the most important thing is to *listen* to other people. I think my job is to listen to people to get information at the right time. We now have a new generation of boats with a little finer line of house and hull because one day I was in Hamburg at the exhibition and there were a lot of people, a big crowd around one of my boats, and I went and heard, maybe three or four times, 'I think there are too many big windows,' or 'I think there is no space on deck.' When I went home I thought about those things and developed the new boats with sleeker lines, more comfortable decks, and smaller windows. And the new boats are prettier and more comfortable to use."

On these pages are the Hallberg-Rassys, the most spacious of quality production boats. They are built in Sweden on one of the most beautiful coastlines in the world (see the photo on the title page) where the tides are minimal so the houses are built right on the water, as on a lake. In the title photo is a Hallberg-Rassy 42— one of the larger of the fleet of six boats which start at 29 feet and go to 49. The 49-foot ketch is in the upper left-hand photo beating to windward. With prevailing wind conditions similar to those on these pages, it's easy to see why these heavily-built boats with the tempered glass windshields— standard items on all but the smallest of boats—have become so popular that Hallberg-Rassy is now the largest boatbuilder in Sweden. On the bottom of the left page the 38 is roaring along on a blustery day, while

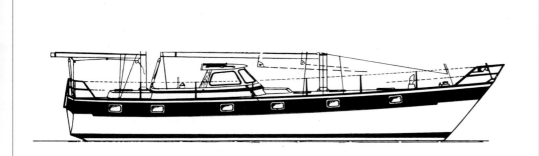

opposite, a reefed-down 35 footer goes to windward. The boats' windward performance is helped by the shrouds being set slightly inboard, and its downwind handling is assured by a moderate keel which you can see in the drawing three pages farther on. Up in the right-hand corner a smiling Mr. Rassy sits in the Hallberg-Rassy harbor. The designs for these strong, spacious, well-appointed boats are his. As these photos show, the height of the freeboard is nicely disguised by a wide sheer stripe into which are set a row of portlights. Locating the portlights down here not only provides ample light to the outboard regions of the boats, but also allows the decks to be flush or nearly flush, making them, on the whole, the most spacious in this book. The photo of the 35 footer shows how well the very low deck house is designed. The bulk of the cockpit coaming is lessened with the use of colored stripes.

Once you get close to the Hallberg-Rassy boats, the difference between them and standard production boats becomes obvious. The vast amount of beautifully layed teak on both deck and house are standard, as are such performance-oriented items as boomlifts and boom vang tackle. The photos on the tops of the pages are details of the new 38 footer. The top left shows the pulpit shaped to receive the mast (set on deck so it can be easily lowered). Note vast decks, inboard shrouds and the massive

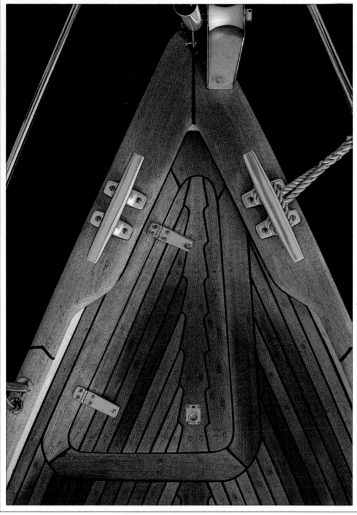

windshield whose center piece opens. To its right is a photo of the *solid* stem of the stanchion. As I said in the text, that piece doesn't just sit there, but continues down into the solid bulwark. The tube stanchion then slips over the stem. For a test of its strength, read the text. The top right-hand photo shows the massive mooring cleats mounted cleverly on the bulwark, out of the way of toes. The teakwork over the anchor well could not have been designed better; but don't forget that this is a country that has been building beautiful wood boats for centuries. The big boat below is the *42*, the small one the *31*.

"I must say to you I have a problem getting information from people," Mr. Rassy said, "because most people are too nice to say to my face what is wrong with my boats. It's easy to say what is good but hard to say what is bad. But I must get more information. That way our boats will keep getting better and better every year."

HINCKLEY

J ust where on earth am I supposed to start? Do I start half a century back talking about Henry Hinckley founding the yard up in Maine, or start instead with his Bermuda 40—without question the greatest fiberglass boat of all time—which Bill Tripp designed twenty-six years ago and of which they still build two or three a year because people just keep ordering the damned things, or do I start in the mold shop where the quality of workmanship is as good as you can find, or instead in the woodshop where it's even better?

There is, quite truly, enough stuff here to fill a book, so with your kind permission I'll just ramble back and forth, all the while trying to tell you why these boats live up to their legendary name. I'll avoid the obvious things like the indisputable beauty of the lines of all the Hinckleys, and the immaculate finish and visible high quality, and I will try instead to cram in many facts, the details hidden beneath the surface which add up to a great boat, so you will understand why, if you ever buy a Hinckley, you can, in time, pass it on with great pride to your son and then he on to his son who will still be getting as great a yacht as it was the day that it was born.

Before I talk about construction I'd like to talk about design, for that seems to be one aspect overlooked by many. I must confess I was at first, like many, so taken by the quality of Hinckleys that I completely neglected to think about performance, thinking that with a boat as beautiful as this who cares how she sails. That, I assure you, is not at all the thinking at Hinckley. The new generation of boats—the Sou'wester 42, 51 and 59—are all designed by McCurdy and Rhodes whose philosophy is that "a sailing yacht has no reason for existence if it cannot make an efficient job of translating the power of the wind into the most thoroughly enjoyable way of moving a boat across the water." At Hinckley that means good seakindly motion and good balance, but it also means *speed*. Jim McCurdy has designed such highly successful racers as *Carina* and has put that experience into Hinckley's new Sou'wester line. The fuller and more powerful aft sections and good beam, along with fine entries, airfoil section keels and centerboards and a wetted surface reduced to the minimum while maintaining good handling, combined with a generous high-aspect ratio inboard footed sailplan, produce boats that sail with great authority and speed.

And the attention to performance is going to be kept because John Marshall has just joined Hinckley as executive vice president. A veteran of four America's Cup campaigns and design co-ordinator for Dennis Conner's current effort to win back the cup, John knows a lot more about what makes a boat go fast than most of us want to hear. He had been head of Hood Sails, so he probably knows a bit in that department too.

But back to boat construction.

Let's start in the mold shop where the hulls are made, where the future of any yacht, great or bad, is founded. The ten men in the fiberglass shop have a total of ninety years of experience building Hinckley hulls and that ought to make them pretty well versed in their daily chores.

John Sweeney is chief engineer at Hinckley. He is a gentle-voiced, calm man, who was a professor of naval architecture at MIT, the kind of man you would have loved to have explain to you the makings of a good boat.

"We use isophthalic resin," John Sweeney began, "because it is good for staving off blistering. We use it for the whole hull. You really only need it for the gelcoat and the next two layers but we use it throughout, just to be sure. For the fibers, by and large, we use unidirectional E glass 1808 which is one 9-ounce unidirectional roving layed across another one whose fibers run at 90 degrees to the first one.

"The layup for the Sou'wester 42 has two mats next to the gelcoat, then two 1808's, then a mat then the Airex core, then another mat, then two more 1808's. We use a thing called 'Morebond' instead of a mat next to the Airex. It's actually a polyester resin-based putty with micro balloons in it. It bonds better to the Airex. Any cored panel will fail in sheer where the two join; in other words, where you have a very weak material, i.e., the foam, joining a very strong one, i.e., the resined glass fibers. What the 'Morebond' is supposed to do is act as a transition material, almost as a shock-absorber, that actually graduates the transition from a very hard hull to a much softer core.

"We turn the Airex with the backing down on a round form so the squares of foam open up, and then we wet it out with resin so the resin actually goes a good way right between the 1-inch squares to even further reduce the possibility of delamination. We then set the Airex into Morebond that has been troweled onto the hull. We squeegee all our laminates, not just roll them, to get all the excess resin out.

"For a centerbond we have about twelve double layers that overlap, ranging from a material width of 12 inches to 50 inches. The centerboard box is fabricated separately, then put on, so you actually have, not a straight seam like most boats have, but a double, almost keyed seam. We have not yet had a single problem.

"For chainplates, we use a great multi-fingered aluminum foundation piece bonded into the hull. The main part is aluminum, but the actual tang that comes through the deck that attaches to the shrouds is stainless. The aluminum is ⅜ inch and is bonded into the hull with three double laminates.

"The lead keel is external to the hull. We have the deadwood, the fiberglass part of the hull come down behind the lead keel and act as a sort of shock absorber in case of grounding so the lead can't kick up through the bottom as easily as on regular fin-keeled boats. And that, by the way, is the major source of damage at grounding: the delamination of the hull right at the aft end of the keel."

Now all of the above is absolutely first class procedure, using the best materials and methods possible for building the hull and keel, but one of the major strongpoints that aids in longevity is the hull-to-deck joint, which is an important stiffener on a boat. I'm going to take a bit of time to talk about this feature, not only because of its obvious importance, but also to give you an idea of how much care goes into the building of the Hinckleys.

The hull-to-deck joint on a Hinckley appears at first glance to be the industry standard deck-bolted-to-flange system, but on closer inspection we find a number of almost unprecedented details. To start with, the flange is a hefty ½-inch thick averaging *6 inches in width* except where the knees for the chainplates are installed. Here the the hull flange widens to 18 inches along a 6-foot run. Some stiffener.

In addition, there is a little lip that rises past the flange, or actually the hull continues past the flange so that the deck fits snugly and perfectly *inside* this lip. Not only does this provide a beautifully finished surface upon which the varnished railcap sits, but it also creates a total confinement within which the deck fits, instead of swimming all around as it can very easily do on most standard hulls where the top of the deck flange is flush with the top of the topsides. For an explanation of how the hull and deck are fitted I turned to Bob Hinckley, son of founder Henry.

Bob is fifty years old but looks much younger with his energy and vigor and eyes as bright as the autumn air. He seems to be a very happy man, and rightly so. He is now president of the Hinckley Company, and I'll tell you later what all that includes. Before I let him begin talking about the deck fit, I'll tell you that many companies just put bedding or caulking on the hull flange, plop the deck on, bolt it down and that is all she wrote. But not at Hinckley.

"To fit the deck," he begins, "we first raise the deck on one of these chain hoists, then we lower it and measure off the bulkheads for trimming. We raise it, lower it, raise it, lower it, up and down like whore's drawers until all the tops of all the bulkheads fit perfectly. Then once the deck gets low enough, we start to grind its edge to fit inside of the little lip that rises above the flange. Once it's fit, we screw it down to check for low or high spots, and if we do find some we pull the deck off and fill the low spots and grind the highs. Then we check the fit one last time, take the deck off, acetone the whole thing so there's no dirt or dust, then lay wetted-out mat onto the flange and lay the deck on top of that, then bolt it down tight.

"It's a slow process fitting a deck this way—takes two days for a small crew—but it's the only way to get perfect results. With the enormous amount of surface contact we have with our 6-inch wide flange, instead of the normal 2-inch or-3-inch ones, as well as that 18-inch flare for 6 feet by the chainplates we get incredibly strong adhesion. Then of course we bond all the tops of all our bulkheads to the deck so we get a hell of a strong joint. I have seen one bad hull and deck damage, a Hinckley 41 that was run over by a barge. The bow of the boat went under the barge and finally popped up again amidships. They were very lucky not to have all been killed."

Hank Halsted, who works for Bob in the brokerage department, was on board that boat and explains what happened. "Well, the deck clamp held reasonably well but the load was transferred aft, cracked the cockpit and popped the bulkheads amidships. Popped them in about 6 inches. The impact was such that one of the Barient stainless steel winches, you know, the old style heavy duty ones, was actually sheered off, cut in half by the barge as it came aboard. I think it was the hull flange in there, the strength of it, that kept the side from caving in and sinking the boat. It was pretty exciting."

"Another thing we do differently," Bob went on, "is that when we install hardware, instead of drilling an oversized hole through the fiberglass and dropping the bolts into them with caulking, we actually tap the holes. That is, we cut threads into the sides of the hole; then the bolt is caulked and *threaded* into place. This goes for all deck hardware, genoa tracks etc. Then of course we still put locknuts on the bottom. And we use cut thread bolts instead of rolled ones. They are a little finer and a little stronger.

"Our masts are made of two joint pieces. We have to join the mast because we can't transport mastlengths over 40 feet by common carrier. We put the joint at the spreaders, which is the strongest part of the mast. There is a big 36-inch-long sleeve inside of it, then we have a great number of *plug welds* to join them. Now these are not spot welds where you apply heat to a small spot on the outer skin and weld it to the inner. This is plug welding, and what that means is that you cut holes in the outer extrusion—in our case we cut ¾-inch diameter holes—and you fill that entire hole up with weld. This way your surface contact is much greater than on a spot weld. Now some people bolt the two pieces together but that means drilling through the inner sleeve which can cause corrosion and other problems. We have about seventy plug welds.

I asked Bob what he thought Hinckley excelled at.

"I think we do a lot of little things well," he said. "Like grinding all the seams on the laminates to get a better successive bond, like fairing in the through-hulls flush with the hull; every little bit helps in performance and I do a lot of racing so I can't help but pass the attention to performance on to others. And the boats all perform well. Did you know that one of our *42's* won its class of eighteen in Antigua sailing week in '85? They came in second overall in the cruising class of sixty some-odd boats. We do pretty well."

There are many barely noticeable things which make the Hinckleys look so beautifully finished—the jewel-like hardware, the perfect gelcoat, the slightly canted hatch frames, and the flush fit portlights that are worked perfectly into the house without any molding or trim. And the portlights are not plexiglass or even Lexan, both of which scratch and discolor in time, but tempered glass which will stay clear forever.

Inevitably we start talking about the famous Hinckley brightwork that is usually so bright you have to squint.

"We have no hard and fast rule," Bob said, "for how many coats of varnish each boat gets because different types of wood require different amounts of varnish to fill the grains. Believe it or not, we have gone as high as sixteen coats of varnish. Normally we use about five to eight. Most of the units of cabinetry are pre-assembled and then spray-varnished in the varnish shop where there is a minimum of dust. We try to do as little varnishing as possible inside the boats, first because there is so little air and not much room and second, because it is faster and hence less expensive to spray it in the varnish shop. Believe it or not, we put in all the quality as economically as we can. Once everything is in the boat we brush on at least one final coat for touchup. We use a phenolic tung oil varnish which is a basic old-fashioned varnish. No urethanes. The only place we use urethane, or rather durethane, is on cabin soles because the holly between the teak will be yellowed by varnish."

The choice of interior wood is up to you. You can choose mahogany, ash, cherry or white painted bulkheads with bright trim—whatever your taste. They will even do teak interiors if you insist, but think twice, because the light woods look much airier.

And what is most heartening is that all this good work is

backed up by Hinckley's integrity of service. Rig Reese, who wears many hats at Hinckley and does the marketing and advertising as well, told me about Hinckley's *unwritten* warranty which seems to go on indefinitely, regardless of how many owners the boat has had. Hinckley will repair any structural or serious cosmetic problem that they have caused no matter when in the life of the boat the problem crops up. But remember when you read this, that all this is *unwritten*. But applied.

"First thing when we bought back the company," Bob says, "there was an old boat built in '65, a one-off, which had its paint lifting. Well, we just brought it in and painted it. That cost $15,000. One expensive welcome. Thank goodness we don't have too many things go wrong with our boats.

"But still, I'd like to build each boat a little better than the last. We have a lot of offshore sailors in middle-management, with a lot of experience, and generally we're a lot fussier than the customers. I mean I'd never build a boat that I wouldn't go to Bermuda in personally. For that reason I like to have total control of the materials that go into our boats. We make all our own stainless hardware, cast our own ballast, have the plywood specially made for us, have our varnish specially made. It's nice to know exactly what we're putting into the boats. People seem to trust us and trust the boats. Over 50 percent of our business is repeat, old Hinckley owners buying new Hinckleys. And they all appreciate in value; you know I have resold a Bermuda 40 seven times, each time for more than the time before. And 70 percent of our charter business is repeat. We have forty-two boats in charter here in Southwest Harbor and fifteen in the Virgins.

"We develop extremely good personal relations with our owners. We have an open factory. If the owners like, they can camp right here in Southwest Harbor during construction and come every day and watch their boat being built. Some of the bigger boats have their captains here to watch construction just so they know how everything goes together, how all the systems work, to get a better knowledge of the boat."

And what the captains will learn is that sheet copper is used to bond all seacocks; that *all* fuel lines are copper tubing, and that parts of the tubing that are likely to be chafed are covered by protective sheathing; that all wires too are sheathed for protection; that the screwheads in the Lexan hatches are countersunk and the holes bunged with Lexan just to look well finished, and that the stanchions are all 14-gauge stainless steel of the highest quality.

They will also see centerboards which work not on a cable but a more positive worm-gear system; they'll see foam being placed between the bulkheads and the hull to lessen read-through; cockpit locker lids with a heavy hidden mechanism to hold them open so they don't come clonking down on your head; and maybe even the monstrous stem iron that is cast of solid stainless and takes a good man two solid days to polish to its Hinckley glow.

And if they go into the shop where the engines are prepped, they'll see Henry Ward with a stethoscope listening for knocks and pings and abnormalities.

Hinckley puts all new engines on a dynamometer and runs them for ten to twelve hours, sometimes more if a problem is suspected. Then they retorque the heads, readjust the valves, and run it for several hours more. The machine determines how much power it puts out. They check for oil leaks, fuel leaks, anything. They spend about twenty-four to forty-eight hours on the engine before it goes into a boat. They change the alternator bracket because they like to use 105 amp alternators instead of the 55 amp that come with the engines. With these you don't have to charge your batteries forever—especially the lighting battery—to get them back up to a state of charge. They make belt tighteners themselves, just a simple turnbuckle really, but it saves you messing around with a screwdriver—which is not much use with the double belted alternators anyway. And they build their own engine mounts sometimes.

"We try our best," Henry Ward says modestly, "I mean machinery is machinery that eventually and inevitably breaks, but we do our best to try and delay that as much as possible. We like to put constant velocity joints on the boats. The constant velocity system uses a thrust bearing so all of the thrust on your shaft and your prop is supported by that thrust bearing. This allows us to use very flexible mounts on the engine to better isolate the vibrations from the hull. Now it's actually the floppy mounts that reduce the vibration and it's the constant velocity joint that allows you to have floppy mounts. You can only go so soft with your mounts with a rigid shaft assembly before you start tearing out your cutlass bearing. It is actually better for your engine too. We also use isolation mounts with rubber-to-rubber contact inside, not steel-to-rubber." These dozens of seemingly small but time-consuming details make Hinckleys live up to their legendary name.

I asked Bob how he invisioned Hinckley's future.

"Well I can see our service facilities doubling over the next five to seven years, but we don't intend to increase our production any. I feel good with twelve to fifteen boats a year, and if we do some big custom boats in the 80-foot range then we'll just have to build fewer boats. We just don't want to expand our production facilities."

And aside from the fine production, Hinckley emphasizes their truly special services. Along with the vast maintenance yard, they have their own insurance company to clear up the owners' problems quickly, with understanding of costs. They have brokerage and a charter service, and even a travel agency to get you to your boat or a charter boat no matter where in the world it may be. They also run a captain and crew referral service for owners who want their boats moved around, and a service department which flies anywhere in the world to help you. If you're in the Virgin Islands, they have a well-equipped service facility there with spare parts and all.

Rig Reese had a good point when he noted that with the Hinckley service system, owners can have the builder looking after the boat *all* its life, instead of having many different yards doing so many improvisations from one year to the next.

When I asked Bob Hinckley about his personal goals, he said, "I hope just to keep learning. There are so many mistakes you can make in boatbuilding that you can only pray

that hopefully you won't make them again. Sometimes you're thinking of doing something, or worse, already begin to do something, and you catch yourself and realize, My God! I made that same mistake twenty years ago!

"I'm fifty years old. I started in the business when I was twelve, and there hasn't been a day I haven't learned something important."

I t's always great fun to write about Hinckleys because one is never at a loss for interesting and beautiful things to talk about. The photos on these two pages will attest to that. The top left photo is of a

Sou'wester 42 going smartly windward in the Virgin Islands. She's a fast and amazingly well handling boat from the boards of McCurdy and Rhodes, who also drew the new *51* which you see in the adjoining shot of the boat almost jumping out of the water. If you look closely, you'll see the shape of the rudder and

centerboard in the water. The McCurdy boats not only sail well but are also very beautiful, as the drawing on the last page and the photo here show. The hulls are extremely graceful and the decks and houses (for lack of a better word) perfect. The aerial shot in the lower left corner is of the Sou'wester 59, which is a floating palace, while the yawls anchored in the sunset are my all-time favorite fiberglass boats, the classic Bermuda 40's. All the boats carry the Hinckley trademark of classically elegant design and excellent crafts-manship. Hinckley does not push "woody" tradition beyond absolute practicality. Indeed, they even discourage people from having teak decks layed over their perfectly tooled fiberglass ones, rightfully arguing that they would be basically creating hundreds of leak-inviting holes. Great designs, top quality and plenty of common sense seem to be their goals.

The interiors of the Hinckleys further reflect good taste and amazingly high quality, but nowhere do you see a trace of overkill. As Rig Reese, Hinckley's head of marketing, said: They really do try to produce the very best boats without spending a penny on something unnecessary. If you look closely, this becomes obvious. The woodwork is simple to the point asceticism, especially in an all ash boat where the bulkheads and trim are the same color. The trim is as uncomplicated as possible, but, as

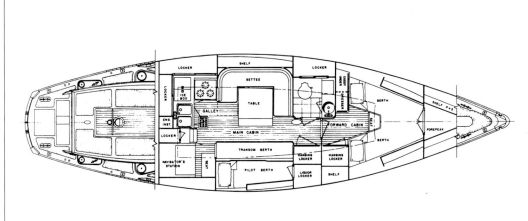

you can see, it would be very hard to improve upon (but since the spaces are large down below, I would like to see a few more hand-holds). The choice of wood in the Hinckleys is up to the owner. Bob Hinckley told me how much he liked a cherry wood interior they had just done, but my favorite still is the white paint and mahogany trim as in the right-hand lower photo. While you're looking at that, feast your eyes on the chart table; it's the nicest design and detailing I have seen. The picture is of a *42* with an aft cabin, whose forward bulkhead the chart table adjoins. The forepeak on the *42* is enormous and so full of stowage that when I spent a week on one I barely filled up one-eighth of the drawers and I had about twenty pounds of camera gear with me. Bob Hinckley has done a lot of offshore racing and it shows in the Hinckleys, in the excellent sea berths and well layed-out work areas.

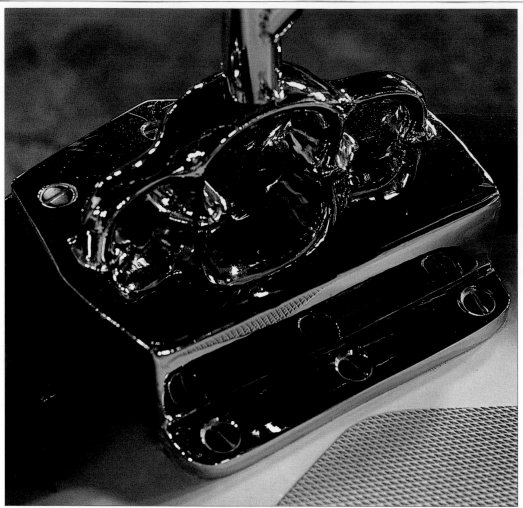

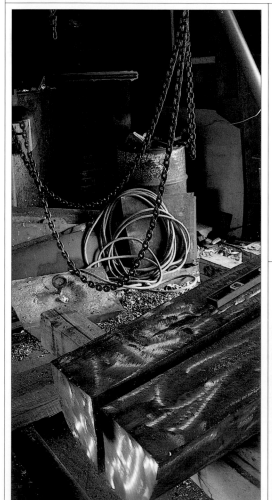

Now for the goodies—all the fine tidbits that add up to these excellent boats. Top left is the fairlead in the stern. These are heavy bronze casting swathed in chrome. Note in the same photo how good the non-skid pattern is. To the right is a track recessed into the deck mold so your toes stay where the Good Lord meant them to be: on the ends of your feet. Next right is one of the most thoughtful ideas yet: tank vent-holes drilled into the pulpit uprights so they will be almost unnoticeable. Next is the truly amazing

Hinckley stem-fitting of *cast* stainless steel. It alone is enough to make you want to own the boat. To polish and fit it perfectly to a boat takes a good man about four days. The bottom left shows the Hinckley ballast casting shop where everyone volunteers to work during the bitter Maine winters; and to its right is the enormous aluminum chainplate base, a massive grid, shown inbedded in the hull under layers of roving. The next photo with the fuel filter shows the meticulous copper plumbing that all Hinckleys have for fuel systems (certainly more damage-proof than even the best rubber hoses) and last but not least, some tidbits in the varnish shop, where Hinckley uses its own tung-oil-based varnish, laying on as many coats as it takes to get the perfect Hinckley glow that will, on a well kept up boat, last for many years. The closing photo on the next page shows rightfully proud co-owners Shep McKenney and Bob Hinckley.

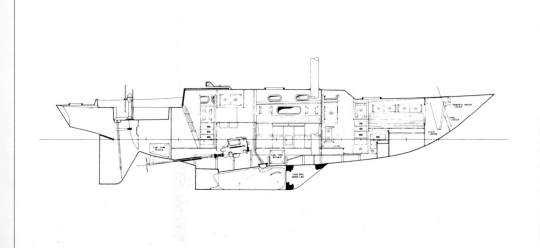

T hen we walked outside into the cool autumn sun of Maine and shook hands and parted, but Bob Hinckley called after me, ''We'll just keep building better boats, I promise you that.'' □ It's damned hard to see how.

P.S. As an objective writer, I feel obligated to mention the bad things about boats as well as the good, and after a few days of pondering I came up two things I don't like about Hinckleys. First, I loathe the carpets they use to line some lockers, and second, I'm absolutely appalled by the fact that I don't own one.

MORRIS YACHTS

I t's always a pleasure to visit with Tom Morris in his boatyard on the shores of Southwest Harbor, Maine, where things change very little from one year to another, the trees get a bit bigger and the people a bit wiser and another long cold winter comes after the summer and the fog. □ If there is such a thing as a perfect boatyard then Tom's has to be it. It has small shops and wood-burning stoves made of pipes and oildrums, and lofts and attics chockful of the magic things that go into a boat, and an office like a pigeon coop perched high on the roof, and outside you can slide the boats down tracks into the water where rocky islets, boats and gulls are scattered on the bay. It's a perfect place to be a kid, even if you're sixty.

And if there is such a thing as an ideal boat-builder it would have to be Tom. He is quiet, pensive, unhurried, thinks things over well, never tosses out answers—the kind of man you'd like to have think and care about your boat as she's being built. And then there are the boats.

The spotlessly clean shops are full of glistening little yachts, some half finished, some nearly done, and some only a gleaming, bulkhead-stiffened hull, but all of them beautiful and built like solid rock. What astonished me at the shop was that regardless of what stage of construction a boat happened to be in, from the lamination onward, every step, every detail, was done with such care and perfection, as if *that* very thing were to be the final touch. Now in a few cases it was, but most often not—most often it was to be covered later with a cabinet or trim—but in spite of that the work was finished to perfection. It is care such as this that gives you confidence in a builder, because you know he's building a boat not for show but for longevity, and in a boat that is to sail the seas no step should be slighted. For just as the framing of a wood boat must be a work of art upon whose each joint and fit the entire ship relies, so a boat built of fiberglass needs care with every step if it's to do service well and safely through the years.

The first important step of course, is to have a good design and Tom has not one but *four* good ones now, ranging from 25 feet to 36, all of them pretty and all of them fast and all from the drawing board of downeaster Chuck Paine.

It may strike some people odd to have so many small boats under 36 feet while most other quality yards *start* at 40 feet and work right up to millions of dollars, but this perhaps is one of Tom's secrets for success. For although there are many builders on the east coast building high-quality big ones—Shannon, Cambria and Alden, to name a few—there is only Tom Morris who offers the very best of construction in a variety of small yachts. And that's great for those of us who don't have three hundred thousand restless dollars in our pockets when we go looking for a boat.

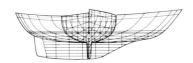

Those of you who like Tom's yachts but need more room below, take heart, for preliminary drawings have been done for a 42-footer, and for those who think Leigh too small at 30 feet and Justine too big at 36, there may soon be a new 32-footer on the way.

Chuck Paine has to be respected for both his knowledge and his vision, for not only does he design his hulls using the latest computer technology, resulting in fast and powerful, yet well handling underbodies, but he has also eclipsed many designers by developing his *own* trademark of crisp, clean, classic lines.

He has certainly gained the respect of his fellow designers, as witnessed by Robert Perry's analysis of Justine. "The design of the Morris 36," Perry said, "is as perfect as I have seen. I could own this boat with absolutely no change. On looking at the lines, I'm first struck by the pleasing balance in this shape. This will be a fast cruising yacht. The wetted surface is low, the entry reasonably fine and the diagonals are fairly symmetrical fore and aft. The sail-area-to-displacement of 16 I think perfect for an offshore boat of this type. There is a word 'yare' that was used to describe a boat where everything was perfect. . . . I think we have a yare boat here."

Can't argue with that.

On the *36,* Tom has begun using Henry Scheel's patented keel, and from all the reports I have been able to gather the keel works exceptionally well downwind because of the tracking its length provides, very well to weather, and of course with its shoalness will open up a lot of gunkholes. Since it has no moving parts, it is certainly less hassle than a vulnerable centerboard with mechanisms that can jam or break. Besides, you don't have to worry about letting the thing up and down. The draft on the *36* has been made moderate and thus the CG has been kept almost the same as with the deep fin, giving the boat virtually the same sail-carrying ability. If you're still skeptical, then let me tell you that Nautor now offers this keel on their Swans and you know what sticklers they are for performance.

The rigs are as modern as the hull shapes with high aspect ratios, and chainplate footings placed well inboard for sheeting the headsail flat. The sizes of the rigs are moderate as befits cruisers, and the sail-area-to-displacement ratios average around 16, which makes them decent light air sailers but still ideal for comfortable cruising without the need for early reefing if the wind puffs up.

On deck, the boats are elegantly simple, with crisp clean lines and excellent proportions, houses that are never too long or ungainly for the hull, decks that are always wide enough, and cockpits that are thoughtfully proportioned. There is just enough wood trim to give the boat some charm but not nearly enough to make it look like it was designed by a fan of pirate movies. All the boats except *Linda* have 3- to 4-inch bulwarks to keep footing on heeled wet decks safe, and all the bulwarks are topped off with nice slim teak caps.

One of the consistently high points of any boat of Chuck's are the cockpits. They are extremely comfortable —you can sleep in *Linda's* although she's only 28 feet overall—but what's more important, the seats are always well sized, with good back supports, and the wells are narrow enough so that you can brace yourself on a heel instead of sliding helplessly forward and ending up on the cockpit sole or lying flat on your back with your toes extended praying for *rigor mortis* to set in and relieve you of the pain.

I'll talk about the interior layouts in the captions with the photos and the drawings but for now I'll say that belowdecks the boats are bright and airy with white bulkheads and cabinetry, and highly varnished teak trim that is minimal and functional, such as drip-troughs under portlights that double as grabrails and another set of grabrails overhead just to be sure to keep you safe in any seaway. The portlights are all small opening ones for strength and security, and together with the many hatches offer good ventilation.

All the boats show complete understanding of a sailor's needs, for instead of succumbing to temptation and leaving vast wide open spaces just to make the boats look big at boat shows, Tom has put in thoughtful things like bookshelves, small lockers, and footwells at the ends of berths for bedding; things which make a boat usable and livable. On one of his Justines I saw a perfectly beautiful ship's tool box made of teak, with a sturdy bar handle, and a bottom lined with felt so as not to scratch or damage anything, and all necessary tools in their own compartments. Now that is the sign of a builder who understands how a boat is used and what a boat will often need. It is this awareness and inventiveness, along with the beauty of the boats and the fine craftsmanship, that make Tom Morris's boats some of the very best.

And if you thought the boats sounded good up to now, wait until you read the rest, for Tom Morris's construction is truly beyond reproach.

"We use isophthalic gelcoat," Tom says slowly, and all the while you can tell his mind is considering all the facets, "because it cuts down blistering. We have also begun using vinylester resin (the most water resistant there is) for the mat backup to the gelcoat for the same reason. But you know what I think? I think that blisters are caused by airpockets which result from poor lamination. I can honestly say that we have never had a blister in any of our hulls save one which was not laminated at our shop. And we have boats down south in warm water, which is supposed to accelerate blistering. We've had people come in and say that our glasswork is the best they had seen anywhere. Maybe that's worth more than the iso. For the laminates we use unidirectional roving. After the double mat we put in four layers of mat and roving, then one more mat because we found it better to bond the cabinetry to. I like using the three light mats to start with because many of our owners want dark hulls, and this assures us that we'll have virtually no readthrough from the rovings."

Following the careful laminating, the strongest point of Tom's construction is his fanatical insistence upon bonding every piece of cabinetry, every shelf, every knee solidly into the boat so that the whole thing becomes an enormous *monocoque* or honeycomb.

"People just don't understand how much strength you add to a boat using this honeycombing," Tom says adamantly. "I think one of the causes of hull-to-deck joints leaking on boats has to do with molded interior units—liners and such. Almost no matter how you try to reinforce a liner, you just don't get the stiffnes you get from these honeycombed plywood boxes. So if the hull isn't stiff, everything is constantly flexing, the hull-to-deck joint included, and eventually it just starts to leak. So when people ask me how we do our hull-deck joint, I show them the through-bolts in the flange and say, 'That's half of it.' Then I point at all these plywood boxes bonded together and I say, 'And that's the rest.' I mean I really look at that thing as a bunch of box beams. That is exactly what they are."

And so as not to compromise the shape of the hull after molding, Tom installs all the bulkheads and cabinetry before taking the hull out of the mold.

"This way we get the exact hull shape each time," he says. "We get a perfect fit for the deck and have a steady platform to work in. We, as most people, prebuild the interior cabinetry in small modules, so if our bulkheads are perfect every time, then our cabinetry will be perfect as well. Also, and it's no small thing, it helps to bond the bulkheads in while the hull is green, and with our pre-building of the cabinetry—we build the cabinets before we even mold the hull—we can bond it all into place while the hull is still green."

And when Tom says, "bond the cabinetry," he means, "bond the cabinetry" because as I said, every edge of every piece is bonded in, *both sides*.

"For bonding in the bulkheads," he explains, "We use biaxial roving which makes for a very strong bond because both sets of fibers (running 90 degrees to each other and 45 degrees to the hull and bulkhead joint) are countering the load on the bulkhead at any given time. With the old style of woven roving if you messed up a bulkhead you could generally take it out by peeling out the bond. With the new biaxial you've got to go in there with a cold chisel.

As if all that didn't create a strong enough boat, they place foam strips every 16 inches against the open hull to form the base for the ribs that they screw the ceiling pieces onto. Two layers of roving complete the ribs, hold the screws in well, and also add a bit more stiffness to the hull.

"I don't know," Tom said, "I just think every little bit helps, so why not do it. We ran a test on a hull once after it was all finished, with the cabinets in but without a deck on, which, don't forget, adds a lot of stiffness. We used a 50-foot tape to measure from stem to stern while the hull was still in the mold, then we picked up the hull, bow and stern. The flex in the hull loaded like that was only 3/16 of an inch. Now you know that most boats bend a lot more than that even *with* the deck on. This thing is *strong*," he said, and he pounded his fist against the side of the hull, making a sound like a cement wall being hit.

"We had an Annie run onto a granite breakwater this summer. She had external ballast so the ballast took an enormous amount of abuse, got chewed away to a depth of about ¾ of an inch, but all the bonding along the center seam was fine. That's because the boat was stiff enough to absorb the shock as a unit instead of the keel area flexing by itself and breaking through the bottom. With a poorly built boat that's what happens when you ground, the keel comes for a visit in the cabin."

To stiffen the boat more, Tom builds floors of ¾-inch mahogany ply with a stiffening cleat on top, and these are bonded completely to the hull—up one side and down the other—together making a box-beam of the bilge. To create a stiff light deck, endgrain balsa is used as coring, with solid glass replacing the core at chainplates, cleats, and tracks. The cabin top has a layer of ¼-inch plywood bonded to it and then formica bonded to that, making for a very clean easy to maintain finish that looks very much more substantial than the supple finish of soft plastic material many builders use on the overhead. And the plywood, that was just a base, is fit in there like a glove. That's a Tom Morris boat.

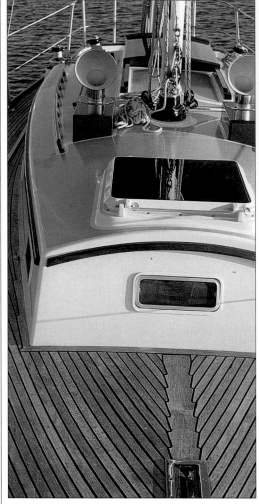

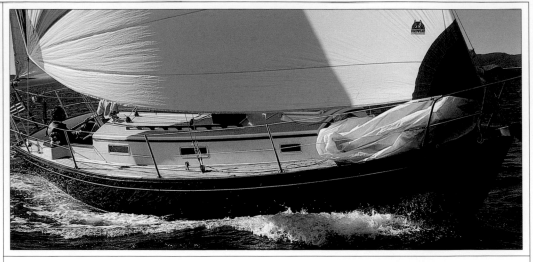

Tom Morris' yachts have an unmistakable sensibility—clean and trim and as lively as a spring breeze. On these two pages are three of his four designs; the fourth, Frances, a 26-footer, is shown in a drawing three pages further on. The next in size is the new 28-footer called Linda (all the boats are designed by Chuck Paine, who likes to give his boats names instead of numbers and what a nice tradition that is), shown in the three photos on the left-hand page. With her slim lines and excellent detailing you have to keep

reminding yourself that she is under 23 feet on the waterline. Chuck designed her as a serious offshore cruiser, yet her lines and weight distribution were computer optimized to provide good performance for club racing or coastal cruising. With a sail-area-to-displacement ratio of 16, she should be a good all-round sailer in any weather. Her forefoot is cut away right back to the mast so she should tack and maneuver well. The photo in the top right corner is of the 30 foot double-ender Leigh, whose underbody is much the same, and the other two photos are of the largest boat in the fleet, the *36* called Justine. Her underbody is shown in the drawing to the right. In the middle of the top row is Tom Morris at the helm of a Linda in Southwest Harbor, where he has run his yard of twelve men since 1972, turning out his distinctive, solidly built, fast yachts that any serious sailor should be proud to own.

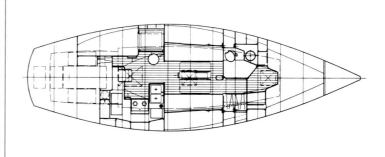

I know this is unjust, but these two pages show the interiors of only the 30-foot Leigh and the 36-foot Justine. The two large photos on top show perhaps one of the best small yacht interiors of all time: the all-white finish detailed to such perfection that no trim pieces are needed to hide the joint of bulkhead to housetop or bulkhead to cabinside or cabinet to cabinet; the beautiful oval passageways; the myriad of small cabinetry even beside the quarterberth; the solid, filled-and-sanded overhead and the minimal trim work, all show great thought and care and excellent design sense. The other five photos are of the *36,* and while they are not as striking as those of Leigh, they show the same good sense throughout. The highlights are the two different chart tables. I especially like the one with the seat.

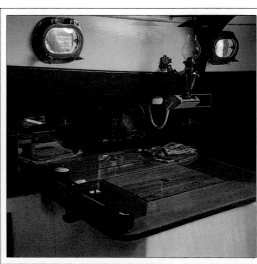

And now my favorite part—the odds and ends. Might as well start in the top left corner where you can see the half-finished interior of a Linda, looking immaculate at every stage. The copper strapping bonds all through-hull metals together to prevent electrolysis. Just to the right of us is a drawing of Linda and below us is a boat Tom built long ago that I liked so much I just couldn't leave it out. Next to it is Chuck's drawing of Frances and her tender, and across the page in the large photo is Tom in one of his shops with the

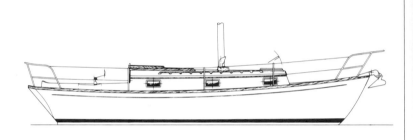

wood fire burning and the winter sun gone down. Above is a detail of some fine cabinetry from a Linda, while the next two photos show the pride that the craftsmen (the owner of the toolbox is a craftslady) take in their trade. The lines drawing at the end shows the hull shape of Tom's boats, resembling the canoe shapes of the most modern racers. In the last photo (you'll have to flip the page to find it) is one good reason why the boats of Tom Morris are as well built as they are. It blows like hell sometimes up in Maine and it doesn't pay to get caught short in some flimsy bit of fluff.

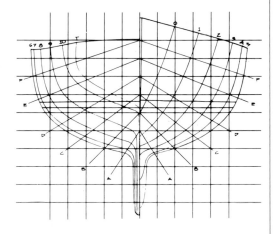

Swans are not only sleek and beautiful but very fast as well, as proven by the races they have won over the years, and in spite of that, down below they feel as good and as comfortable as home. The quality of workmanship is nearly without flaw, and as if all that weren't enough, they have established a reputation of being virtually indestructible. Skipper after skipper I have talked to confess to abuses they have put their Swans through, from murderous Fastnet races to knockdowns and hard groundings. But the Swans just took it, and took it and took it some more.

A dear friend, Eric Swenson, who raced a Swan 47 for seven years including the disastrous '79 Fastnet, and who is well known to be very hard on machinery of all kinds, once did a keel test for Nautor in the fog off Cape Breton. He ran aground onto granite with a two foot sea running, and stayed more or less aground for about twenty minutes. I say more or less because each sea lifted the boat right up a good 2 feet, then brought her thudding down onto the rock. When they managed to find their way back into the channel and finally anchored, they went down to see the damage, and found the keel chewed up but not an open seam or cracked joint anywhere. And no leaks.

"A hell of a boat," Eric said in admiration. "The only thing that went wrong in seven years was that the toilet paper holder rusted."

The reason for this indestructibility is well summarized by Olle Emmes, a gentle, friendly man, the manager of Nautor, who has been with them for seventeen years. At first he was at a bit of a loss when I asked him what made Swans so good, then he thought for a moment and said, "I suppose it must be that we don't like to compromise. We never want to compromise in strength and quality, neither to save money nor to accelerate performance.

"We try to find the best materials we can and then we do the best job with them that we can. And I have to say that it is the tradition of this area—a respect for quality of workmanship that is inbred in everyone—that allows us to achieve such quality in our boats."

And that is without exaggeration, for I heard at Baltic, whose top people all began at Nautor, that in the beginning Nautor wasn't really aware of the quality of its boats. It was the buyers and the journalists from around the world who first brought the news that the Swans had become the world's very best yachts.

Ingmar Granholm, a naval architect who has been with Nautor almost eighteen years and now handles Nautor's marketing, (how many other boat companies do you know that have a naval architect in that position) further explained Nautor's philosophy and approach to quality.

"I think we have learned to understand that boat building is a very old industry *and* a very old art. If you try to change it too rapidly or too drastically I think you would be going against its nature. I don't think it's possible to make drastic changes against the nature of something. It has to be a slow methodical change.

"One typical example of not compromising is that our smallest boats have exactly the same quality as the big ones.

We just cannot say, 'Well, let us leave out some of the quality and then lower the price and we'll reach a bigger market.' We can't do that. We don't want to do that. I think many people take a very large step when coming up to their first Swan and we want to give them the best quality we can.

Olle Emmes: "There are a lot of things about us that we would like people to know. For a long time our fiberglass quality and finish quality were so much better than those of other boat builders, but now more and more people have begun to do quality finishes. Unfortunately many of those are only nice finishes without the step-by-step structural integrity of construction. I think for us the important thing, and it seems the most difficult thing, is to inform the people who are looking for a sailboat that to us every step of construction is vital. They have to understand that it is all those little steps that make for a strong safe reliable boat: Layup, plumbing, electrical; everything.

"We talk about this problem of communication day in and day out, and it is a difficult one because you just cannot expect a surgeon or a violinist to come here and be familiar with all the different phases of boat building and appreciate what we are doing. It is too much to ask. Communicating step-by-step, *invisible quality* is very much a problem.

"I think also, that when we improve on something, which we try to do every day, we don't talk about it too much because I think that it's a natural thing for us, for people, to want to make improvements, to want to create a better and better whatever it is they create. We just assume that people understand that we are doing the best job we know how, and *that* to me means doing a better job every day. We learn so much every day that it would be foolish, it would be unnatural not to want to put that into our work. And quite honestly sometimes we forget about the things we do well because we become 'home-blind.' You know what I mean?"

The history of Nautor has been for the most part without the great financial problems that beset many other builders, mostly because it seems that there is always a market for the best of things, but also perhaps because after a great fire just before Christmas of 1969 one of Finland's largest paper companies, Oy Wilh. Schauman AB, pulled Nautor from the brink.

"The fire put us into a very difficult financial situation," Olle Emmes said, "So Schauman actually came to our rescue and I think for the most part it has worked out very well. Of course we have to fill out a lot of forms for them but it's nice to know that you have resources for tooling new boats and a sort of father to fall back on if things get very bad. And I think it's also important for our clients to have such a big company behind us. Boatyards all alone can be very vulnerable, but with Schauman we are assured good continuity. There are three hundred and thirty people working here now very steadily, building about fifty boats a year. We are, like everyone else—going up in total tonnage but coming down in number of boats. We used to produce one hundred boats a year but they were small, a lot of *37's.* Now we are even building a 102 footer and our new production boats seem to be getting bigger as well."

"We usually start a new design," Ingmar Granholm said,

"when we find that a boat gets too old and we cannot incorporate into it all the new ideas we have come up with over the years. When we begin work on a new boat design, we study very carefully what people have learned about boats of that size, the good things, the bad things, because once the boat is actually designed, you really cannot make major changes because they seem to set off a chain reaction and very soon the whole boat will be bastardized. It will simply not be as pure and good as initially intended. So I think it's important to think the problems through thoroughly from the beginning, to *engineer* the boat and not just modify it later by taking bits out here and there.

"I think we spend more time engineering than any other yard in the world. That is why it takes us so long to come out with a new design. And yet we are receptive to customers' requests; this doesn't mean that we will necessarily end up doing anything. It just means that we do listen and evaluate suggestions and requests. The owners can tell us exactly what they want, what their ultimate expectation is, but not necessarily how to get there. That gives us an opportunity to come back and show them how we think we can make it work. Sometimes we get owners in here who think they are the world's greatest boat builders and try to tell us to do this and that without having the faintest notion about stress and strength problems. We have ten people here in design and engineering. After the designers, like Frers or Holland, give us the designs, we do all our own detail drawings, stress tests, everything. All the Swans are built with a Lloyds' Hull Construction Certificate. This means that the premises, the raw materials and the scantling are approved and checked by the Lloyds' surveyor who also pops in and checks the boats at irregular intervals."

We started walking through the yard with Ingmar, and seeing all the meticulous work on the beautiful hulls of the mold shop made me feel like a kid in the world's biggest toy store. The hulls of the Swans are solid fiberglass without cores, but both strength *and* lightness are maintained by stiffening the hull by means of a grid of longitudinal and lateral beams, a grid which creates individual panels no more than half a square meter in size.

"We do not use a core," Ingmar said. "We have tried and tested it but we found that the danger of separation was always there and we really didn't gain anything weightwise. With the method of the closely spaced stiffeners we can build a single-skinned boat as strong and as light as a cored boat. The subject of sandwich hull cannot be dismissed with a few words. The larger a boat gets the more sensible core construction becomes, but doing it with guarantees involves expensive materials and methods. It is certainly possible to build a light, smallish yacht with 'normal' materials and save weight, but will the hull withstand extreme conditions? What happens if you hit a floating object, a log or something? And what is the lifetime of such a vessel? To build a sandwich construction as light or lighter than a single-skinned reinforced one, means thinner skins and that needs no further explanations. How come you rarely find a yacht approved by a classification company, built in sandwich? If you do find one, compare the weights of the hulls.

"We do a lot of research in association with the Technical Research Center of Finland on everything from hull panels to rigging. We test things for a long period before we change anything because when we do make a change, it must be for the better, not the worse. We found that one of the most important things is to bond in the bulkheads while the hull is fresh and the laminates still green. This way we get a chemical reaction—and therefore a better bond—between the hull and the bulkhead bonds instead of just an adhesive reaction. We don't have a choice with bonding the tops of bulkheads to the deck, because we put in much of the furniture before the deck goes on.

"We also think a hull should cure in the mold for some time, so its shape is settled and it won't move and distort. Of course putting the bulkheads in while the boat is still in the mold is one way of holding the shape and the other is putting in the grid-works. We do floor grids, hull grids, bulkheads, while the hulls set in the molds. We once pulled a boat before those things were in and found that as the hull sat in the cradle we got some deformation, just from its own weight. You just keep learning all the time."

And learn they do. They use fine roving near the surface, then coarser roving later which helps them achieve one of the finest hull finishes in the world. They use isophthalic resins and epoxy to prevent blistering and, to pad the odds even more, they use clear gelcoat—which is less porous than the pigmented stuff—below the waterline.

The hull grid system creates as stiff a boat as possible as discussed above, and also provides backing for bulkheads and major pieces of furniture so they don't print through the hull. Print-through is not only unsightly but it creates a weakening hard spot in the skin as well.

Now that others have done years of testing on the shoal Scheel keel for cruisers, Nautor has started using it and Ingmar says the owners are very satisfied. They claim they can't see any significant difference upwind, and downwind they actually do better because the longer keel helps them steer a better course.

The deck is reinforced with high-density closed-cell PVC foam, which adds great stiffness yet does not deform when subjected to heat buildup from the sun, like Airex tends to do.

The mast step in the newer boats is incorporated into a complex metal floor grid which stiffens the hull against the torquing of the keel and spreads the load of the mast as well.

One of the most impressive things about Nautor is that they do everything themselves, from the fabrication of all metal parts to the anodizing of their aluminum. And they anodize absolutely everything inside and outside the boat in the best way possible. For example: They designed their own toerail and have it extruded especially for them *but* they take delivery of it unanodized. The toerail is then fitted onto the boat it's intended for, pre-bent and screwed down into place and bent some more if it needs adjusting. *Then* once it's perfectly fit, it's removed and sent down to be anodized. This way there is no chance that the anodizing will crack while the rail is being bent, or get scraped or gouged while the rail is wrestled with during fitting. Certainly this is a very time-

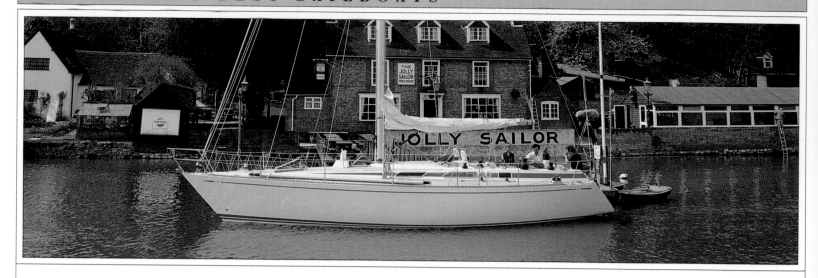

I t's accepted industry-wide that Nautor was the first in the world to build top quality fiberglass boats, and they certainly have not changed course. The lines—drawn by the world's best: Sparkman & Stevens, Ron Holland, German Frers—are the most beautiful in contemporary designs. I like Frers' *46* and Holland's new *43* the best. The underbodies are designed for top speed *and* good handling, with deep fin keels (although the shoal Scheel keel is available as an option) and highly efficient spade rudders. The decks are designed for function without compromise, yet hidden inside the Spartan lines are some of the most luxurious interiors in the world. All Swans, even the smallest, the *371*, have very usable aft cabins which—as you can see in the drawings of the previous pages—by the time you reach the *59*, become almost

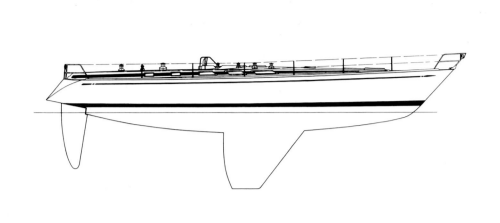

palatial. The exterior photos on this double spread depict three of the Nautor line of nine boats ranging from the 37 footer to a *76,* which when launched in 1980 was the largest serially produced cruiser/racer in the world. In the top left corner is Ron Holland's *39.* Below and in the top right corner is the beautiful Frers-

designed *46* with its elegantly faired-in stern, and beside it is the *651* on whose vast decks the crew of eighteen almost become lost. On the two following pages are some of Swan's legendary interiors. Simply put, the joiner work is second to none in both execution and imagination. The attention to detail is best exemplified by

the fact that Nautor has experts buylng whole teak logs which they then mill down (and reject 30 percent of the resulting lumber). The veneer is hand chosen to be perfectly matched for each bulkhead and is then laminated onto the plywood in the parent company's local plywood division.

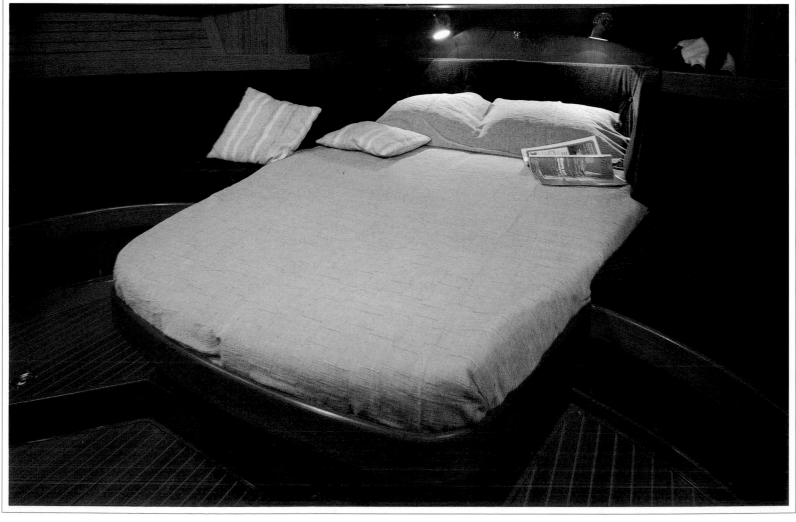

With-
out doubt, the most
outstanding
cross-section of
cruising boats in this
book is built by
Pacific Seacraft.
From the Bruce
Bingham designed
20-foot Flicka (top of
right hand page)
seen snuggled under
the palms in the far
reaches of the South
Pacific, to the largest
of the line, the
Crealock 37 (above)
anchored off the
autumn Connecticut
shore, they are boats
of great character,
practicality *and*
integrity. The other
boats include the
Crealock 34 (shown
coming and going
on the bottom of the
left-hand page) and
the little Dana 24,

beating smartly in the bottom right-hand corner. The rest of the line is made up of the Orion 27 and the new Crealock 30, which is just being born. I included the color cutaway drawing on these pages to show you that underneath the classic teak caprails, bronze portlights, and gentle lines, lie lean modern underbodies. The drawing is of the Crealock 37. The sizable skeg will make steering downwind an exhilarating adventure instead of a version of out-of-control downhill skiing. As the photos show, the Crealock boats have extremely pretty canoe sterns and graceful bows, and *all* the boats have lively sheers. Pacific Seacraft builds the boats with solid hand-layed-up hulls, and although much attention is paid to good performance, an equal amount of thought is given to the displacement needs of a serious cruiser, which will need to carry substantial quantities of anchor chain, food, supplies and water.

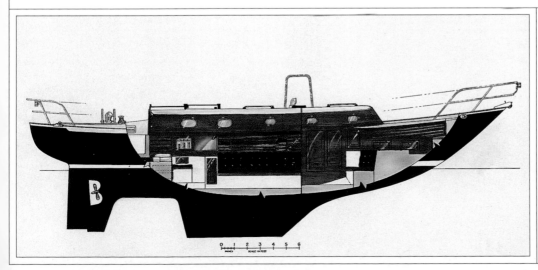

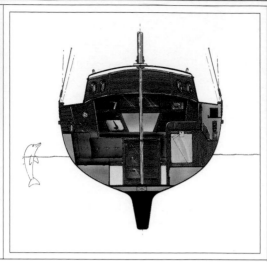

The two photos and two drawings on this page are of the Dana 24. The ingenious table stows by sliding underneath the berth. The photo below is of Flicka's unbelievably large interior. That's a

20-footer you're looking at, with full headroom. The 27 foot Orion designed by Henry is represented in the sailplan and the two photos on the top of the opposite page. The first photo shows a unique *and* serviceable chart table that, through some miracle, Henry managed to tuck in behind the angled galley counter.

Observe it hiding behind the sink in the adjoining photo. The drawing and the photo to the right are of the Crealock 37's unimprovable interior. The highlight is the forward cabin which has a settee, a berth with—finally —lots of footspace and a huge hanging locker. The big photo at the bottom of the page is of the Crealock 34.

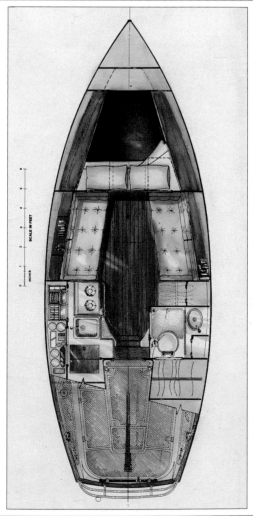

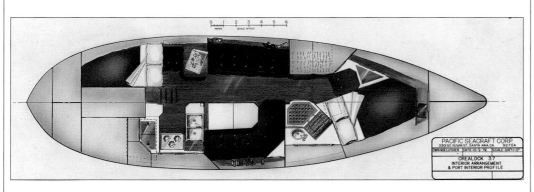

PACIFIC SEACRAFT CORP.
330 SO SUSAN ST. SANTA ANA CA.   92704
DWN W.R.LUTHER   DATE 10-5-79   SCALE 3/4"=1'-0"
CREALOCK 37
INTERIOR ARRANGEMENT
& PORT INTERIOR PROFILE

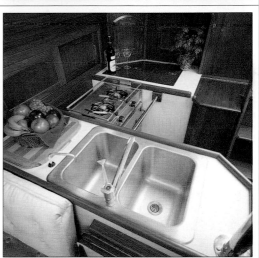

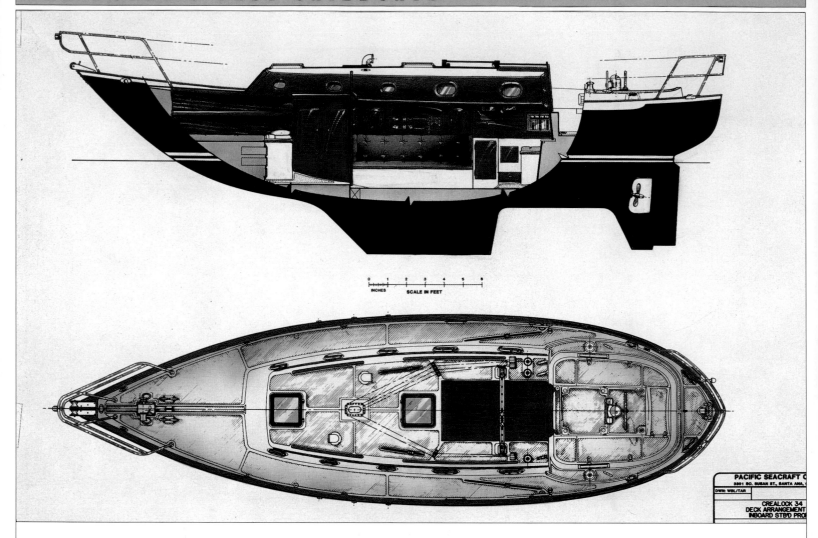

INCHES   SCALE IN FEET

PACIFIC SEACRAFT C
3901 SO. SUSAN ST., SANTA ANA,
DWN: WBL/TAR

CREALOCK 34
DECK ARRANGEMENT
INBOARD STB'D PRO

As I've so often said, small details make great boats. In the cutaway drawing of the *34,* notice the rudder elevated a couple of inches above the skeg so that in case of grounding the rudder won't be damaged.

Note also all opening bronze ports and louvered doors for ventilation. In the drawing below, look at the curved cockpit coaming corners which make leaning back on a heel extremely comfortable. Also note that all lines lead aft for safer sail handling, and be aware of double anchor rollers for use and stowage of

ground tackle. The photo shows a nifty fairlead with the L-shaped base that is about as effective for guarding your caprail against rope-chafe as you can ask for. Across the page, note the small manageable sails of the *34,* and in the photo beside it, the angled head (we sure cover a lot of ground fast here) which allows for the

large space in the forepeak. In the galley, a space behind the sink is made to hold snug an inexpensive, easy-to-clean, unsinkable garbage bin. The tightly-closing lid is made to double as a chopping block. Below it is shown the "keying" of the caprails, which greatly helps in permanently locking

together two pieces of the rail. Next, there is simply no better way to design a cockpit than with a removable sole giving access, air and light to the engine below. Also note stop-blocks beside controls which prevent the levers from snapping off when you stomp them. Pacific Seacraft gets the award for thoughtful design.

That is Pacific Seacraft in a nutshell. The boats are pretty and strong and simple without pretension, and they are affordable and reliable long distance cruisers. My best regards to Bill Crealock for his designs and my hat off to Henry and Mike for building such fine boats. I bet they go to sleep at night with great grins on their faces. Heaven knows they've earned them.

SAM L. MORSE CO.

Some boats look elegant and lean, like the lady of your dreams, and some boats just look fast and mean, then there are boats that look like true friends, and Sam Morse's little cutters seem like the best friends you can find. ☐ I might as well start off by telling you that the Bristol Channel Cutter and the Falmouth Cutter are the most beautiful 28 and 22 foot fiberglass sailboats in the world. There. Now that we've cleared that up we can begin at the beginning.

The designer of both boats is Mr. Lyle Hess, whose accomplishments include *Seraffyn*—the boat Lynn and Larry Pardey sailed around the world without an engine—as well as a new boat designed for the Pardeys. The most reassuring thing about all of his designs is that each new boat is more beautiful than the last. And that may be because Lyle Hess is one of the last of the old school of designers, like William Garden and Bill Crealock and the eccentric Ray Bolger, who believe that sailboats are mystical, and magical, and among the—sadly few—truly beautiful creations of man. Aside from that they all believe that sailboats have to sail well and take just about anything the sea decides to give.

Now you might rightfully think that to incorporate all the above in a design is no small task, but I think as long as a *good* designer is given rein and not hobbled by racing rules and market surveys and the need to cram four hundred berths into a floating thimble, then, if the man is honest, listens to his heart and respects the sea, he'll find it pretty hard not to draw a fine boat.

But first and foremost a boat has to be beautiful, if for no other reason than to avoid insulting the sea. And to get a bit more selfish, I must tell you that for me one of the great joys of sailing is coming upon beautiful little yachts in hidden harbors, something that happens too infrequently nowadays. The two little yachts of Lyle Hess that Sam Morse builds in the old Westsail yard in Southern California help to keep a flickering flame burning.

Lest you mistakenly believe that these sweet-looking yachts are clunky old dears who can't get out of their own way, let me tell you that one Bristol Channel Cutter sailed from Dana Point California to Nuku Hiva in the Marquesas in twenty-two and a half days, or an average speed of 5.8 knots over 3,150 nautical miles. One day she made good 180 miles or 7½ knots, and for a 28-foot boat that's as good as you can get. Apart from that, the boat is stiff and heavy, with an even, gentle motion, thanks to her heavy displacement of 14,000 pounds for a waterline/displacement ratio of near 340 which is about as heavy as you'll find on a boat that sails so amazingly well.

Her sailing ability comes from her extremely long waterline of 26 feet 3 inches—if you want to be generous, then think of her as a 34 footer without the overhangs—and her deceptively full lines aft which give her good stability and lots of sail carrying power. Yet her fullness aft does not indicate a clumsy boat as many an old boat tended to be because they carried their beam too far forward causing bloated bows. If you look at the lines of the Bristol Channel Cutter, you will see she reaches maximum beam well aft of mid station, and her entry lines are all straight, very much like the best of modern cruisers.

As to how well she handles, all you have to do to answer that question is read the Pardeys' books, for they sailed her without an engine all over the world, which means a lot of mean tight tacking in mean tight harbors, and they came back to the same design again.

Mr. Hess designed and styled his boats after the old Bristol Pilot boats and Itchen work boats which in turn were designed to handle nasty steep seas in a sea kindly fashion. And if you think that these little boats are just for old-fashioned dreamers who never sail anywhere, then look at the photo with not one but *two* Bristol Channel Cutters anchored in the Solomons in the far reaches of the Pacific.

They make ideal long-distance cruising boats for a good number of reasons: First, they look just perfect in far distant harbors; second, their heavy displacement results in a very comfortable motion despite their small size, a motion much less wearing on the crew than the bobbing skidding sliding hopping motion of a light boat; third, their construction—of which I'll say more later—is excellent; and last, because their design shows good common-sense and utter simplicity.

The long keel gives you good tracking and relaxing turns at the helm, yet the whittled forefoot makes her a decent handler in tight quarters. The cockpit is comfortable but small, holding but 700 pounds of water if filled to the brim. The decks are broad and, with the outboard rig, uncluttered for safe sailhandling and movement. The enormous rudder makes her respond quickly, and since it is aft hung, is easy to repair, and even easier to add a self steering vane to. Better still, she's steered by a tiller that needs almost no maintenance, and very seldom fails. Her rig, although big enough to move her well in light airs—sail area to displacement ratio of almost 16.5—has a total sail area of less than six hundred square feet, still small enough for a couple to handle with ease.

And perhaps this won't mean much to some, but when sailing her I felt as though I was handling a little ship that moved through the sea as if she'd done just that for centuries. Those of you who have sailed in boats that felt like pingpong balls and mushed to and fro like a bowl of melting Jello—causing you to look anxiously back to see if the rudder was still there—will know exactly what I mean.

The one objection that some have is that the bowsprit is narrow and long without a platform or a pulpit—hardly a place of comfort and security for changing headsails in a blow. True enough. But Sam can add little "ears" to the sprit, making it nearly 1 foot wide and much safer to stand on, and you *can* get a furling jib and never go near the blessed thing again, or you can avoid being out there in a blow if you change your headsail early. And if it's a question of a *real* blow then you'll probably want only reefed main and staysail anyway, meaning you just want the jib down and out of the way, a feat which can easily be accomplished if you have a net of some sort strung between the whiskerstays, for then you can just net the jib and lash it to the bowsprit. It might get a little salty overnight, but then that's the sea.

Meanwhile back on deck. Thanks to the dead-parallel cabinsides, the side decks are astoundingly broad—2½ feet in one spot—which, with the very high 8-inch bulwarks, make for a comfortable cradle in which to sunbathe. The bulwarks alone are beautiful enough to make you want to have the boat. They are not a part of the hull as is customary, but are made of solid planks slightly raised off the deck, supported by through-bolted wood posts on 20-inch centers. What this means is that the entire deck is one long scupper, guaranteeing you quick drainage in any seas, and assuring that there will be no puddles of water left anywhere, no matter how badly she may be loaded out of trim.

The entire top of the little forward house opens, making passing of sails a sailor's dream. The split trunk cabin may cause some to object to the loss of space belowdecks, but the deck in between makes for a low safe place to stand and brace yourself while handling the halyards. And I almost forgot; there are good coamings around the cockpit to keep the water out and the small of your back braced.

But let's talk about belowdecks. Good design and common sense are very evident here. Too many designers and builders simply refuse to believe that some people are seriously interested in sailing long distances with a crew of two, requiring but two good berths, and ample living, working, and stowage space belowdecks. Or if not involved in voyaging, that there are many couples with one child or no child, who seek peace and solitude, who do not jam their boats full of friends and aquaintances but take refuge in the company of only their dearest, and go and hide and watch mother nature unveil all her secrets.

The Bristol Channel Cutter has the ultimate small yacht layout for world cruising for two. The galley to port is ideally sized, with the sink near the centerline and the stove outboard with some bracing to be had against the companionway ladder. As with many small boats, the icebox is found opposite the galley, in this case under the chart table. This is just as well, for as you are preparing food in the galley, you won't have to sweep the counter clean to get into the icebox. The traditional drawback such an arrangement used to have was that the lid was set into the center of the chart table and the cracks and trim surrounding the lid made the use of pencils and dividers a forecastable nightmare. *But* Sam has saved the day. He has transformed the *entire* chart table top into a lid without the cracks and trimpieces that used to change the simplest course line into the sign of Zorro.

The salon is exactly like it says in the Sailor's Bible, "Two settee berths, dropleaf table, footlocker over end of berth." The pilot berth to port opens into a big double and that's nice indeed unless you're a loner, and even then it's good to have in case you change your mind. With the deep broad bilges of the BCC accommodating the fuel and water tanks, there is good stowage beneath the berths.

So far, you may say there is nothing truly spectacular about this layout and of course you would be right, but I think it's rather hard to improve on a layout that has served small yachts so well for nearly a century. But what lies forward of the main bulkhead of the BCC definitely falls under the heading of "remarkable."

Customarily you have a cramped head to one side and a pigeon hole to the other with a V berth forward which can be utilized only by the most dedicated and astute of leg braiders among us, normally followed by a sail locker too small for a hanky and a chainlocker that barely holds two links of chain. As a blessed change, the BCC has the following solution. The area forward of the main bulkhead, running the full width of the hull, is an open space incorporating a head, two vast lockers to starboard, either hanging or not

—the choice is up to you—and miracle of miracles, a true, honest-to-god workbench off to port. For those of you who tend to belittle the importance of a workbench on a small cruising yacht, let me tell you that Eric Hiscock, who has cruised almost as much as the rest of us put together, once remarked that after his berth his most cherished place aboard was the workbench.

The workbench on the BCC is of perfect standing height and nearly 4 feet in length. There is good headroom here, and don't forget that the hatch above you opens to give you all the light and air you could wish for; a true blessing indeed for either working at the bench or sitting on the throne. The area beneath the high bench is full of lockers and drawers, and the head has a lid that flips down over it, making it a place to sit while you're working, and even better, a place to kneel when you're trying to rummage in the good-sized sail locker, which is accessible through a large opening in the bulkhead directly forward.

The remarkable thing about all this is that all these functions can be performed here, utilizing only the very small surface of the shower grate as floorspace. Now *that* is intelligent, ingenious, designing.

If you're not converted yet, then let me tell you how she's built. A good indication of the solidity of this good yacht is that in spite of her 28 feet she weighs almost 9000 pounds *without ballast.* And let me tell you that ain't all wallpaper. What that means essentially is that she's built like the proverbial brick relief station. Her laminates are all hand layed up and the schedule goes like this: white gelcoat, dark gelcoat (makes it easier to see air bubbles and dry fibers during layup) then mat and cloth, then four layers of mat and woven roving, finished up by a mat and cloth. In all you have six structural layers.

The glasswork is done by Crystaliner, who have over twenty-five years of experience building fiberglass hulls. They used to do all the glass work for Westsail, and they do very good work indeed.

The main bulkheads are all of sturdy ¾-inch plywood, and what is remarkable about them is the bonding. Whereas many builders use only a piece of 4-inch fiberglass mat tape to tab the bulkheads in, Sam Morse uses cloth and mat and roving a full 12 inches wide. What that means is that the potential of bulkhead delamination is cut down drastically. But Sam Morse is a worrier and he likes to do things better than mere humans, so to reduce even further the chance of failure, he drills 2½-inch diameter holes through the bulkheads in the area of the bonds to come. When he lays in the wet bonds, he actually joins the bonds together through the holes to "lock" the bulkhead in. This makes it almost impossible for the bulkhead to pull away, or separate, from the bonds.

Apart from that, Sam bonds every piece of furniture in place—there are no liners in the boat—making a hull of great strength even stronger. The deck is fastened in the industry-standard through-bolted flange method, with 5200 sealant in between. The work throughout is excellent, completely befitting a world-class yacht.

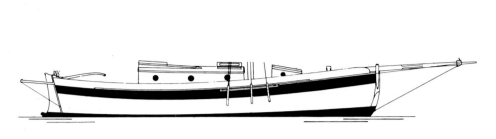

I t's hard to write about Sam Morse's boats without being seduced into staring at the pictures for hours. They are the *most* romantic little offshore cruisers being built today. When you read the text, you'll discover what kind of fine timing they have achieved doing ocean crossings. If you look at the opening photo on the previous page, you'll see a little Bristol Channel Cutter leap joyfully over the sea. Her almost plumb stem and chopped broad stern give her a long waterline and good power, and her sail area of nearly 600 square feet moves her very well. Her standard rig has a modern marconi main; not the gaffed one you see in the photo in the top right corner, but the picture was too pretty to leave out. Her split deck-house leaves good deckspace to work the sails without limitations to the interior.

The interior is as perfect a creation as you will find on a 28 foot boat, and that is another thing that makes the Lyle Hess-designed Bristol Channel Cutter stand out. The best general angle is in the photo directly below, where you can see the galley to the left, the chart table to the right, and an ideally sized salon forward. The footwell in the starboard berth is first class for stowage *and* for acting as base and safety bar for the cabin heater. The pilot berth to port is a deceptive little critter, for it slides

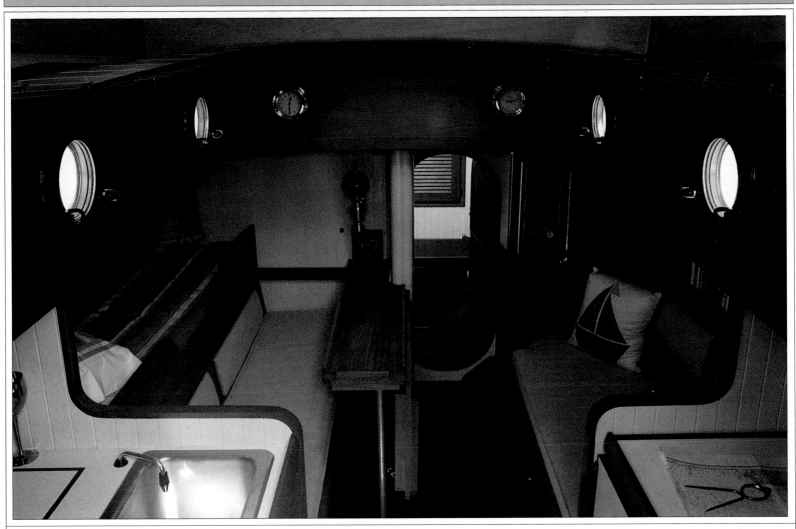

out to form a double, whose inboard half is spacious and airy. If you look closely, you'll see the heavy teak track running to the table's edge. I spent almost half a page talking about the forepeak in the text, so I'll skip it here and point out a couple of other things. The drawing is of the smaller Sam Morse boat called the Falmouth Cutter— 22 feet on deck. There are plans for it in the back of the book. Now look closely at the photo to its right and you will see (you might need a microscope) that the front of the chart table, which is also the icebox, has a hinge-down countertop extension stored against it. In the *up* position, this piece closes the space between the chart table and the galley counter, giving you as much working space as the kitchen of the average suburban home. Bravo Sam Morse! The little jewel in the bottom corner is an 8-inch brass vent Sam uses to circulate air in his lockers. The man has class.

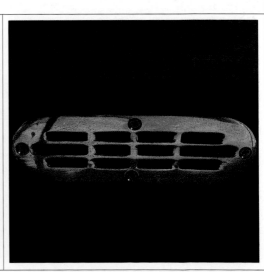

Okay. Here are the goodies. To the left, the hefty taffrail ends are being glued in place. In the upper corner the tongue-and-groove pieces of the main hatch are being fitted, and to its left the samson posts are capped off by massive bronze caps with the boat's initials emblazoned upon them. Directly below, you can see the fine curved cockpit coaming and cast-bronze winchbase. A commendable idea is the double compass setup which lets you steer a course on either tack without having to revert to the wretched lubberlines. I never could subtract in a nightwatch coma.

Above, note the forward hatch—almost a companionway—pumping vast amounts of air and light belowdecks. A great little boat. Quit pondering. Go and get one. I asked Sam to describe his philosophy about his boats, and he told me the following: "When my wife Betty and I got into this back in '75, we wanted to build a really good boat, not the super hyped 'incredible' and 'awsome' quality of so many boats being advertised, but something much more than that. The true quality of a really honest boat—the best you could build. Like the one or two things you have owned for so long you've forgotten, things that still work, still do the job, just as they were meant to. Like the little CO_2 soda maker we've had for years, made in Sweden, that still works as well as ever although it needs a new gasket now and then. Just a good honest piece which someone made to really last and give someone his money's worth—nothing's ever broken, nothing's fallen off, still looks good on the bar. It's a simple device and that's important. We want our boats to be like that."

So that in short is the story of the Bristol Channel Cutter. Perhaps, to create singularly beautiful little yachts such as these, it takes a pair of incurable old romantics like Lyle Hess and Sam Morse. They are, without doubt, an endangered species. Who will come to take their place, God only knows. Perhaps no one. And a sadder and more dreary place will the world be for all that.

SHANNON

I have always been a fan of honest boats, boats that do one thing remarkably well instead of boats that try to be all things to all people, only to end up as everybody's nightmare. And my favorite boats are still long-distance cruisers that can sail the seven seas ably and with good speed, built without compromise in construction or design to serve her crew well regardless of the weather. □ Walter Shulz's Shannons fit that description to perfection.

Walter and his boats are a study in contrast. At first glance you see fine traditional features like gentle sheers and sturdy bowsprits, bronze opening ports and hefty teak caprails, but on closer scrutiny you find center-board underbodies that go to weather well, high aspect mainsails and stainless steel rod rigging and, best of all, foam-cored hulls built with the most sophisticated gelcoats, resins and fibers in the industry today. If that's the kind of boat you're after, Walter Shulz's Shannons are pretty hard to beat.

Walter learned about boatbuilding the best way possible, by working in a yard that repaired all sorts of boats, giving him an overview of why some sailboats stayed together while others fell apart.

When he and his friend David Walters started Shannon in 1975 their objective was to build the best, most solid cruising boats possible. And that they did. No detail in a Shannon is left to chance; if something can be slightly altered from the norm to aid the structure, it's done; and if something can be done to extend the life of the boat, it's never missed regardless of the cost. Indeed at Shannon, as at the classic yards of Hinckley and Nautor, most of the things that put the boats among the very best are "the invisible components" hidden beneath the surface. It is these things that really count, and it is these things that I'll talk most about here.

Mark Perry, a perfect example of the serious, intense Yankee, is the manager of the yard. He has been at Shannon since Day One and has stayed with them as they grew from a handful of workers to a hundred and seven strong. He spent the day guiding me through the yard and not once did he slough off a detail; indeed, the smallest bit of what most call engineering but he calls "common sense," he understood and explained.

We started in the mold shop where Steve Butterworth, who is at least as ardent about boatbuilding as Mark, is the foreman. "We lay the hulls up in one piece," Steve began, "using a two-piece mold in order to get an internal hull-to-deck flange. It's a lot more work but it is worth the effort."

"To get a good layup, we believe you can put in only one layup a day, let it go off, grind the next day to take off any imperfections *then* put in the next layer. The first day we shoot the vinylester gelcoat (that's as impermeable as you can get, hence the best against osmosis blistering) then one layer of 1 ounce mat. The second day we grind the seams fair and check for any air pockets, then we put in 1.5-ounce mat and a 2.6-mm coremat (a thick compressed layer of short fibers) to stop any readthrough from the pattern of roving. That cures, and the process goes on day by day. Depending on the model size, we use a computer-analyzed schedule using combinations of double bias roving (usually called biaxial) that's patterned at 45 degrees diagonally, unidirectional roving, Airex core, E-glass filaments and conventional roving. Then the entire inside of the hull is covered with a coating of fire retardant resin with a color pigment. The computer readout tests say this type of laminate schedule is almost 40 percent stronger than conventionally layed up

hulls using only mat and woven roving, yet they're 15 percent lighter."

"Another important thing is," Mark took over, "that the unidirectional roving runs from one side of the hull *across* the centerline and up the other side. The internal molded lead ballast is then put in over this, so all the load is taken by these continuous long fibers running athwartships." (Now *that's* good engineering. F.M.)

"At the sheer, the layup is almost ¾-inch. At the bottom the layup will be close to 2½ inches. We've had boats up on coral reefs, rock breakwaters, hit big boulders, and never had any structural failures. Don't forget people take their families aboard our boats on long distances." And at the word "families" a kind of gravity came into an already serious voice. Then he said, "All these steps are very important to us."

Into this already monstrously strong hull they put two massive longitudinals averaging about 8 inches in depth. These are of 1½-inch wide solid mahogany glassed over with mat-roving, mat-roving, then double roving at the end. These laminates run 18 inches onto the hull past the mahogany. That is the same bonding they use to attach the bulkheads to the hull and to attach the plywood knees for the chainplates to the hull. When the bulkheads go in they go on foam backing. I asked Mark why they bother putting in foam when they have the Airex already.

"Well, he said, "To us it's just as important not to put a hard spot against the inner skin as it is for most people to protect the outer skin. A hard spot weakens the laminate. We're not stopping readthrough but it helps a little structurally and *that* is very important to us."

And you thought *I* was a maniacal overbuilder?

"Before we glass in bulkheads," Mark went on, "we use small tabs of fiberglass bonding to position the bulkheads. We just want to make sure we get them perfect. If not, we cut the tabs and reset the bulkhead. Then after the first final bond, we drill through the laminate and the bulkhead on 10-inch centers and a roving is put through it, then it's resined to the hull just to stop the bonds from ever pulling away from the bulkheads. Then we finish bonding the bulkhead in. All hulls are built the same, from the 28 footer to the 50 footer."

Shannon has an abhorrence of drilling into the skin inside the Airex core so they set ribs on the hull at 16-inch centers made of Klegecell foam, and screw into the glass bonds that they put over them. And they don't even like screwing into the inner skin of the deck, so they put wooden battens of ½-inch plywood around all hatches and portlights and every 16 inches between them, and laminate over them with mat and cloth. If you don't think that all these little bits and pieces add additional strength and stiffness to the boats, then think again.

Another thing. With all these ribs and ceiling strips, you now have yourself a ventilation system that goes right through the whole boat, down to and through the bilge, so you get constantly circulating air that not only helps to prevent mildew from forming but also acts as insulation much as an airspace 'cold-roof' does in a house.

The deck is bolted to the massive hull flange; Caulk-Tex bedding compound is used to bed the two together. Then they do something unique. They put a strip of epoxy-sealed wood under the flange so that the nuts can, as Mark explains, "bury themselves in there. We found that with glass, being as hard as it is, sometimes even a lockwasher will, in time, work itself loose. But if you bury the nut in the wood, the wood will have more give and hang onto the nuts a little better." Nothing wrong with that for sure.

"And you still use lockwashers and locknuts even with the wood?" I asked him.

A look of complete horror spread over Mark's face. "Of course!" he blurted. "You kidding me?"

"Chainplates are very important to us," he said as we went on a little ways. "We use the plywood knee with foam between it and the hull, then it's held there by mat, cloth, roving, mat, double roving, mat and roving." I just shook my head and started laughing. Mark didn't even blink, just went on talking. ·

"If we have a situation where the chainplate is attached to a bulkhead, the bulkhead is reinforced the same way as the knee along the entire outboard foot-wide part of it. Bulkheads are from ½ inch to 1 inch thick depending on where in the boat they are. These are fir plywood which, after being bonded into place, are covered over by *solid* teak or mahogany or oak strips, depending on the customer's choice. So the main bulkhead ends up 1¼ inches thick. The furniture is built the same way; ¼-inch ply covered over by ⅛-inch strips of solid wood. The teak and holly sole are again a solid ⅝-inch thick. We use the solid wood finish everywhere so that if you nick or gouge a piece, it will still be repairable instead of being totalled as would a piece of thin veneer. This kind of damage happens over the years. We build our boats to be around for a long time." *That* may be the understatement of the decade.

And that's not even close to being everything. A cabinet of drawers on a Shannon is not just a four-walled box with frail runners for the drawers. No sir. Instead, each drawer slides on a full plywood shelf. This kind of honeycomb structure, which is in turn bonded to the hull, creates a hull that would laughingly meet the specifications of an icebreaker.

"All structural framing in the boat," Mark said, "is solid mahogany. Okay?"

"Okay with me," I said.

And when Mark says solid he means *solid.* The subframe they use is not made of the normal ¾-inch cleatstock, but rather knot-free, hefty 2 by 3's. In other words, it's lumber slightly lighter than you'd use to frame the average three-story-tall house.

As I listen to the tapes I made on the visit to the factory, I constantly hear myself muttering "Good God," or "I don't believe it!" or often just irrepressible laughter that burst out of me when I sighted something else that was so completely thought out and superbuilt.

A heavy fore and aft bulkhead, bonded to the hull as above, divides the chainlocker and also acts as a base for the staysail stay. With the division, you can nicely separate the lines for the twin anchors, which any serious long distance cruising boat will have.

With the massive structures used for the cabinetry and with even the smallest cabinets bonded inside and out, you actually end up with minor structural bulkheads on about 20-inch centers. The heavily glassed-in knee to which is bolted the chainplate for the uppers is nearly 3 feet in height and over an inch in thickness by the time it's finished bonded.

The floors are made of solid mahogany 2 by 3's, 2 by 4's, and 2 by 6's all let into each other, and all heavily bonded in.

Another precaution, which I have seen taken on very few boats, is that all material which will be exposed to the ample bilge is thoroughly coated with a long-lasting wood preservative to guard against rot. Even the bottom of the ½-inch plywood subfloor gets a good dousing of the stuff—an archaeologist's dream come true.

The bedding logs for the engine mounts are almost truly logs. They are made of 4-inch wide by 16-inch deep laminated white oak, and they receive the same entombing to the hull as do the chainplates. These heavy wood bedlogs absorb much more vibration than a fiberglass pan.

The scarfing in the toerail is about 2 feet long. Compare *this* to the completely butted up wood toerail of many wood trimmed quickies.

For added waterproofing, the caprail is grooved underneath to hold the bedding compound and ensure a leakproof joint. For the one-hundredth time Mark said, "That is very important to us. Very important."

They use enormous bronze check valves on sink drains, and if you don't know what those are for, then you've never cleaned three-day-old scrambled egg tailings from a sink that floods itself on every heel.

And something else. The threads of the bolts are first wrapped with a piece of polysulfide; *then* the normal caulking is put in *and* around the hole, and then the bolt is set in place. Cleats, genoa-tracks, and winches are all double-caulked. "We don't get deck leaks." Mark said. "That's very important to us."

With eight thousand manhours in a 43 footer, and six thousand manhours in a 37 footer, one can easily see where all the hours go and why one hundred people put out only fifteen boats a year. All this caution and use of good sense germinates from Walter Schulz, who seems to view boatbuilding more like a lifestyle than a career. Walter is almost as serious as Mark; he speaks articulately, slowly; thinks things out.

"We try to make sure that good boatbuilding won't die out," Walter begins. "I'm on the advisory board at a boatbuilding school and I've worked out a program with two vocational schools to convert some of their carpenter apprentices into boatbuilding trainees, to give them basic entry level skills, with regard to boatbuilding. Then we pick the best of those kids, put them on a part-time schedule, and train them here. The best of them we keep.

"During the summer months, every Tuesday night, we take the kids sailing to teach them how to sail. I mean how can you build a boat if you don't know what it has to do after it leaves the shop? This to me is one of the great oversights in this industry. We have boats being designed by people who only race around buoys, for that's where the fame and fortune is, and then we have boats being built by people who, through no fault of their own, shackled by their socio-economic background, never got *near* a boat let alone learned to sail one. So we teach them. Then the best from the school end up on long cruises moving the boats up and down the coast for the boat shows. The guys love this. And I'll tell you something; when it's blowing 40 knots and the rail is down, and the rain falls in sheets, and a guy is there, right there to see it, then you can be sure that when he gets back here and he's caulking a bolt or leaning on a nut or doing the hull layup, he'll understand *why* all those things are as important as we say they are."

Walter doesn't just know how to handle employees, he knows what his owners want.

"Let's face it, the people who come to Shannon to have a boat built have usually owned two or three production-built sailboats. While they might not know exactly what they want, they sure as hell know what they *don't* want in their next boat.

"When I sit down with them to design an interior or a machinery layout, I have to be prepared to justify every item whether it's engine access or location of the towel racks in the head. Most of all, they want to be sure they can get to every pump, winch bolt, and electric wire without using a chainsaw. For instance, every tank—fuel and water—is removable on a Shannon using simple hand tools. And we never use fiberglass tanks. They're all 5052 alloy for fuel, and stainless for water. Each tank has an isolator valve in case they pick up any bad fuel or water. "People want a boat that is easy to sail and comfortable for long passages. But they don't want a slow tub that can't sail to weather. At the same time they want flexible interiors that won't cost them an arm and a leg, to meet their individual needs. They want room for all sorts of gear, electronics, machinery, and equipment. They want the performance of a racing boat with the storage capacity of a barge."

With two hundred Shannons sailing all over the world, it seems that Walter has found the right combination.

"Another major item at Shannon is the cockpit layout. By the time people get here they know how critical a cockpit is for comfort and safety. I spend as much time designing the cockpit as I do for the rest of the interior. We had five complete cockpit layouts built on the 43 tooling before we built the mold."

Standing on the dock at Shannon's boatyard a few miles from the building facility, he pointed to the bowsprit on a Shannon. "Look at the bow platform. It may not seem like a big deal, but if you're going to go anywhere in a sailboat you need at least two anchors of a different type ready to let go at a moment's notice. If your C.Q.R. is dragging in the middle of the night you need to get a second anchor out quick. I'm always amazed when I see people with only one anchor in the bow and the other one buried in a cockpit locker. I've dragged anchors too many times to be able to sleep with only one anchor to depend on.

"Also I never built a boat without twin headstays. With them you can wing and wing or have roller furling on one and standard hank-on jib on the other. I mean what the hell do you do when you roll up your furling jib? How can you run up a smaller headsail? I copied the system of Chichester's boat when he was in Newport long ago. As soon as I saw that on *Gypsy Moth* I said to myself, 'That is going on every boat I build.' "

Looking over the Shannons tied to his dock, Walter said, "You know it's really great fun and I'm damn lucky. By the time we get a boat layed up for a specific owner, we become friends. I get a lot of credit for design work, but I have the most valuable resource in the industry—*owners.* The best ideas found on Shannons are the culmination of all the input from the people I build boats for. I could never have designed the galley layout in the *37, 43,* or *51* without tremendous input from women. A man just doesn't have as much feel for what works or for space utilization in a galley. Also I get letters and postcards from my owners telling me about their experiences and giving me more ideas about equipment and layouts. On top of it all, they are our only real sales force. Most Shannons are sold by word of mouth."

Walter found a lot of his ideas through aviation.

"I'm a tinkerer. I'm a pilot and I've lifted a lot of technology out of the industry. Our hydraulic bow thruster is a direct adaptation of a hydraulic landing gear from a Cessna 401. I was hanging around a hangar one day watching a mechanic working on one. I looked at this nice little pump he was using and that was enough for me. After we installed one of those, one of the magazines said, 'Walter Schulz is on the frontier of hydraulic research for sailing yachts.' Hell, all I did was pick up some old pump from a plane. I just figured that if the pump can lift something up it should be able to turn something as well. It doesn't know what it's doing, so why not use it broadly? We can run hydraulic generators, desalinators, windlasses, winches, compressors to fill scuba tanks, bow thrusters, air conditioners etc. All just running the engine at idle."

When I suggested that he go into manufacturing these units, he just shrugged his shoulders and said, "Ferenc, I'm a boatbuilder. I just do this widgetry stuff because it's fun."

But even with his widgetry he is very cautious.

"I guess I'm careful because I've seen so many badly built boats cause problems during all the years I've spent in yards doing repair and warranty work on production boats. But no matter how well we build the boats, I still worry. Every boat Shannon launches, I launch with a few drops of blackberry brandy, some on the bow for good luck and a few drops in the water for the gods. I learned that from an old Swedish boatbuilder I worked with when I was still in high school. The old guy went and poured a bit of homemade brandy on the bow of a boat we had just repaired, then went and poured a bit into the sea. I asked him what the little show was all about and he says, 'I don't know. But my grandfather did it and his grandfather did it and I always do it and every boat we have built have always floated.' So ever since then I personally launch each Shannon with the little ceremony of the blackberry brandy. And all our boats have floated."

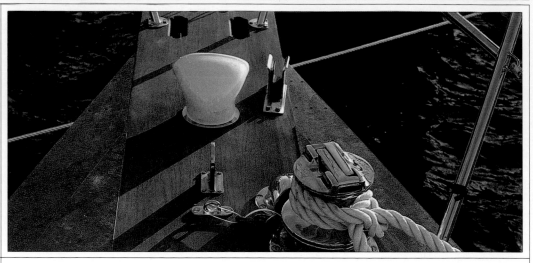

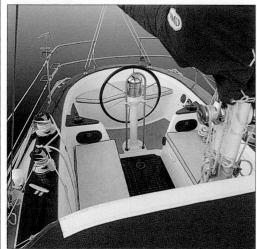

I know there are a lot of photos on these two pages, but then there are a lot of good things to point out in these boats. The first photo in the top left corner is of the *38*, which comes as a full keel or centerboard (see drawing), while the smaller boat in the bottom corner is the *28*, the smallest in the fleet that goes to 51 feet and includes the 43 foot ketch you see clipping along below. But the highlight in the Shannons is the attention to detail, not just in execution but in planning as well. In the small photo to the left, it's

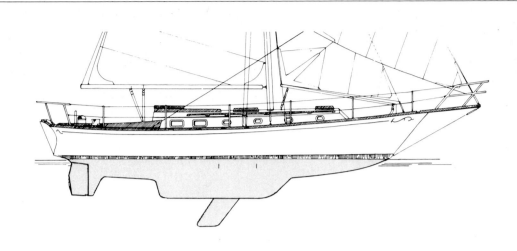

the cockpit of a *50;* you can see the *symetrically* curved coaming behind the helmsman, which means that regardless of the angle of heel, the helmsman will be kept equidistant from the wheel *and* comfortable, instead of being scrunched up in a sharply angled corner. The outboard portions of the helmsman's cockpit-sole slope upwards to provide solid footing on a heel. The cockpit grate can be raised level with the seats so that, with the aid of cushions, the cockpit becomes a large outdoor double berth. In the photos across the page see the arguably best nonskid pattern in the industry; the plethora of vents; the lexan for additional light on the dorade boxes; the heavy teak strips on the hatches for safe footing; the good nonskid on the seats, as important as good nonskid on the decks; and the second steering station under the dodger. Above, notice massive brass plating to protect the platform.

The great attention to detail continues down below. The strips of wood you see on the faces of cabinets and bulkheads are not veneer, but solid. The teak and holly sole is also solid (not plywood) as is the framing around the cabinetry. The overhead in the boats is lined with white tongue-and-groove patterned fiberglass, which not only looks first class and is child's play to keep clean, but is also much more fire-resistant than the foam-backed soft plastic overheads, which are normally the first to catch fire when a stove flares up or a lamp

overheats. All locker doors are louvered for ideal ventilation; all portlights are solid bronze opening type with double dogs, and the cabin lights are solid brass. In the photo above right, you can see an aft cabin of the *51* center cockpit. It's the size of an average bedroom. Note easy access to both sides of the huge berth; drawers

and lockers everywhere for stowage; a big hatch above for ventilation and light and grabrails on the overhead. At Shannon every exterior grabrail is matched by one inside. In the left-hand bottom note the tiled shower (interior finish is always owner's choice) and the abundance of

electronic equipment. At Shannon they have had much practice in installing everything from desalinators to food processors and garbage compressors. The drawing shows the layout of the *50* aft-cockpit, and the photo beside it shows an ingenious, swing-out cabinet for the radar.

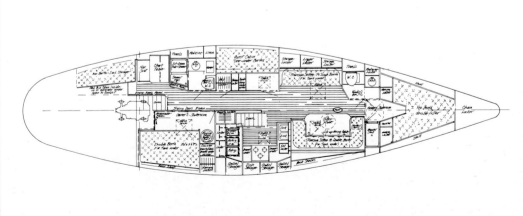

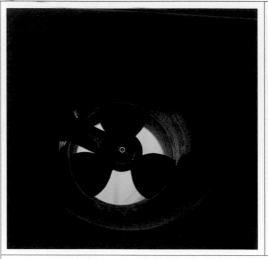

For more amazing details, see the masterpiece of a ...osquito screen top left; the hydraulically driven bow-thruster used on the 50's for easy maneuvering; the massive anti-snag rail around the cowl vent; the work it takes to fit a bronze fairlead in a toerail; the drawers built with let-in sides and partitions; and in the large, bottom right-hand photo the remarkably honeycombed sub-cabinetry. All drawer openings have solid pieces of plywood for reinforcement, creating an almost indestructible beam structure. In the photo bottom left,

note the ladder rungs grooved to prevent slippage; the galley searail doubling as a beautiful grabrail; the cover over the stove (which creates more working surface) lined with stainless steel *and* the tiny searails even around it. The stove has not only a solid bar in front for safety but also a nicely sewn belt with clips to hold the cook safely in place at sea. Shannons are serious offshore cruisers. Manager Mark Perry (upper corner) and owner/designer—concerned as always—Walter Shultz (next page) make sure that the boats are made as safe and as useful as humanly possible.

"I like to build the boats as well and as strong as I possibly can." Walter said. "At any given time there are a number of Shannons doing a circumnavigation—right now there are five—and I like to hear where they are. I like to keep track. Before I go to bed I listen to the weather, and when I hear that there is such and such a storm blasting where one of the Shannons is cruising, I can smile and feel good and sleep well that night. I get a great kick out of that. □ "And this may sound egotistical, but I'd like to have every boat I build still be afloat the day I die. Have my boats outlive me. I'd like to leave something good behind."

SWEDEN YACHTS

There is something refreshing going on in Sweden. □ In a world awash in a sea of junk, awash in things thoughtlessly designed and pathetically made, things that are soon cast aside to make room for *new* things that are very seldom better, it's like a breath of fresh air to find yourself in Sweden. □ The Swedes seem to understand that life won't last forever, that it's all too short for many of the good things and certainly *much* too short to be wasted making bad things that will just have to be fixed or redone six times over when they could have been done *once* if done right in the first place. And so the cars they build last for decades, their houses still stand into the next century, and their faucets all work and their doorknobs all work and everything feels solid as if carved from solid rock.

Jens Östmann engineers the boats of Sweden Yachts as if he wanted them to stay afloat until eternity. The designs are elegant and simple with no flimsy fragile pieces anywhere, and the construction is so thoughtful and precise that if anything will ever go wrong with these boats I would be most surprised. And for what you get, the prices are so reasonable that a boat from Sweden Yachts must be one of the last "good deals" in the world.

Most of this is made possible by Jens Östmann's planning. His thoughtfulness and simplicity and engineering make a boat from Sweden Yachts one of the most intelligently built boats in the world.

He was our host last fall in Stenungsund on the northwest coast of Sweden and we could certainly not have asked for anyone more kindly and sincere. He was in turn serious and jovial throughout the long hours in the yard and out sailing and afterwards, proving our suspicion that Sweden was a special place indeed.

There is a very definite system of boat construction going on in Sweden. Of the three Swedish boatbuilders in this book, none molds its own hulls; they are molded nearby, in a region where people specialize in fiberglass. Everyone seems to do what he does best. I mention this here, because a yacht is made of many parts, rigging and hardware and mechanical gear among them, and it's reassuring to know that every piece that goes into the boats of Sweden Yachts is made by people who are experts at their work.

Peter Norlin, who is an expert at designing some of the fastest boats in the world, designs the hulls for Sweden Yachts, all of them state-of-the-art IOR racer cruisers with powerful hulls and highly efficient high aspect ratio keels and rudders. The 38 footer we sailed in Stenungsund had something that every racer/cruiser would vie for: a very efficient, and also very shoal, wing keel à la Australia II. It is not surprising to find that Sweden Yachts keeps an eye on the Americas Cup, for they in fact built the Swedish challenger *Sverige* that participated twice at Newport.

The rigs—as sophisticated and efficient as the keels—are tall to move you well in any air, and items like boom vangs, adjustable backstays and halyards led aft, are all standard on all Sweden Yachts boats. And yet as impressive as the sleek long-tailed hulls of Peter Norlin are, it was the decks and interiors designed by Jens Östman that I found most striking.

His pure clean lines and planes are almost unnerving. The house rises without a ridge as if growing from the foredeck and the house sides sweep boldly aft in a beautiful curve, then turn unnoticed into coamings. There are no bumps for winchpads or lumps for blocks, just beautiful clean lines and smooth surfaces. The severe and bulky look often associated with high coamings is eliminated by a shallow step where the house becomes the coaming, and again as it fairs into the transom and becomes open at the stern. The cockpit can nicely handle seven people if need be, and in Sweden family and friends are a big part of sailing so the need comes often. The cockpit seats and coamings are all teak-lined.

The teak decks and teak cabin tops—standard on all Sweden Yachts—are clean and wide, broken only by the hatches and the genoa tracks which have fairing pieces on either side to keep you from stubbing your toes.

All the above things are "standard" on a Sweden Yachts boat, as is spinnaker gear and even pressure water, but even more important are the basic items, which are some of the very best: hull and deck joints, chainplate reinforcements, floor grids, and the most thoughtful of hardware installations in the teak deck and cabintop.

After knowing all that, you would not be blamed for being amazed at the low price of the boats. I certainly was. As a matter of fact I was downright suspicious and kept looking in nooks and crannies for bad workmanship or cheap materials that help save cost, but they simply were not there. Only at the end of my first day's survey was I finally convinced that it is Sweden Yachts' forethought, engineering, and efficiency that allow the boats to be made for such good prices. Halfway through my first factory tour, I turned to Jens and said, "Okay, how do you do it?"

"Well," he said smiling, "I'll give you an example." Then his eyes lit up mischievously and he asked, "What did you notice in the galleys?"

"Which boat?" I asked, "The *36, 38 or 41*?"

"All of them."

"They are very efficient," I said. "Good size. Nicely locked in by the engine housing so you don't get thrown around in a seaway. Good storage, nice set of four or five drawers."

"But what did you notice that one had but not the others?"

"I can't recall," I said.

He broke out laughing, "Very good," he said, "That's because they are all the same!"

I didn't believe him. He went and brought out three sets of blueprints and by god he wasn't kidding; the galleys in the three boats were completely identical. I was flabbergasted. That was one of the most intelligent ideas I had ever heard.

"We simply found," Jens explained, "that there are minimal requirements that you want to have in the galley of a comfortable cruising boat: sink, stove, icebox, stowage, counterspace, elbow room. So I designed a comfortable and efficient galley. Then we realized that just because the boat gets a few feet bigger, it would be silly to add a couple of inches here and there just to make each galley seem different. Why not save money by having three identical galleys to fabricate —no confusion, no mistakes, no three sets of different pieces —and pass those savings on to the customer."

This simplicity of thought seems the foundation of Swedish engineering. When we went to look at our first Saab — which we tried, to no avail, to destroy on the worst roads of Canada and Mexico—we were shown a simple looking, beautifully *aerodynamic* car. That was twelve years ago, long before most car makers had even heard the word. When we asked to see the other models, the man pointed at the car in front of us and said, "You sir, are looking at the entire line." This concentration of doing few things but doing them extremely well makes Swedish products not only good values but a true joy to own.

"Now of course," Jens went on, "That galley alone is not

enough to make our boats 20 or 30 percent cheaper than other luxury boats, but it is a start. I like to think out every boat completely, engineer every detail before we begin building until I have found the most efficient method of using the best construction. If you prepare enough, then you don't end up making expensive changes and modifications or maybe even repairs. This is how most people think in Sweden. Maybe with the long winters we got used to sitting and figuring things out.

"So what we end up with is a boat built as simply and as well as possible. We don't use four or five needless pieces that will have to be trimmed and fussed with if, with a little forethought, we can use just one or two instead. I think we build boats in a very traditional method where simplicity was always stressed. And good engineering helps the owners of our boats as well, for fewer things fail on a well engineered boat and if things *do* fail they are much easier to repair. I am not saying we use cheap solutions because you can see we don't. We just make everything as useful and as practical as we can.

"My main concern is to start a design by trying to establish what makes for a good comfortable salon, or navigation table, etc. And that you can only do by going to boat shows and being aboard your boats and other boats—without telling anyone you're the designer—and just listening to all the comments, sarcastic or otherwise, and really thinking about them. Then of course you have to be open to change and not believe that just because you are the designer you are right. And then you have to go, I believe, and design whatever it is you are going to design with as few pieces as you can, and keep working at it until you are truly happy and confident that you have done your best. And you have to design things so they can be finished to as high a degree as possible outside the boat because, as you know, to try to do things inside a boat is awful. It's chaos. Everything is out of angle; you slide down the hulls; there is no room to move.

"I think a boat should have all the basics in it but these basics should be well executed and good looking. Like a traditional yacht."

And Jens of course is right. If all boats were built this way instead of—as too many are—having things added and fudged on just because someone forgot to think about it initially, we could all have a lot more fun sailing our boats instead of spending time on frustrating repairs.

"The other thing we do," Jens went on, "is to have our hulls and decks molded by an outside fiberglass specialist. They are given exact orders on which material to use in any given area, how to roll it, how much resin to use—everything. They have been building fiberglass hulls since the 1950's and have such good experience at it that I feel it is a much better method for a new company like ours." Sweden Yachts is ten years old. In Sweden that is considered rookie status whereas in many other countries they would be considered at least veterans, if not experts.

"And do not forget that here in Sweden we have very rigid regulations for health and safety in industry. To build a proper laminating shop with proper ventilatilation, which means changing the air completely every few minutes—you

can imagine what sort of a heating system you have to have to support that—would mean a great investment, the cost of which would have to be passed on to our customers. You would have to build I think two hundred boats a year before that can be economical. We don't want to do that. We are happy with our sixty boats a year. We want to build a very fine boat, and I think you can see that we do, but we want to do it as economically as possible. And we don't compromise one bit of quality or performance or even experimenting; our wing keel is proof of that.

"And one more point. With the subcontracting of hulls, masts and such, we know exactly at all times what the cost of each boat is, and we know exactly what the cost of each part of each boat is. When you try to do everything in house, you end up with a lot of people running up and down stairs doing at best maintenance, and at worst, nothing. This way we can keep a maximum of control with a minimum of people. We don't even have anyone to look after our stockroom. It is an open house. Everyone goes and gets what he wants and each man is given responsibility for what he uses most of. So a deck fitter is responsible for making sure that there are enough cleats, winches whatever. That really helps with our overhead."

"You don't have any theft problem?" Candace asked amazed. "When we were building our Westsail, one of the running jokes at the company was that by the time workers quit after a year they usually had a whole Westsail going in their living room."

Jens smiled a little smile and said very humbly, "There is no such thing here. The number of things that get carried off here in a year I would happily carry myself to the worker's house in my hands."

Then he went on. "We have one foreman here only. One foreman for the whole shop. That way we have no friction between departments, no one can blame anyone else; everyone is responsible for everything. That of course means that everyone employed here has to be skilled enough and intelligent enough and conscientious enough to look after himself. We have very good crews here. Most of the people who started here ten years ago are still here. I think we have exchanged fewer than 3 percent a year. And most are young people, that's the funny thing about it. But they are well paid and we have a very modern factory. It's a good place to work."

That's the understatement of the year. The place looks like a hospital. When one man sabersaws a hole for a portlight, another kneels right next to him vacuuming away the fiberglass dust before it can spread into air and lungs. Compare this to some companies where the air is so full of ground glass that it looks like a minor blizzard and you can easily see why people enjoy working here and why they do such fine work.

"But of course you can see," Jens said, "that with this method of operation we have a very definite upper size. We can only run a shop this way within limits to avoid getting into hierarchies and confusion. So we must be careful of growth. As it is, we can run a financially solid company that does not have to make wild guesses in the dark and wake up broke one day. We like to have a certain stability which I

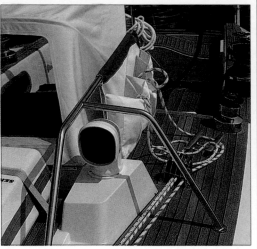

The perfect designs of both Peter Norlin (hull) and Jens Östmann (deck) are evident on these pages. The long Norlin stern adds power and grace, while the impressively clean cabin-side lines give great beauty to the deck. In the right-hand photo above, you can see (or rather can't see) the deck house fairing into the deck without a trace. Note also the well-placed and guarded vent on the foredeck. The adjoining photo shows how prettily the house-sides become coamings. Note also massive stainless support for safe commuting in and out of companionway, and nifty canvas pouch for stowage of lines. All the teak decking you see (including the house top and the cockpit seats) is standard on the Sweden Yachts boats, as is the rod-and-block boom vang and adjustable backstay. What else can you ask for?

Now feast your eyes on the interiors. (As is traditional in this region, they are of mahogany.) The drawing is of the *38,* as are most of the photos. The galley could of course be from any of the three boats because, as I elaborated in the text, they're all the same. Note nice touches, like the many drawers and the chrome and rubber non-slip on the rungs of the ladder. In the adjoining photo is the electronics panel. It hinges down for easy servicing of equipment and wiring, and can be removed almost as simply for safe winter storage of expensive gear. In the next photo to the right is the very solid and comfortable swiveling navigator's seat; the two doorways to the *two* aft cabins, (not bad for a 38-foot boat) and the very well done, luxurious upholstery. The overhead is nicely done with sturdy panels. Grabrails are everywhere. The engine is as accessible as any I have seen, and there is access to the gearbox from the aft cabin.

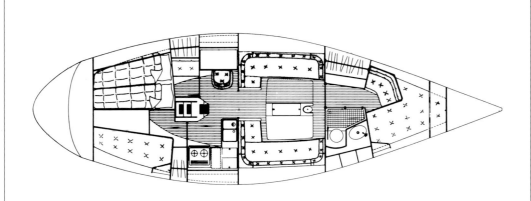

R eady?

Top left: Under helmsman's seat is bilge pump and fire extinguisher. To the right is a massive eye bolted to two keel bolts, which can be used to haul the boat with a simple hook and ordinary crane. (Hook comes straight down through hatch.) Next is the Sweden Yacht's wing keel— to my knowledge the very first to be offered on a quality production boat. Next right is the out-of-the-way-and-weather windlass in the anchor well, while to its right is the interior of the Sweden Yachts-built Twelve Meter *Sverige*. Below

that are the cleverly counter-sunk holes for hardware bolts. The countersunk shoulder leaves room for a ring of caulking to form a sealing ring around the bolt. Below that is a boat sitting in the test tank drenched with spray, and next to that is the deep and wide reinforcing gridwork in the boats' bottom. Next is a boat

headed for baptism and beside that is Jens Östmann holding—believe it or not—a chainplate support. Above him is the immaculate and ultra-efficient Sweden Yachts plant complete with a forest of overhead vacuum pipes, overhead crane; the works. First class place, first class people, first class boats.

I'm sick of this. □ What ever happened to the good old days when you could get a nice flimsy, thoughtlessly built fiberglass boat, and sail it, aglow with the excitement and fear of chainplates tearing loose and the mast crashing down and bulkheads popping out and keels just drifting off, and best of all, whole decks peeling off like the lid of a sardine can. □ Those were the days. □ What's the world coming to? Those guys at Sweden Yachts have taken all the wholesome panic out of sailing. The biggest thrill on their boats is a lightbulb burning out.

TED HOOD'S
LITTLE
HARBORS

Perhaps more than any other designer of our time, Ted Hood has changed sailing for the good. And he hasn't just made sailboats faster or bigger—the two things which assure designers all the headlines; but he has done something more important, more commendable. Through his inventions, like furling jibs and furling mains, he has made sailhandling easier for us all, but even more importantly, he has enabled many an older sailor to keep sailing through the later years in life. And those are perhaps the very best years of all, when all the striving is left behind and there's more time to reflect, more time to enjoy the magic of the sea.

Ted Hood seems a restless man, always on his way to something else or somewhere else, which might explain how in a career of some thirty-five years, he has managed to design boats, make sails, run a large boat service yard, invent and build a myriad of gear, and somehow endlessly, wherever on earth he could, build some fine yachts of all shapes and sizes.

The line of Little Harbor Yachts consists of pretty centerboarders designed on the old Hood philosophy of high performance with moderate to heavy displacement, principles which in many minds contradict each other. But if you hear Ted Hood out you might just see the light.

He now spends his time looking after the design office, the big service yard—where they'll repair and rebuild for you anything from any stage—and his own boatyard in northern Taiwan where, under his son Ted's direction the graceful and solid Little Harbors are now built.

My first reaction after hearing about the Taiwan yard was to scratch the whole show off my lists of *bests,* but I have always admired Ted Hood's work and felt obligated to give him a fair shake. After a day and a half of crawling through the boats and talking with him, and talking with other builders to fathom their opinions, I was, as you can see by the chapter here before you irrevocably converted.

"Boy, where do I start?" he smiled a little shyly. "We built wood boats in Japan back in the sixties. After that we went to Holland where we found a little yard owned and run by Frans Maas, near Amsterdam. We started there with steel boats with fiberglass over. We sent Frans very detailed plans of joints, hull-to-deck, hatch details, we worked with him from boat to boat. We got along well. Seemed to understand each other right from the start. Got to the stage where we didn't have to give him details anymore, just sent the lines, didn't even get a price back until a few weeks after they started on the boat. We had a very good working relationship. But then his costs got out of control in 1972 so we just had to stop.

"So we tried other places in Europe but the costs were too high. We built a half dozen custom boats ourselves. After years of putting it off, I decided if we were going to design and build quality yachts with completely custom interiors, we best find the most economical place to do it. In 1978, I flew over to Taiwan, Korea, Hong Kong, to visit various yards. I fould Taiwan to be the best. I still feel it was a good decision. The bad decision was that at first we picked an existing yard with its own way of doing things and it turned out to be the wrong yard. We tried to change things, but we had no direct control over the work force. Production scheduling and quality control didn't exist. You have to get people to understand your particular way of doing things. So we moved into our own yard, an empty place, got our own people and started up. After the initial start-up pains, the general quality improved quickly."

He tapped the wood table for good luck, then he went on in his strong yankee drawl.

"Now, after just three years of having our own yard, we have people who can really think on their own. Bruce Livingston Jr., our general manager, and Vinnie Yuan, production manager, take care of daily operations. We also have six or seven good young foremen, all trained by us, who can really think things out. Half the time they think up ways of doing things that are much better than any of ours here. They're steady and darn hard working people and they'll stay with you as long as you give them enough overtime. We are getting so steady and confident that we're getting into large one-off boats. We also have a couple of naval architect graduates there who can really think things out and do good working drawings.

"You have to build a good-size boat in Taiwan with high labor content to make it pay, otherwise you shouldn't be building a boat over there. The shipping is just too costly. Instead of cutting corners in production, we add man hours wherever there is room for improvement. For example, the *53* has more than sixteen thousand man hours. So you end up with a boat that is still moderately priced, but we feel that the general quality and attention to detail is superior.

"The big problem is getting people to appreciate a good quality boat. Many simply do not know the difference. They are not interested enough to be educated in good quality. Now people say we here in America are getting quality conscious and they use the example of how popular cars like BMW's and Mercedes are getting. Well hell. When a guy buys a Mercedes does he really buy it because he appreciates the quality or is it just a status symbol to keep up with the guy next door? Does he know any of the details of the Mercedes? The little non-rattle, the smoothness of the transmission, or how evenly the brakes engage? Maybe a bit, but not enough to spend three times more than he would on an American car. And some of the people come and look right at the things, the wiring, the plumbing, the bulkhead bonding, the quality of the woodwork, they look right at it but they simply don't see it. And if they don't care about the difference in quality enough to recognize it, then boy I'm the first one to say, 'You're wasting your time tooking at our boats.' Now Swan was one of those to start doing high quality production boats and I'm glad to see a lot of people starting to come along.

"I guess you'd have to say our boats are designed to be different. They are heavier than most but I tell you they sail well. We find we can design a heavy boat that goes just as fast as a light one and carry a lot more gear besides. We tested a maxi. One maxi was 88 feet, the other was 80 feet, and ours weighed 160,000 pounds against 80,000 pounds. Both have identical IOR ratings, and all the tank tests said that ours was just as fast through the water in all conditions except for surfing down waves in 30-knot winds. Then the lighter one would get surfing faster, but under other conditions they were the same. And this is using 20-foot models which give you very good accuracy.

"And where do you think we were the fastest? In light air. The heavy boat was the fastest in light air against the others. We had the best sail-area-to-wetted-surface ratio, and the lowest prismatic coefficient. You have to have a low prismatic to go fast in light air. High prismatic is good for high speeds. We have low prismatic so we go fast at slow speeds, and for a boat like that that's 10 knots. Most of the time that's what you sail at. We have less wetted surface because our lines go more directly, more straight down to the keel instead of the great surface that the flat bottom boats have. We have a more straight line with our slack bilges than their almost 90-degree turn. All this is more important than the total weight. Wetted surface causes the most drag in light air, so all this is more important than reducing weight.

"In straight acceleration we lose, but if the wind dies you can coast a lot further so you have to count that. I'm not saying that one completely balances out the other because the heavy boat will fall a bit behind in a tacking duel. But take the twelve-meter rule. It's a known fact that a twelve meter is faster the more you sink it in the water. Because of that they say that if you're going to sink the boat into the water you've got to take some sail area off to make up for it. So obviously no one can do it in twelves because you'd have to take so much sail area off that to get the same twelve meter rating you'd be no good in light air. Now in IOR rule, or for a plain cruising boat, it's a different thing. The IOR rule says if your boat sinks in the water you can actually add more sail area for the same rating, because a heavier boat needs more sail so you can have it for nothing. If you analyze that, the only time a heavier boat won't go is if you take sail area off. Other than acceleration, the weight doesn't hurt. In the old days they used to sink the eight meters as deep as they dared; they'd completely fill the bilge, and in light airs they were faster than if it was pumped dry. Now that was a fact. Full-sized experiment with real boats. Faster through the water because of less wave-making resistance.

"The argument against this is that bigger sails are harder to handle, but then you're only talking about 10 or 15 percent. When you double the displacement you don't double the sail area. On the maxis we were testing we doubled the displacement and raised the sail area only 15 percent.

"That's not to say that all heavy boats will go fast. You have to have the right prismatic, the right hull shape. We get stability from a fairly narrow hull that gives us a lot of displacement and interior space, but with a very symmetrical streamlined hull. So we can build a good solid boat and the boat will still go fast. Plus we can load the boat up with water, gear, and fuel and it will then sink a little deeper in the water, and go even faster. Just like a twelve meter without the punishment of the rule.

"Look at that old centerboarder I have out there, that one tonner built by Maas in '72. It still wins races. When I bought the boat back, my crew came down before I did and cleaned it out, stripped all the gear off, all the spares. They even took the companionway ladder out. Well, I came down to the boat and looked around in shock and asked, 'Where is all my gear!?'

'We're saving weight!' they said.

'Yeah, but the boat'll go slower!' I said. 'Bring the gear back on!'"

The one-tonner debuted at the SORC '73 and got third overall. Next year Ted built a similar boat that won the whole thing, including the tough St. Petersburg/Ft. Lauderdale race. His designs have won the big St. Pete race four

times. That must be a record.

"The big advantage of centerboarders," Ted said, "which nearly all my boats are, is their sea motion. You don't get that big chunk of lead deep down there jerking you back and forth. You can heave-to much more comfortably in a centerboard boat; you don't trip over the keel, you just mush comfortably through the water.

"And I don't care what anybody says, you're not going to win races when you're dead tired. My little one-tonner is much more comfortable than a Maxi in the Gulf Stream, where the waves get steep in rough weather. You can sleep in her, whereas you can't sleep in a maxi. In a maxi you hit a wave and you nearly get pitched out of the cockpit. You have to hang on to the wheel or you get catapulted right out. The light boats are just too tough on the crew. Especially when they go and set the crew out on the rail. Who needs that?"

"What size and weight would you consider a good size for a couple of people?" I asked him.

"I think it takes more brain power than body power on a big boat," he answered. "You just have to think a little more ahead."

On Stoway mainsails:

"I find I actually sail twice as much with furling gear and a Stoway main. I stop in little places, sail up to the mooring, have a lot more fun. I can stop for lunch somewhere, drop the hook and have the sails stowed in thirty seconds. Before, that was a big deal, now it's fun. As an example, we recently designed and built a custom 60-foot sloop for Dodge Morgan with extensive roller furling gear. He just finished a single-handed, non-stop voyage around the world in record time. In this heavy displacement keel boat with all the latest equipment he was able to average over 7 knots for the trip. Without furling gear, I really don't think he could safely handle a boat that size by himself.

"But there is a funny thing going on now. There seem to be fewer and fewer experienced people around. People seem to be scared away by all these write-ups about Grand Prix racing. They all think that sailing has to be competitive, expensive and dangerous so they get themselves a power boat, turn the key and drive away instead. I guess they feel safer with less hassle.

On genoas:

"I'm against a cruising boat having any kind of genoa, any overlay. Well maybe a couple of feet but that's all. Big genoas put big loads on the gear; you have to have big winches to crank, lots of slapping, miles of sheets to mess with. The racing rules say that high aspect is 50 percent faster, they charge you twice as much for your height but not for the length of the foot. The only reason big genoas are used is that the rules don't charge you for it. You get a little bit out of it so you put it on. If you had to pay for the overlap, you'd never see a genoa on a racing boat. The little bit of power you gain when you go from a 110 to a 150 genoa you can parallel by adding 2 feet to the height of your mast. Off the wind the area of a big genoa doesn't do you any good; you just back-wind your mainsail. You have to overtrim your mainsail because of the backwinding. Besides, a 110 is the biggest sail you can efficiently wing out with a pole, so you get just as much projected area with a little sail downwind.

"Look at it this way: Going from a 100 percent to a 150 percent genoa gives you 50 percent more sail area *but* you only gain about 5 percent in power. For all that agony. And you can get most of that back with 2 feet added to the mast and end up with much less sail area and much less mess. Plus you'll tack faster with a smaller headsail. What you'll have is more efficiency and less load on yourself and on the rig. And those big genoas are dangerous, especially on a cruising boat, because you can't even see where you're going. You want a high enough clew and not much overlap so you can see under it."

In answer to my question of how much stability you sacrifice by putting a couple of extra feet on the mast, Ted said, "Nothing. You lose on the weight of the mast and the windage of the mast, but the overlap of a big genoa makes you heel a lot more than it drives you forward. Makes you wonder, doesn't it?"

That's putting it mildly.

So all that thinking and all that experience go into his Little Harbor yachts. And when you couple that with the reasonable labor rates of Taiwan what you end up with is very beautiful boats for reasonable prices. But hidden under the civilized mild-mannered topsides are racing developed keel centerboard configurations with balanced, air foil rudders with a thin trailing edge.

The tooling on the boats is truly first class, and perhaps so because Ted and his son are always in Taiwan to start a project off.

"It's not just to get a perfect mold," Young Ted said, "But because there are so many fine decisions to be made at that stage."

When I asked him what sort of things had gone wrong in the years before they got their own yard, Ted just smiled and shook his head. "You name it," he said. The problems that did crop up were corrected in their Marblehead yard and the owners are quite happy, as witnessed by the annual Rendezvous which East Coast owners of Little Harbor Yachts attend.

And things are running smoothly in the Taiwan yard where the lastest technology is applied to the boats. They use isophthalic resin for skincoats to prevent osmosis. As an extra precaution, they—like Nautor and Baltic—use no pigment in the gelcoat below the water line, because clear gelcoat is less water-permeable than pigmented. The fiberglass hulls are layed up by hand with an Airex Foam core to provide more strength as well as sound and thermal insulation. Ted pioneered the use of Airex for yachts in 1969 and prefers it over balsa because a finished panel is not quite as brittle, and therefore less likely to delaminate under impact. They use "Knytex" biaxial roving/mat throughout to eliminate "print-through" common on dark hulls.

"In decks," Young Ted explains, "We use Divinicell coring because Airex is not as heat resistant and thus there is greater potential for more sag and creep. This is important when you're in a place with lots of sun."

"To get good adherence of the Airex in the hulls, we grind to remove any high spots before we lay the Airex core into wet mat. Once the core has set up, the whole thing is tapped with a hammer to make sure that everything has bonded and there are no voids. The hulls are layed up in one piece. While the hull is still in the mold, we set the major bulkheads onto a foam spacer to keep the hard edge of the bulkhead away from the hull. The main bulkheads that carry the chainplates are 1½-inch thick, the rest are ¾ inch. We bond the bulkheads to both hull and deck with double mat and roving.

"After the bulkheads are in place the hull is removed from the mold and lead ballast is cast in place around the centerboard trunk. Then we encase this whole area with about ¾-inch solid glass so that if you ever ground the boat and eventually wear through or destroy the outer skin, this second bottom will still keep the boat afloat."

"The watertanks are integral with the internal parts all gelcoated, then a prefabricated fiberglass lid is bonded on. Once all the fittings are on, we pressure-test the tanks. It's nice to have integral tanks, for you really increase the amount of tankage by not wasting space around them."

Just as much thoughtfulness goes into other details. The bronze through-hulls are contersunk and flush. A small but reassuring detail is that all the bronze seacocks are labelled with hard plastic tags so you'll never have to wonder what exactly it is that you are closing or opening.

The wiring is wisely encased in a coiled plastic conduit, like sheathing, for protection against chafe or nicks.

The hull and deck joint is through-bolted. The flange in this case is 5 inches wide and the deck is set into a heavy epoxy paste, then bolted on to it at 4-inch centers and even 2-inch centers where the genoa track is located.

The construction throughout is as heavy as the displacement of the boats. Great massive stainless steel stops are bonded heavily to the underside of the cockpit to act as wheel stops for the steering quadrant.

All shelving and cabinetry is very well bonded in even the most obscure places and the only complaint I have is that the edges of the bonds aren't cosmetically perfect, something that a five-minute grinding job could correct.

And there are nice touches everywhere that certainly only inexpensive labor can make affordable. I'll emphasize the stowage place under the cockpit because if a place so out of sight is well done you can imagine how good the rest is. Back here the dropboards are reinforced with a layer of fiberglass, top and bottom, to provide good protection and longevity for the wood. Nice bits of grating act as covers over seacocks and water filters to protect them from being damaged by heavy objects or fouled by lines, while still allowing for quick inspection of the hardware's position and condition. The emergency tiller lives down here in little chocks, and is itself so beautifully made of polished stainless steel and laminated teak that one might almost be perversely tempted to hope for a steering malfunction just so the tiller can be brought out of hiding.

I won't go on. You'll have to look at the pictures and read the captions for the rest.

Ted Hood's boats all have an elegant simplicity as the photos on these pages show. There are eight Little Harbor designs from 42 to 90 feet and of course there is no limit if you want a custom boat

designed. A perfect example of Ted's lines is seen in the 50 above and to the left, where the beautifully propor-tioned house is feathered to wafer thinness over the last 8 feet. The moderate stern of the 50 can be seen in the top right photo. Back in the photo to the left, note the maze of cowl vents, all with guards.

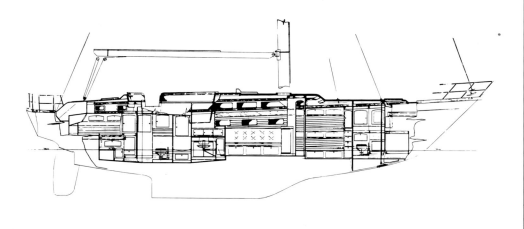

In the cockpit photo below, the cowl vents aft (and forward) assure complete air circulation below. The massive steering pedestal supports a cockpit table and the Stoway sail controls.

There is no question that the fine finishing achieved in the Little Harbor yachts would be impossible to duplicate without the economical advantage of building in Taiwan. The first photo (most of these were taken in the *53*) top left, should be enough to convince you of that. Look in the bottom right-hand corner and you'll see a piece of inlay work that would take the average wood butcher like yours truly about a week to do. Note also the complex angled cabinetry and fine trim around the doors. The two adjoining photos show large louvered doors, and, above the berths, the space-saving and very useful "airplane compartments." These are of plywood, molded to a curve. The bottom of the left page shows the ultimate in round-table dining, including the optional spinning center portion, which rises to reveal a small condiment

rack. At the top of the right-hand page, you can see the well proportioned fore-and-aft galley; the shaped armrests at the ends of the settee, and the companionway ladder with curved rungs to give you level footing on a heel. The detail of the ladder below shows that the rungs are strips of teak and holly, requiring hours and hours of labor. In the next small photo, showing the rest of the galley, look at the bafflingly complex inlay of teak and holly *plus* a border trim on the sloped portion of the cabin sole. Fine craftsmanship at its very best. The drawing is of a custom Hood 80 footer.

The top left photo has a closeup of some of the teak and holly sole. Note how the whole sole is made of a series of hatches, giving you access to the entire bilge. Note also that each hatch is framed out with covering boards. In the photo below, the small settee hinges up to reveal the most accessible engine in captivity. Below that is some amazing grateman-ship. The drawings are of the 46, left, and 53, right. The series of cockpit shots, above, show the cockpit seats with teak grabrails. Behind these are compartments for

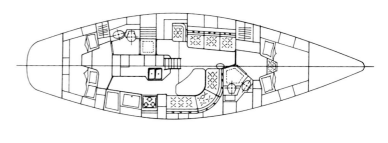

The staff of three in the design shop is normally occupied with custom boats and developing new Little Harbors. The two photos below show the modern facility where the hulls are hand layed-up in one-piece molds. The laminates run fore-and-aft and athwartships inside and outside the core. The photo on the right shows Ted Hood inspecting an almost finished 53. With their fast centerboard designs and the painstakingly detailed construction, the boats have earned their way into the group of ''best.''

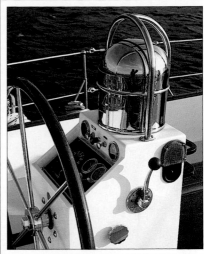

line stowage. In the close-up of the cowl vent, note the cowl's shape. With the tapered head fitting flush around the throat, line snagging would be nearly impossible even without the guard. The last photo on the top is a close-up of the strongly built console. The cockpit table is supported by a leg, adding further strength. Below the table runs a bar against which you can brace your feet when the boat is heeled or rolling. The wiring photo shows a very cleanly layed-out wiring system, unlike the masses of spaghetti one too often finds. Note myriad of tie-wraps to hold everything in place.

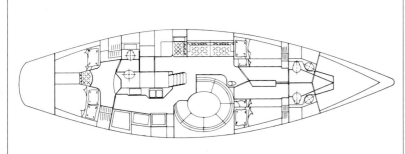

J ust one thing in closing. While most designers are obsessed with striving to be at the "leading edge" of fleeting trends, Ted Hood sits back and stubbornly follows his own instincts and comes up with the truly major changes in the sport. Just think where we would be if others trusted their convictions half as much as Ted.

VINDÖ SWEDEN

I f you were to ask most sailors to tell to you in one phrase *how* they'd like their fiberglass boats built, they would tell you without hesitation, ''Out of wood.'' □ Vindö yachts of Sweden has gone and done just that as far as is humanly possible. They have combined the strength and longevity of fiberglass hulls and cockpits and a partial deck with the beauty of a magnificently crafted varnished mahogany house and teak housetops and teak decks, to create some of the prettiest yachts in the world today.

Vindö started building yachts in 1928 on the island of Orust on the west coast of Sweden, an island where boats have been built since the 11th century. Today there are close to three thousand people working in boatbuilding on Orust, including mastmakers and riggers, sailmakers and makers of Volvo diesel engines, but whatever phase of boatbuilding the people are involved in, they have nine hundred years of tradition to fuel their pride. To help continue the tradition, Orust has established a school of boatbuilding which, with its high standards, is very difficult to get into. Those successful spend their first year in school and the second doing apprentice work in a boatyard.

But those who don't get in don't have to give up the idea of boatbuilding. There are dozens of small yards in the area, some just two-man operations, some very much larger, where there is always room for someone with enthusiasm who wants to learn the age-old secrets of the trade.

The people at Vindö certainly know most of them. Since 1928 there have been close to three thousand Vindös built, of all shapes and sizes. Since the conversion to fiberglass hulls in the early seventies, Vindös have ranged from the little 28 footer, which is without doubt the queen of all small coastal cruisers, to a large 39-foot ketch. As recently as five years ago there were two hundred twenty Vindös being built a year, but then the Vindös' fortune changed. When the big slowdown of the early eighties came, the old family ownership loyally refused to lay off their longtime workers and so kept on building boats when there was no one left to buy them. When the banks finally put a halt to that, Vindö's doors were closed and new owners found.

Sture Björklund, who was manager of a large Swedish shipyard for many years, but whose first love was always sailboats, and Bengt Isaksson are now owners of the scaled down Vindö boatyard with fifteen people working in the shops and sunny sheds just up from the inlet's rocky shores. But of the fifteen who are there, most have been with Vindö over twenty years and the gentleman who builds those magnificent wood houses has been with them now for thirty-five.

And that is perhaps the great secret of the Vindös. The quality of boatbuilding that goes on in this yard would be very hard to find anywhere at any price, but here the wood deckhouses have been built this way for decades, it's all down to an art, so much so that Mr. Abrahamsson can fit one of those amazing curved housefronts in just three hours. It's irreplaceable skills such as these, perfected over the years, that keep the prices of the Vindös surprisingly low.

The other secret, I think, is that the boats are so beautiful. Vindö had the same designer from 1928 to 1978. He passed away at the age of ninety, leaving behind a long line of fine yachts. My favorite is the little 29 footer designed eighteen years ago, of which they have built four hundred sixty-two. This kind of classic continuity is impossible to find in the world today; the only other boat I can think of that has survived the years so well is Hinckley's Bermuda 40, which *aficionados* keep ordering year after year regardless of the price and regardless of its age.

But even at this writing, the little Vindö 29 is an endangered species, for many people would prefer to buy a larger boat of much less quality and certainly less beauty, so unless all you lovers of beautiful sailboats rally, these fine little yachts may just pass into history.

But there are two other very pretty Vindös that are going strong: The amazing 34 footer which, in spite of its graceful lines, has a little private cabin aft, and the perhaps even more amazing 39 footer which is one of the prettiest center cockpit boats created, cleverly layed out, with its huge owner's cabin aft.

The interior drawings speak for themselves, but do treat yourself to a close look at the 39 footer with its long fore and aft galley where you can be luxuriously braced against the lockers in a seaway, the spacious head accessible from forward and from aft, the truly regal-sized dinette with another settee across the way, the chart table of dimensions seldom found even on larger boats, and of course the aforementioned aft cabin with the airy berth the size of a football field. The berth in the forward cabin is of similar size and spaciousness, so that all in all, this is the ideal cruiser for two couples who like a beautiful boat to sail during the days and some beautiful berths to sleep in at night.

Now that we've dashed through the interiors, let's go back out and look at the hulls. As I said, the hull of the 29 footer is an eighteen-year-old design, whereas the other two are only four years old. The newer ones have stayed with the long keels but the forefoot, especially of the 34 footer, has been well cut back to reduce the wetted surface and to increase her ability to maneuver in close quarters. The rudders on the newer boats are also fuller for quicker response. The entries of all three boats are moderate and the buttocks rather full for good power.

The waterlines are long on all the boats with modest overhangs, and the shear is much the same on all three—gentle with a little spring.

On deck the Vindös all stand out, not just because of the beauty of their houses but also because of the spaciousness and comfort of their cockpits. The varnished cockpit coamings are high for comfort and security, and are well rounded in the aft corners for the helmsman to snuggle into. The footwells are narrow enough to brace yourself with your feet, on any angle of heel.

The side decks are of modest width on all the boats but certainly sufficient and safe, with 3-inch bulwarks with teak caprails to keep your feet on deck.

The masts are all deck-stepped with tabernacle bases and the pulpits are all formed like cradles to accept the mast when lowered. This is the ideal rig for cruising the canals of Europe.

If you think I'm rushing through all this to get to the construction, then you're absolutely right, because to me that's the most exciting aspect of these unique little yachts.

Vindö is very flexible in its layup of hulls, and although all hulls are now built to Lloyds of London specs, I would recommend as a good minimal layup for the smaller boats: two layers of mat and roving at topsides, three at the waterline and four in the keel area. For the 39 footer add a laminate everywhere. If you are happy with the rather old method of Lloyds of London rating, then take the hulls as they come.

The ballast is of internally-placed lead castings.

Now, the most interesting part is how the deck and house are made. The deck is actually layed up as traditional fiberglass decks are, with a flange bulwark. Between the hull and deck joint they fill with micro balloons and resin. Then the hulls are bonded with laminates to the deck from the inside to create a leakproof unit. The deck layup continues part way up—about 3 inches—to form the base of the cabinside. This high vertical lip is the beginnings of the house and is a very vital part, for it eliminates the potential deck leaks that old wooden boats had at the joint of house and deck.

The entire cockpit is a fiberglass molding, again eliminating a constant source of rot and leak problems common to most wooden boats, for cockpits undergo a lot of strain from steering systems, jumping bodies and dropped winch handles.

As you can see, so far we are talking about a fiberglass boat that is missing a few details, like cabin sides and a house top but those are coming next. Once the deck and cockpit are securely in place, a heavy layer of black polysulfide—the best sealant you can get—is layed onto the 3-inch high vertical fiberglass lip that's the foundation of the house sides, then the nearly 1 inch thick *solid* mahogany sides are screwed to the lip on 3 inch centers.

Now comes the best part. I always thought that the beautifully curved forward part of the house was some thin veneer which would die an early death. Not so. The entire front piece is a series of *seven* laminates of ⅛-inch-thick *solid* mahogany, layed in a massive jig and glued and clamped together. They are then fit and scarfed, with the most perfectly fitting joints I have ever seen, onto the house sides.

Next, a set of laminated deckbeams are set into the house sides on about 12-inch centers, and a layer of plywood that has been milled to look like tongue-and-groove is glued and screwed onto the beams. The heavy ½-inch teak decking is then layed over that. If you're skeptical in the least regarding this construction, remember that they have built three thousand boats this way in the past fifty-eight years which all worked well just as they were meant to. Ideally the teak should be set into thickened epoxy glue which would create a tremendously strong structure.

Things like the covering boards on the house top, which are actually the corner of the house top itself, are meticulously crafted with beautiful overlapping joints in the corners. All the hatch openings are amply reinforced and generally the house and deck feel enormously solid. We saw a boat that was over twenty years old, sitting in the winter sheds, and except for needing a coat of varnish—just to liven up the shine and for no other reason—the whole structure seemed as if it were only a year old, with not an open or cracked seam or joint anywhere.

The next step at Vindö is to cover whatever is fiberglass with a layer of heavy solid teak. So the fiberglass decks and cockpits vanish under some fine woodwork, and even the sides of the cockpit-well get covered over.

To preserve the teak in top shape, the seats are sloped to let the water run off, but then, just to be sure, there are little copper tubes set in the seat to insure drainage in case the boat is loaded out of trim.

To show what kind of care is taken with details here at Vindö, let's look at how the deck drains. The deck scuppers are *bonded* right into the deck to prevent any leaks into the interior. On most production boats the drains are led directly through the hull at deck level, allowing dirty water to run down the topsides and leave horrendous dirt stains on the hull—and oh, how many cursed hours I have spent scouring the unscourable from ours! But at Vindö the drains lead into heavy pipes bonded right onto the inside skin of the hull, which then lead down to the drainholes in the bootstripe. Now that's good engineering.

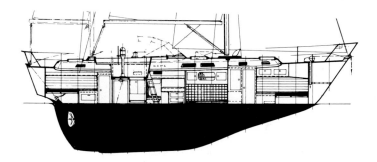

The rest of the boat is as well thought out: the tiller on the *29,* hinges up onto the aft deck leaving the cockpit free; the steering mechanism on the *34* is completely accessible for maintenance and inspection; there are interior red night-sailing lamps all over the boat; and the beautiful good-sized teak and bronze mooring cleats are set up on the caprail where they are out of the way and from where the docklines lead overboard fairly eliminating the need for chafeguards on the caprail.

The bedlogs for the engine are enormous pieces of wood and the engine installation is well done, as is the electrical and plumbing—the seacocks are all bronze. And there are endless hours invested in lining even the lockers with mahogany strips, beautifully dressing and bullnosing the most hidden dropboards, and varnishing them three times, and fabricating teak grates in the head that are works of art.

I must mention one thing that I have seen on very few yachts other than Vindö, and that is the beautiful, solid china sinks in the heads. Not only do they look good when the boat is new, but because they won't scratch or stain or discolor, they'll look beautiful for years to come. All you builders who use the ugly little plastic monsters read and learn.

One question that always comes up with the Swedish yachts is: Why do they all use mahogany instead of teak for interiors and, in the case of Vindö, for all the exterior structures as well? The answer to that is tradition. For over a hundred years mahogany has been the wood used in this region. Besides, mahogany is an infinitely better wood for structural use than teak, since it glues and laminates well, whereas teak, with its enormously high oil content, does not. The mahogany in use at Vindö is bought in solid logs, and only the finest pieces with the best grain and color are used in places where the wood is visible.

Vindö Yachts of Sweden is without parallel in boat building today, with their small and medium-sized yachts with fiberglass hulls, side decks and cockpits, and beautifully varnished solid wood houses. Vindös look exactly

as a good yacht should. They have been building boats for almost sixty years and currently have three models: the little 29 footer, a 34 footer and the 38-foot center cockpit. The workmanship is so precise that a violin maker couldn't improve on it, but then some of the best shipwrights here have been

building Vindös for 35 years. The photo in the top left corner shows the beautiful cabin top covering boards and the curved frontal piece laminated from seven 1/8-inch thick layers of solid mahogany. The photo to its right shows the 34 footer head on, with just a trace of tumble-home. The thirty-year-old photo

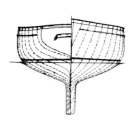

in the bottom
left-hand corner
shows a small Vindö
to the right on the
rocky Swedish
coast, while the
photo beside it is
again of the 34
footer under sail.
The 38-foot center
cockpit is shown in
the drawings. Above
is a good photo
showing the
extensive wood-
work in house and
deck.

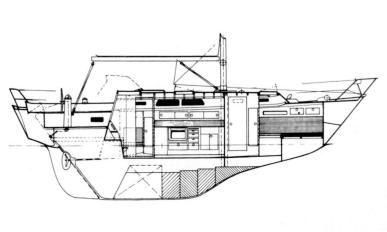

The top left photo shows the laminated front of the cabin top. The entire front is one piece, with the seven laminates I mentioned staggered, so the center seam you see is only one layer deep. The photo to its right shows the solid turtle hatch under which the main hatch slides. It is built as one piece with the curved base for the dodger. In the top right corner is a beautiful mooring cleat set wisely out of the way on top of the caprail. If you look really hard, you can see a strip of brass behind the plate guarding the caprail against rope chafe. Below it is a detail of the lapped joint in the house-corner, while the large photo shows the wood-lined cockpit. I say wood-lined because, to prevent leaks, there is a monocoque fiber-glass molding underneath the wood. A classy idea, to say the least! In the bottom left corner are three

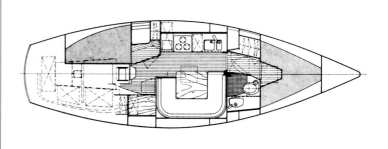

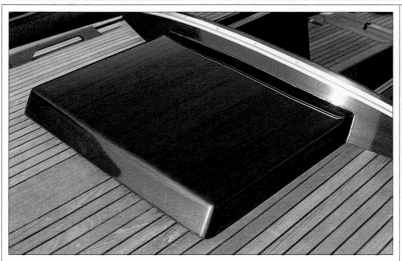

interior shots and a drawing of the 34 footer, showing the lovingly crafted mahogany (the traditional wood in these parts) interior. Note the laminated beams which are the structural part of the house, and the tongue-in-groove patterned cedar overhead over which the teak decking is laid.

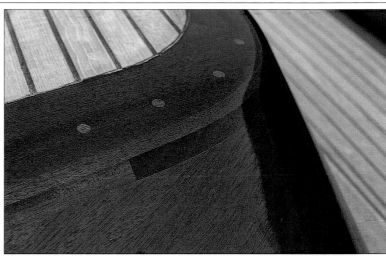

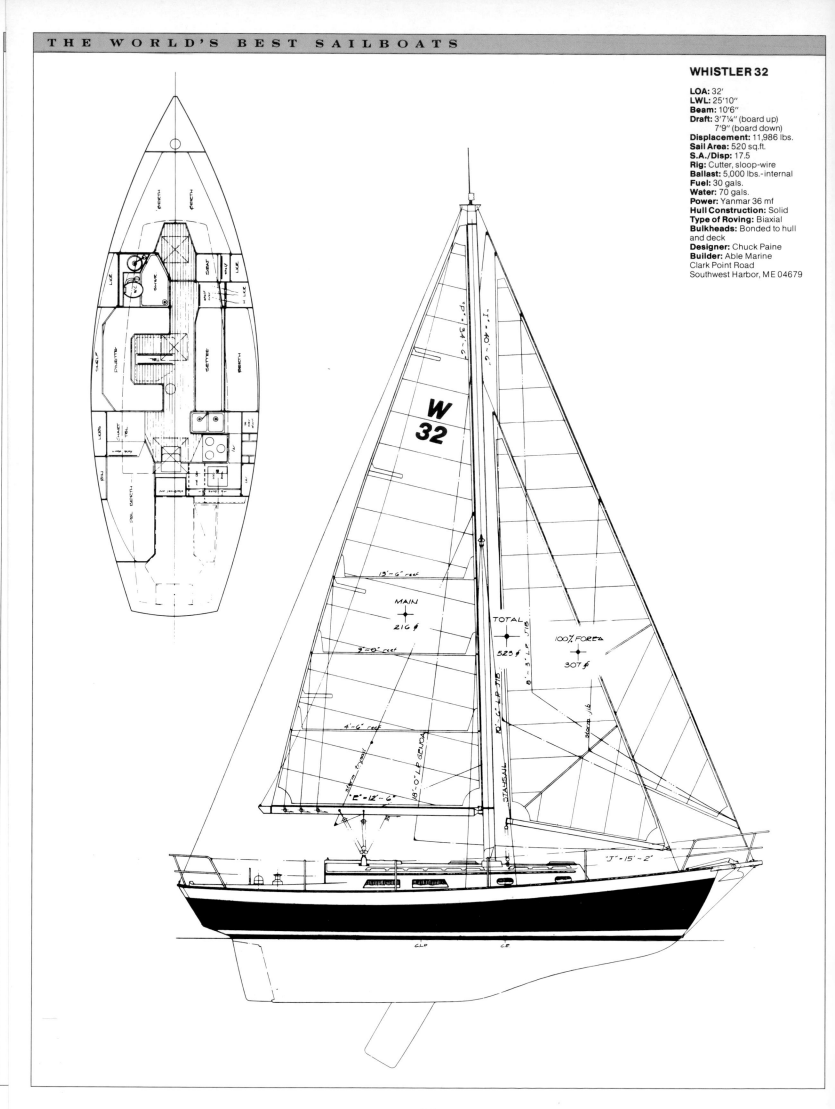

WHISTLER 32

LOA: 32'
LWL: 25'10"
Beam: 10'6"
Draft: 3'7¼" (board up)
7'9" (board down)
Displacement: 11,986 lbs.
Sail Area: 520 sq.ft.
S.A./Disp: 17.5
Rig: Cutter, sloop-wire
Ballast: 5,000 lbs.-internal
Fuel: 30 gals.
Water: 70 gals.
Power: Yanmar 36 mf
Hull Construction: Solid
Type of Roving: Biaxial
Bulkheads: Bonded to hull and deck
Designer: Chuck Paine
Builder: Able Marine
Clark Point Road
Southwest Harbor, ME 04679

WHISTLER 48

LOA: 48'
LWL: 40'3"
Beam: 14'
Draft: 5'10"
Displacement: 35,909 lbs.
(half load)
Sail Area: 1,176 sq.ft.
S.A./Disp: 16.52
Disp./LWL: 281
Rig: Ketch, cutter-wire
Ballast: 13,600 lbs.-external
Fuel: 200 gals.
Water: 300 gals.
Power: Westerbeke 70 or 100
Hull Construction: Core-Airex
Type of Roving: Biaxial
Bulkheads: Bonded to hull
and deck
Designer: Chuck Paine
Builder: Able Marine

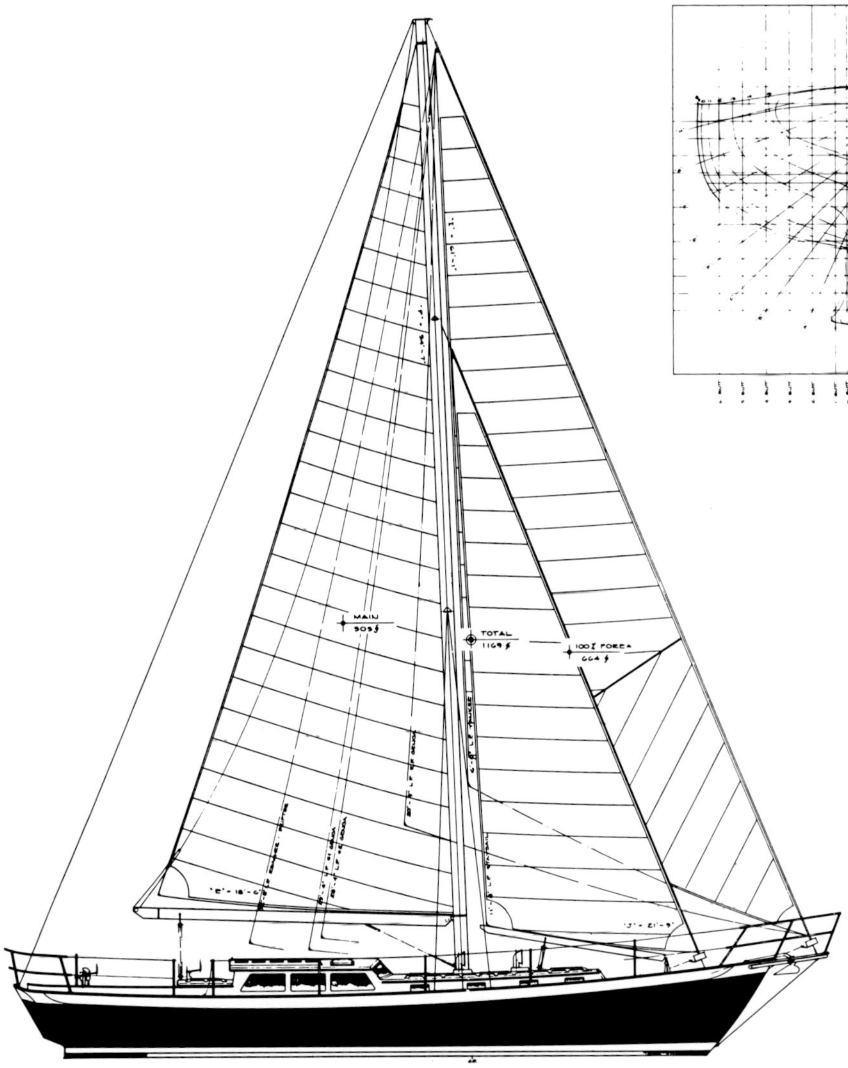

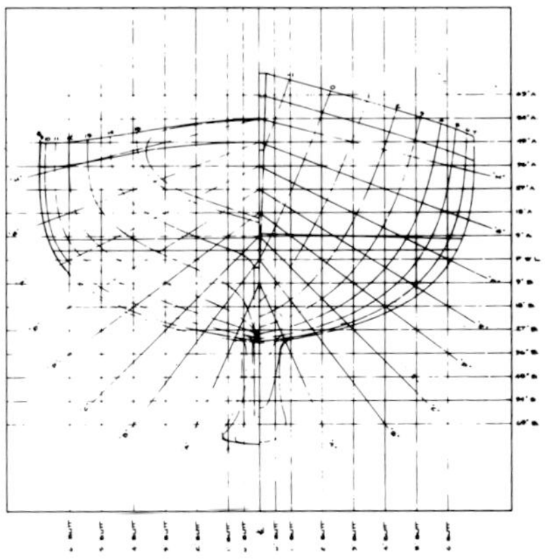

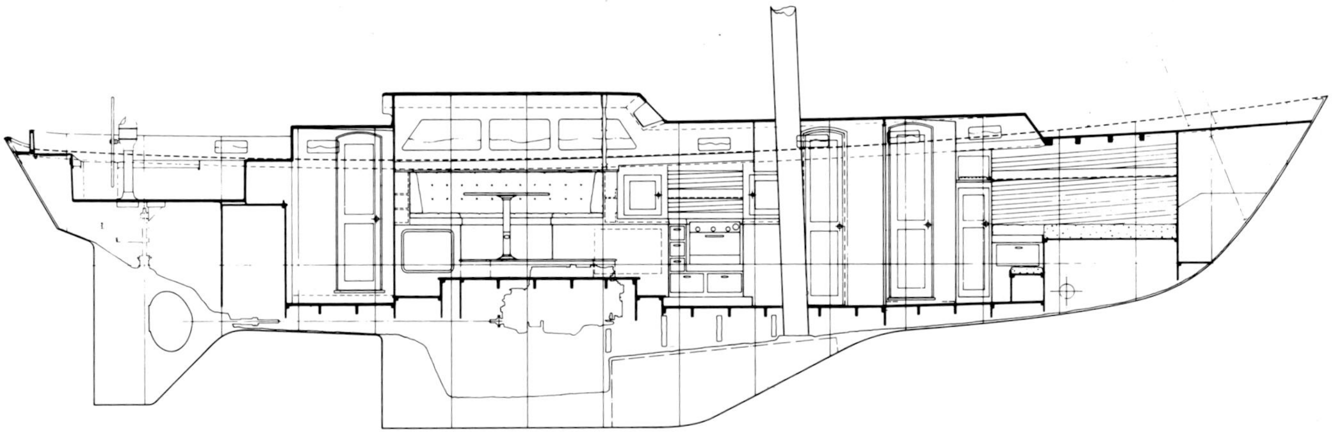

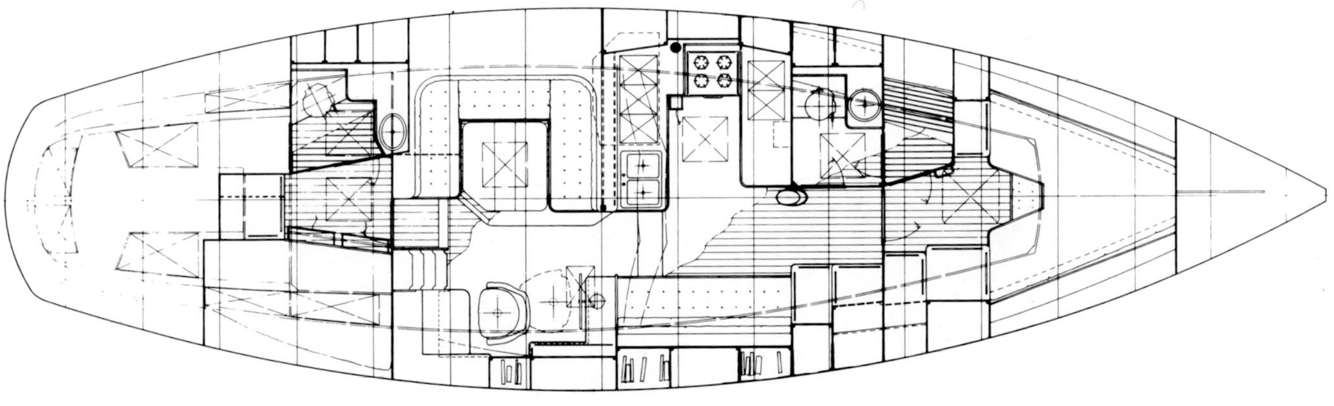

ALDEN 52 CC

LOA: 52'7"
LWL: 40'
Beam: 14'4"
Draft: 5'6" (board up)
10'4" (board down)
Displacement: 37,800 lbs.
Sail Area: 1,170 sq.ft.
Rig: Wire
Ballast: 16,300 lbs.-external
Fuel: 130 gals.
Water: 300 gals.
Power: 73 hp Westerbeke
Hull Construction: Core-balsa
Type of Roving: Unidirectional, unidirectional
Bulkheads: Composite balsa and fiberglass, bonded directly to hull and deck
Designer: John G. Alden Co.
Builder: Alden Yachts

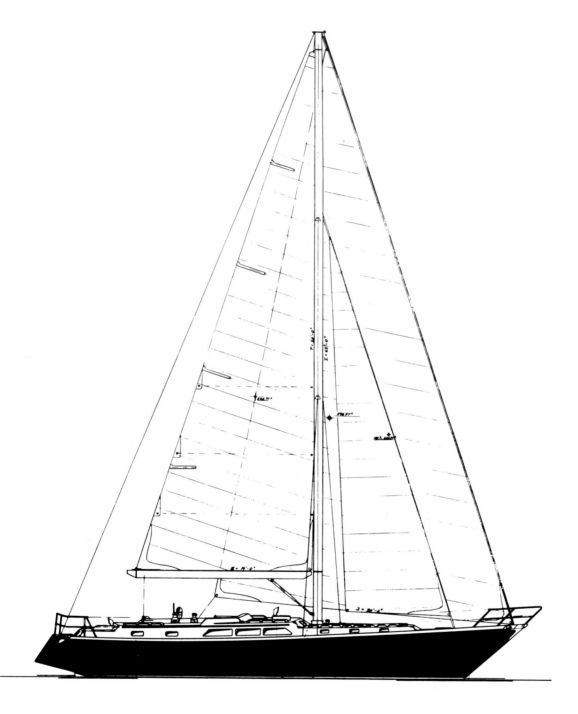

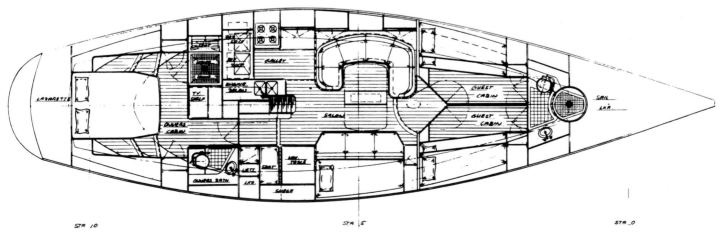

ALDEN 54

LOA: 54'1"
LWL: 40'
Beam: 14'4"
Draft: 5'6" (board up)
     10'4" (board down)
Displacement: 38,000 lbs.
Sail Area: 1,230 sq.ft.
Rig: Ketch, cutter-wire
Ballast: 16,300 lbs.-external
Fuel: 130 gals.
Water: 280 gals.
Power: 70 hp diesel
Hull Construction: Core-balsa
Type of Roving: Unidirectional, biaxial
Bulkheads: Bonded to hull and deck
Designer: John G. Alden Co.
Builder: Alden Yachts

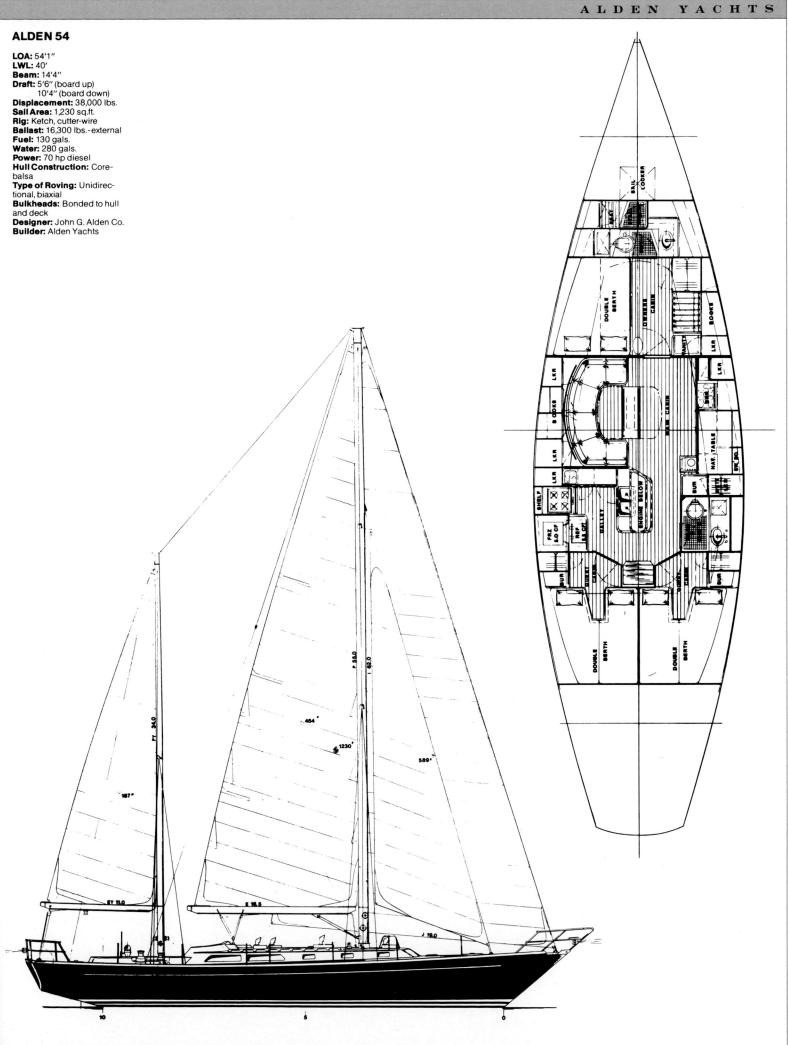

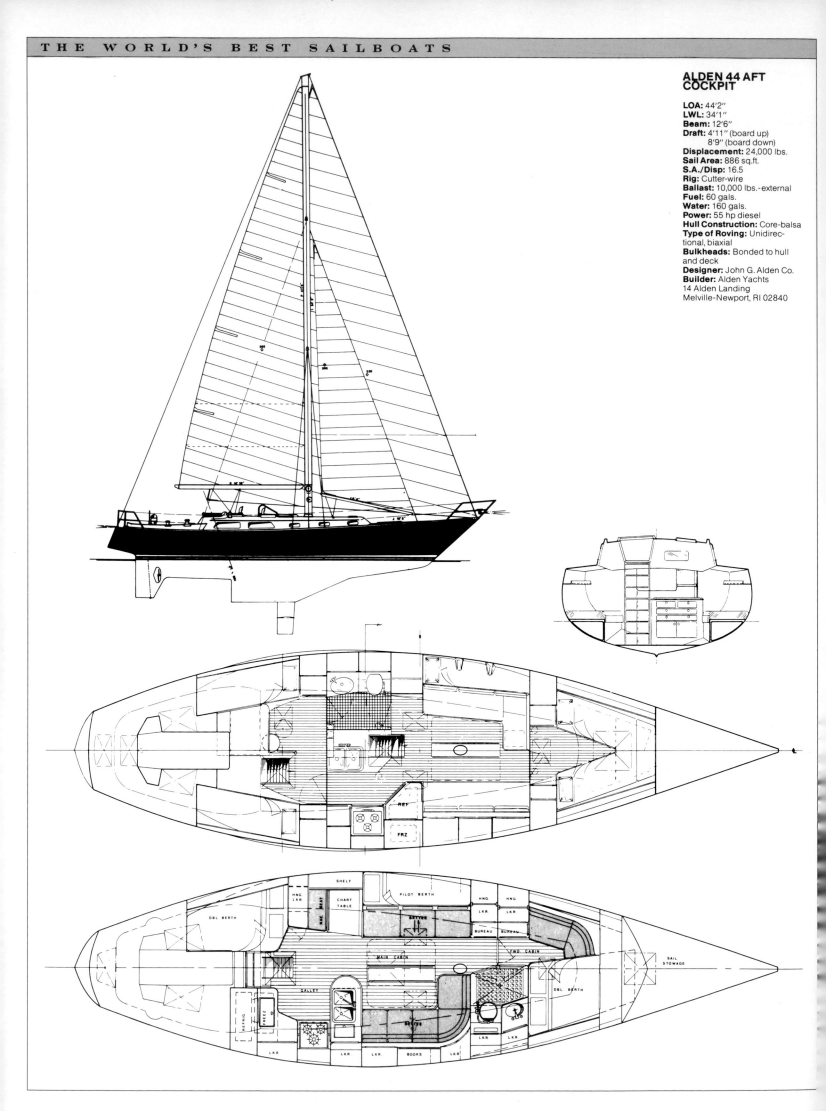

ALDEN 44 AFT COCKPIT

LOA: 44'2"
LWL: 34'1"
Beam: 12'6"
Draft: 4'11" (board up)
8'9" (board down)
Displacement: 24,000 lbs.
Sail Area: 886 sq.ft.
S.A./Disp: 16.5
Rig: Cutter-wire
Ballast: 10,000 lbs.-external
Fuel: 60 gals.
Water: 160 gals.
Power: 55 hp diesel
Hull Construction: Core-balsa
Type of Roving: Unidirectional, biaxial
Bulkheads: Bonded to hull and deck
Designer: John G. Alden Co.
Builder: Alden Yachts
14 Alden Landing
Melville-Newport, RI 02840

ALDEN 50 AFT COCKPIT

LOA: 50'
LWL: 40'
Beam: 14'4"
Draft: 5'6" (board up)
10'4" (board down)
Displacement: 38,000 lbs.
Sail Area: 1,170 sq.ft.
Rig: Cutter-wire
Ballast: 16,300 lbs.-external
Fuel: 130 gals.
Water: 280 gals.
Power: 70 hp diesel
Hull Construction: Core-balsa
Type of Roving: Unidirectional, biaxial
Bulkheads: Bonded to hull and deck
Designer: John G. Alden Co.
Builder: Alden Yachts

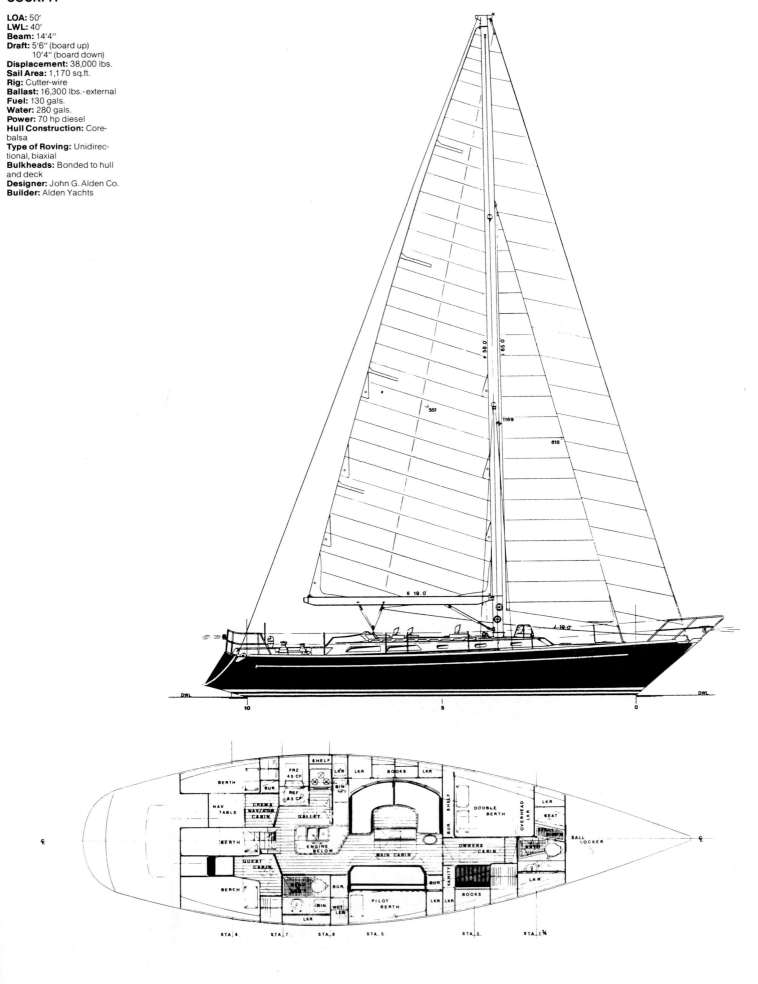

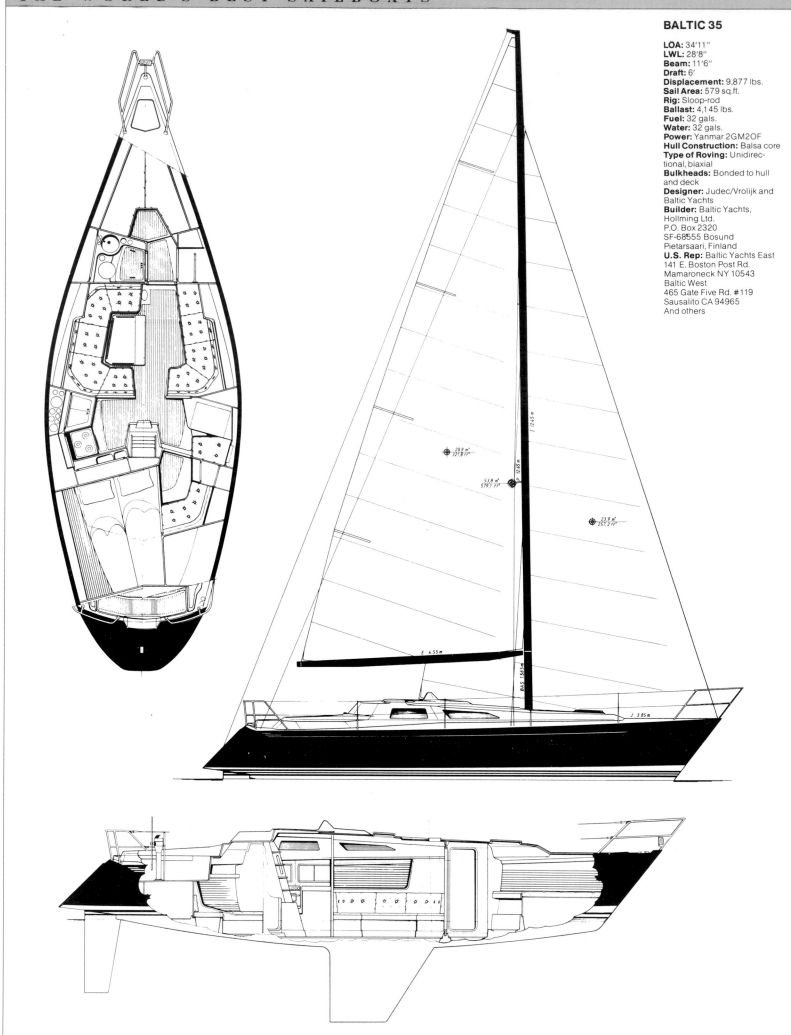

BALTIC 35

LOA: 34'11"
LWL: 28'8"
Beam: 11'6"
Draft: 6'
Displacement: 9,877 lbs.
Sail Area: 579 sq.ft.
Rig: Sloop-rod
Ballast: 4,145 lbs.
Fuel: 32 gals.
Water: 32 gals.
Power: Yanmar 2GM2OF
Hull Construction: Balsa core
Type of Roving: Unidirectional, biaxial
Bulkheads: Bonded to hull and deck
Designer: Judec/Vrolijk and Baltic Yachts
Builder: Baltic Yachts, Hollming Ltd.
P.O. Box 2320
SF-68555 Bosund
Pietarsaari, Finland
U.S. Rep: Baltic Yachts East
141 E. Boston Post Rd.
Mamaroneck NY 10543
Baltic West
465 Gate Five Rd. #119
Sausalito CA 94965
And others

BALTIC 38 DP

LOA: 38′
LWL: 31′6″
Beam: 12′4″
Draft: 7′3″
Displacement: 14,330 lbs.
Sail Area: 743 sq.ft.
Rig: Sloop-rod
Ballast: 6,500 lbs.
Fuel: 26 gals.
Water: 60 gals.
Power: Yanmar 3HMF 3 Cyl.
30 hp
Hull Construction: Core-balsa
Type of Roving: Unidirectional
Bulkheads: Bonded to hull
and deck
Designer: Doug Peterson/
Baltic Yachts
Builder: Baltic Yachts

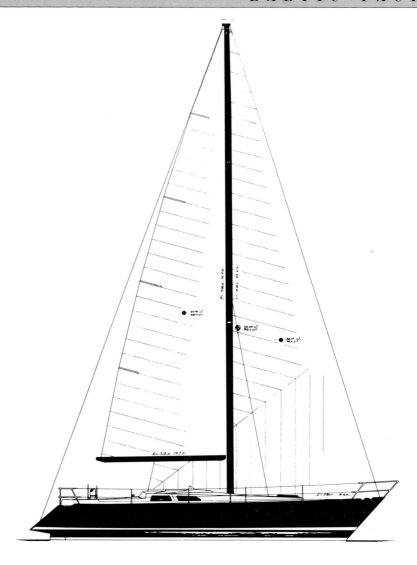

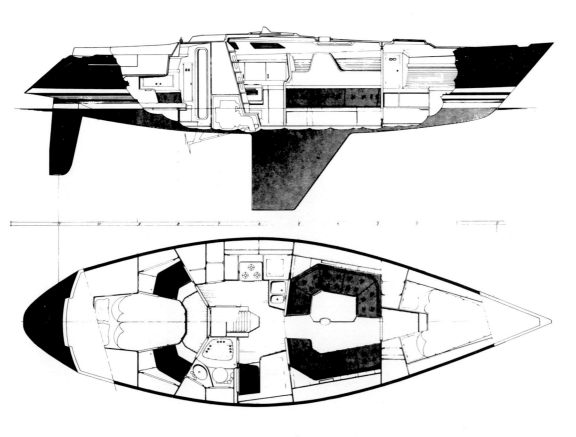

BALTIC 51

LOA: 51'
LWL: 41'
Beam: 15'3"
Draft: 9'
Displacement: 34,390 lbs.
Sail Area: 1,127 sq.ft.
I.O.R. Rating: 40.5 ft.
Rig: Sloop-rod
Ballast: 13,536 lbs.
Fuel: 46 gals.
Water: 180 gals.
Power: Volvo-Penta MD 21 A 61 hp
Hull Construction: Balsa core
Type of Roving: Unidirectional, biaxial
Bulkheads: Bonded to hull & deck
Designer: Doug Peterson/ Baltic Yachts
Builder: Baltic Yachts

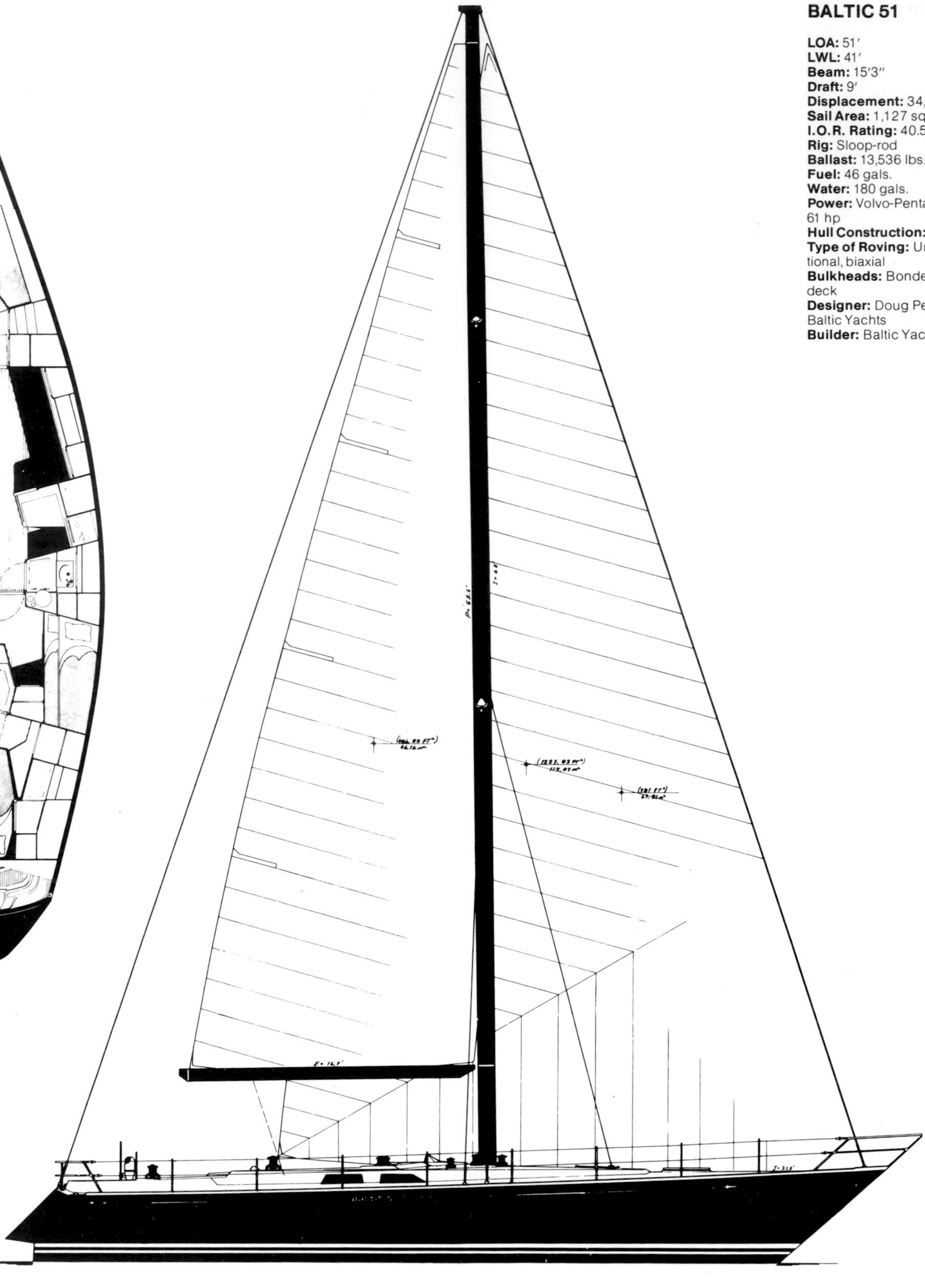

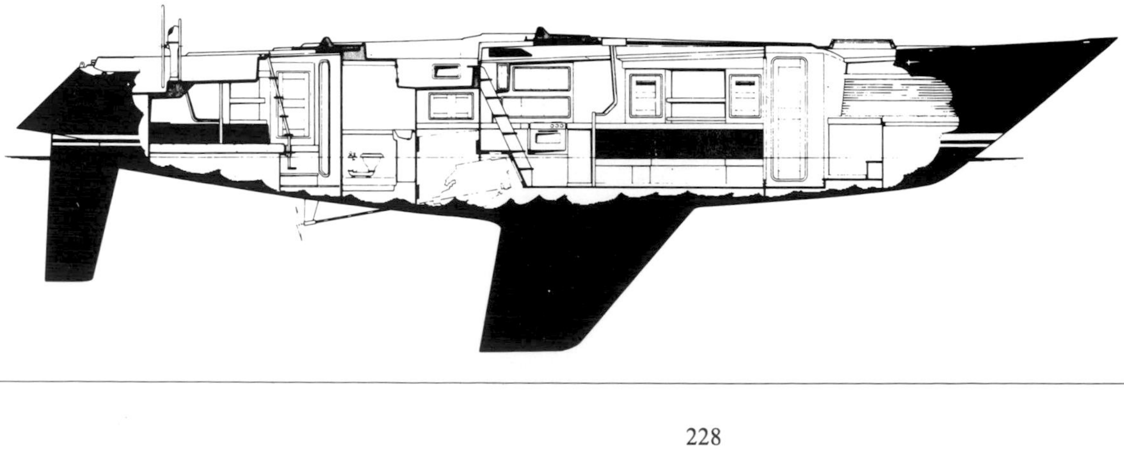

BALTIC 55 DP

LOA: 54'9" 16.7m
LWL: 47'6" 14.4m
Beam: 16'1"
Draft: 9'7"
Displacement: 38,590 lbs.
Sail Area: 1,489 sq.ft.
I.O.R. Rating: 45.5 ft.
Rig: Sloop-rod
Ballast: 16,140 lbs.
Fuel: 85 gals.
Water: 200 gals.
Power: Volvo TMD 30 4 cyl. 86 hp
Hull Construction: Core-balsa
Type of Roving: Unidirectional, biaxial, woven
Bulkheads: Bonded to hull and deck
Designer: Doug Peterson/ Baltic Yachts
Builder: Baltic Yachts

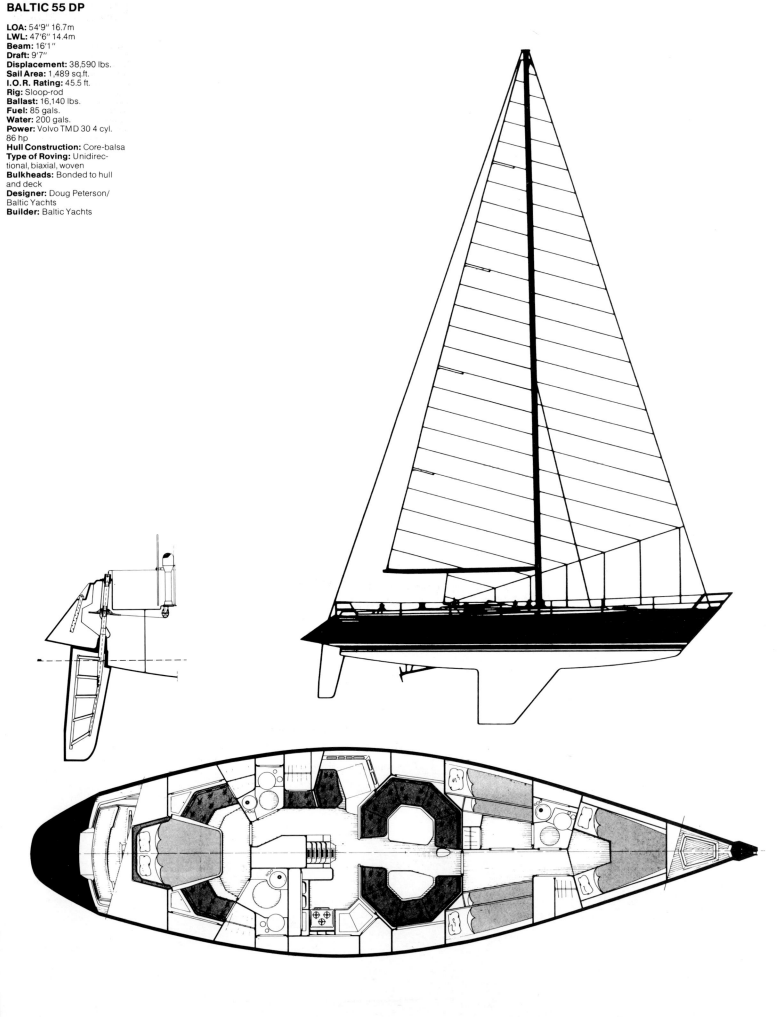

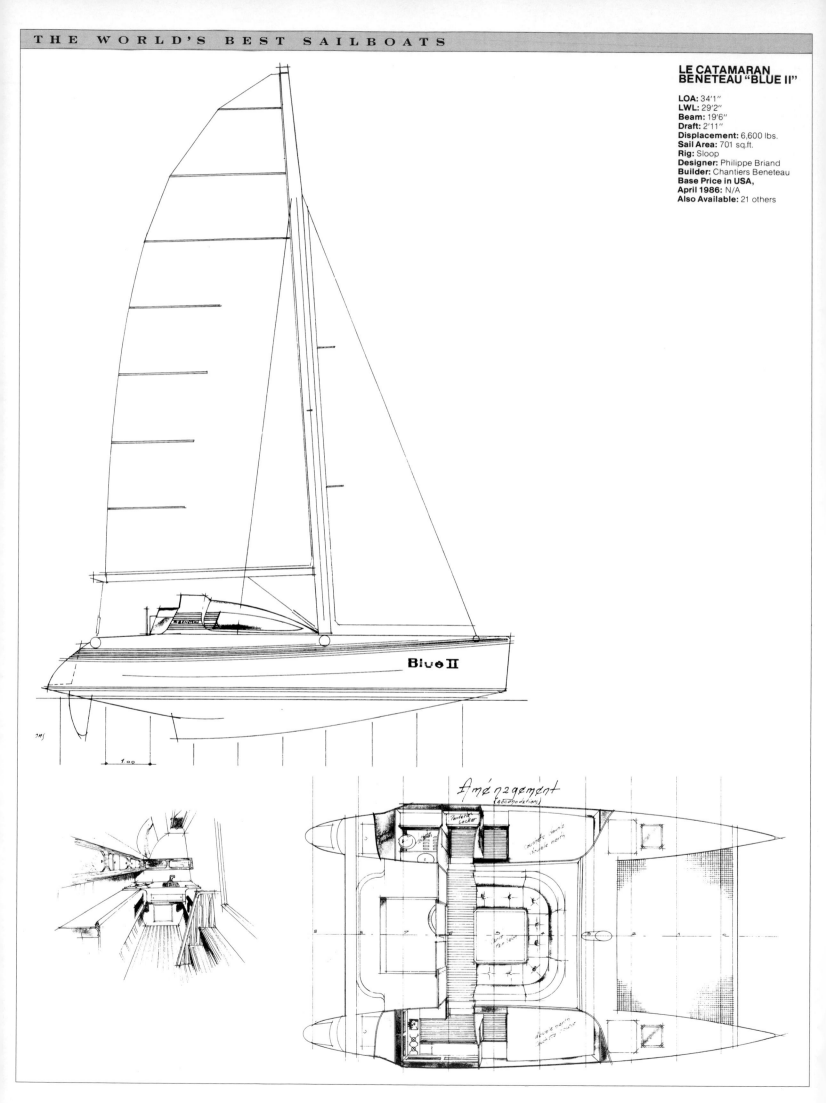

**LE CATAMARAN
BENETEAU "BLUE II"**

LOA: 34'1"
LWL: 29'2"
Beam: 19'6"
Draft: 2'11"
Displacement: 6,600 lbs.
Sail Area: 701 sq.ft.
Rig: Sloop
Designer: Philippe Briand
Builder: Chantiers Beneteau
**Base Price in USA,
April 1986:** N/A
Also Available: 21 others

BENETEAU FIRST 305

LOA: 30'7"
LWL: 26'11"
Beam: 10'7"
Draft: 5'8"
Displacement: 8,242 lbs.
Sail Area: 534 sq.ft.
S.A./Disp: 20.91
Disp./LWL: 189.03
Rig: Sloop-wire
Ballast: 2,976 lbs.-external
Fuel: 9 gals.
Water: 27 gals.
Power: Volvo 2002
Hull Construction: Solid
Type of Roving: Woven
Bulkheads: Bonded to hull, deck and liner
Designer: Jean Berret
Builder: Chantiers Beneteau
Z.I. des Mares
85270 Saint Hilaire de Riez
France
U.S. Distributor: Beneteau
USA Ltd.
326 First Street
Annapolis, MD 21403

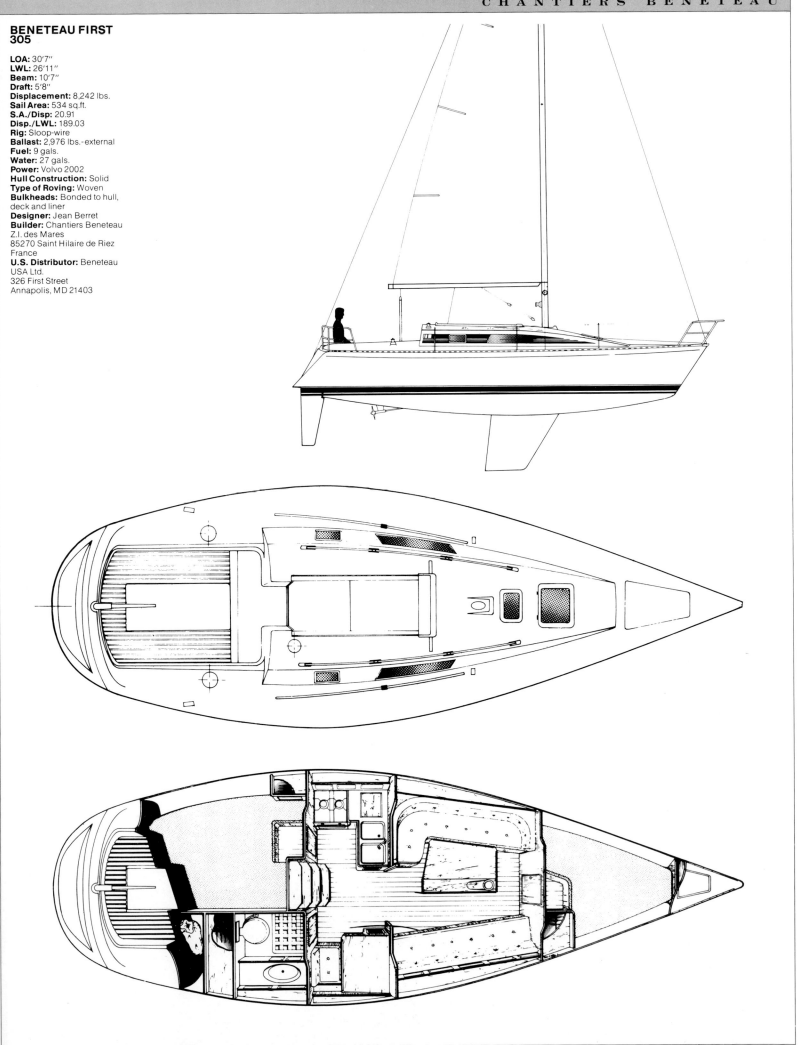

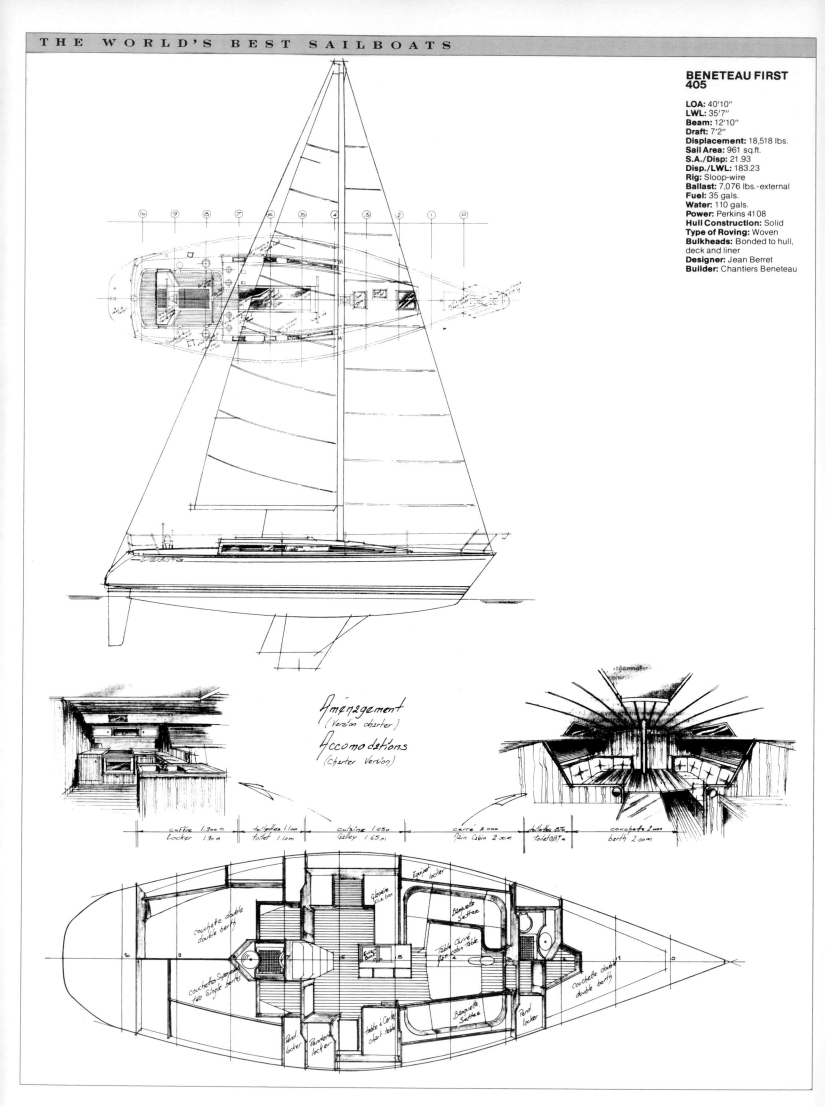

BENETEAU FIRST 405

LOA: 40'10"
LWL: 35'7"
Beam: 12'10"
Draft: 7'2"
Displacement: 18,518 lbs.
Sail Area: 961 sq.ft.
S.A./Disp: 21.93
Disp./LWL: 183.23
Rig: Sloop-wire
Ballast: 7,076 lbs.-external
Fuel: 35 gals.
Water: 110 gals.
Power: Perkins 4108
Hull Construction: Solid
Type of Roving: Woven
Bulkheads: Bonded to hull, deck and liner
Designer: Jean Berret
Builder: Chantiers Beneteau

Aménagement
(Version charter)

Accomodations
(Charter Version)

BENETEAU FIRST 435

LOA: 43'7"
LWL: 36'1"
Beam: 13'1"
Draft: 7'6"
Displacement: 21,825 lbs.
Sail Area: 11,116 sq.ft.
Rig: Sloop-wire
Ballast: 9,259 lbs.
Fuel: 51 gals.
Water: 85 gals.
Power: Perkins 4108
Hull Construction: Solid
Type of Roving: Woven
Bulkheads: Bonded to hull, deck and liner
Designer: German Frers
Builder: Chantiers Beneteau

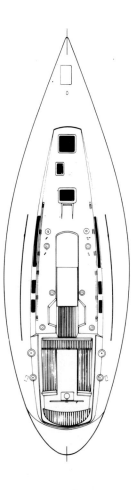

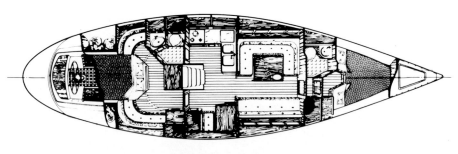

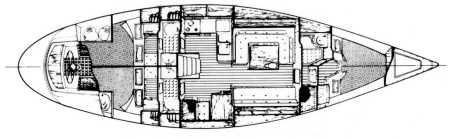

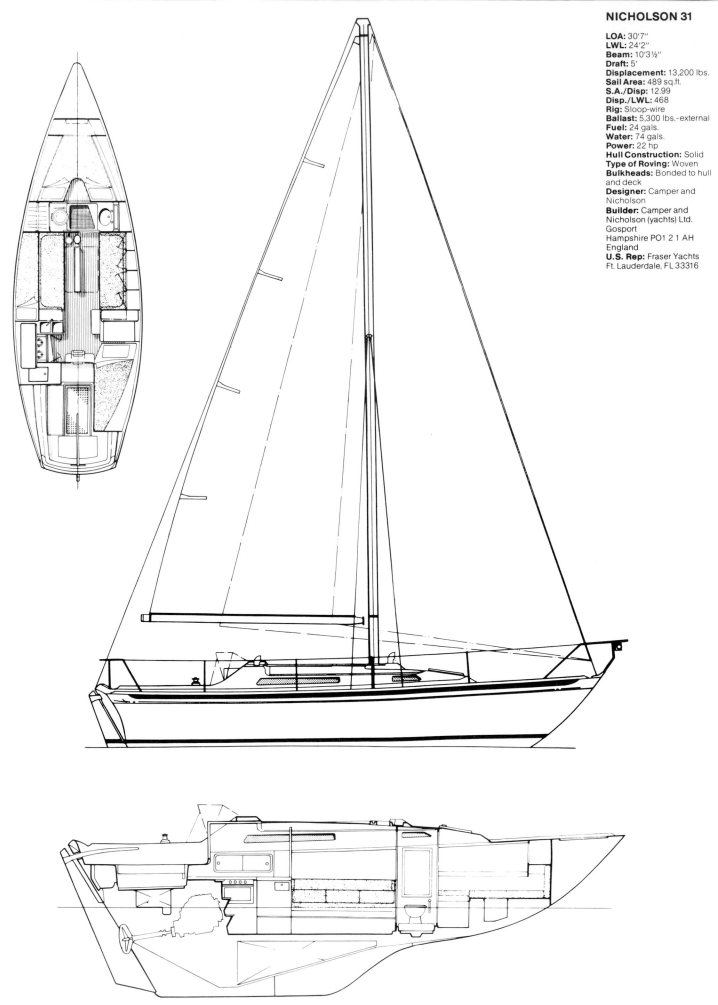

NICHOLSON 31

LOA: 30'7"
LWL: 24'2"
Beam: 10'3½"
Draft: 5'
Displacement: 13,200 lbs.
Sail Area: 489 sq.ft.
S.A./Disp: 12.99
Disp./LWL: 468
Rig: Sloop-wire
Ballast: 5,300 lbs.-external
Fuel: 24 gals.
Water: 74 gals.
Power: 22 hp
Hull Construction: Solid
Type of Roving: Woven
Bulkheads: Bonded to hull and deck
Designer: Camper and Nicholson
Builder: Camper and Nicholson (yachts) Ltd. Gosport Hampshire PO1 2 1 AH England
U.S. Rep: Fraser Yachts Ft. Lauderdale, FL 33316

NICHOLSON 35

LOA: 35'3"
LWL: 26'9"
Beam: 10'5"
Draft: 5'6"
Displacement: 15,800 lbs.
Sail Area: 550 sq.ft.
S.A./Disp: 12.97
Disp./LWL: 413
Rig: Sloop-wire
Ballast: 7,840 lbs.-external
Fuel: 48 gals.
Water: 96 gals.
Power: 47 hp
Hull Construction: Solid
Type of Roving: Woven
Bulkheads: Bonded to hull and deck
Designer: Camper and Nicholson
Builder: Camper and Nicholson (yachts) Ltd.

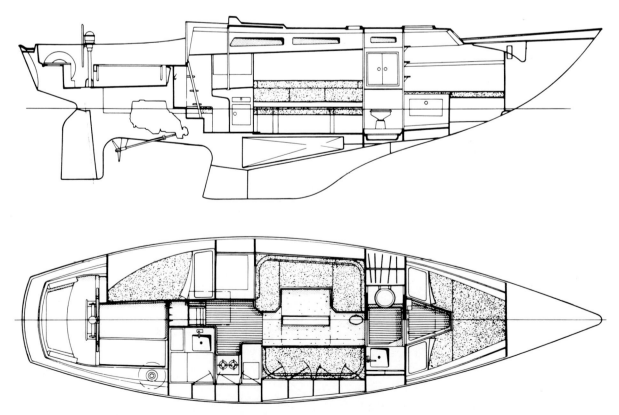

NICHOLSON 476

LOA: 47'5"
LWL: 38'7"
Beam: 13'8"
Draft: 5'10"
Displacement: 29,460 lbs.
Sail Area: 969 sq.ft.
S.A./Disp: 15.09
Disp./LWL: 298
Rig: Ketch, cutter-wire
Ballast: 13,500 lbs.-external
Fuel: 90 gals.
Water: 180 gals.
Power: 72 hp
Hull Construction: Solid, core-balsa
Type of Roving: Unidirectional, woven
Bulkheads: Bonded to hull and deck
Designer: Camper and Nicholson
Builder: Camper and Nicholson (yachts) Ltd.

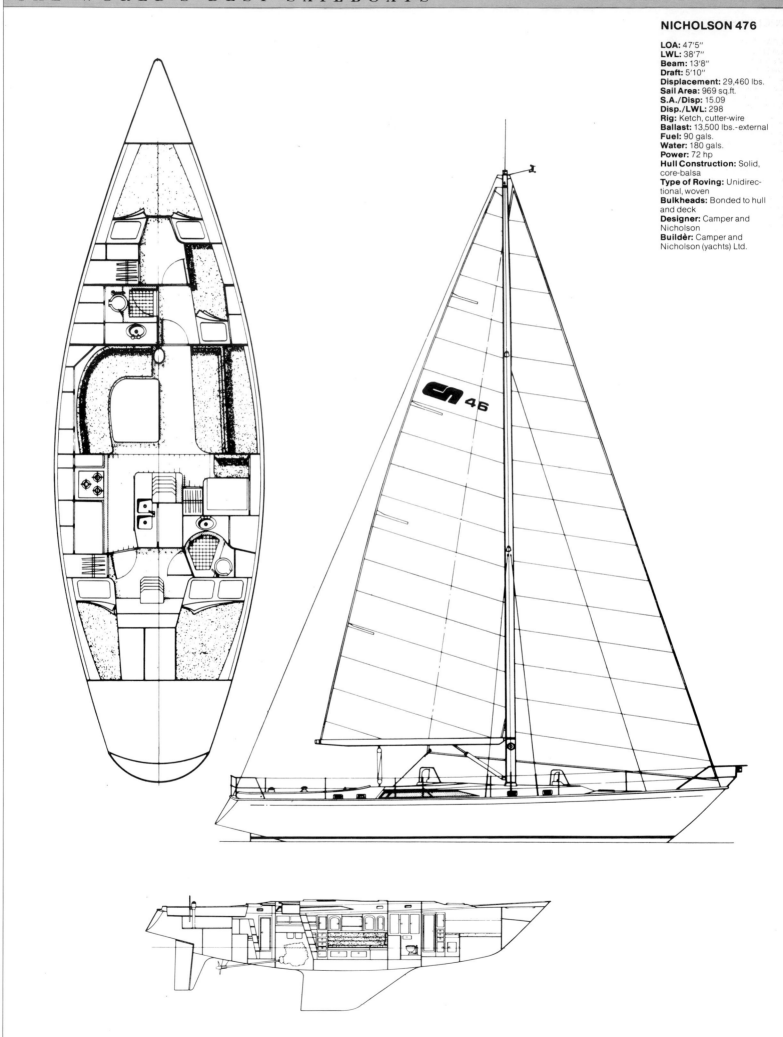

NICHOLSON 58

LOA: 57'7"
LWL: 46'8"
Beam: 15'7"
Draft: 8'6"
      7'
Displacement: 49,200 lbs.
Sail Area: 1,468 sq.ft.
S.A./Disp: 16.22
Disp./LWL: 242
Rig: Ketch, cutter-wire
Ballast: 19,000 lbs.-external
Fuel: 360 gals.
Water: 216 gals.
Power: 120 hp
Hull Construction: Solid, core-balsa
Type of Roving: Unidirectional, woven
Bulkheads: Bonded to hull and deck
Designer: David Pedrick, Camper and Nicholson
Builder: Camper and Nicholson (yachts) Ltd.

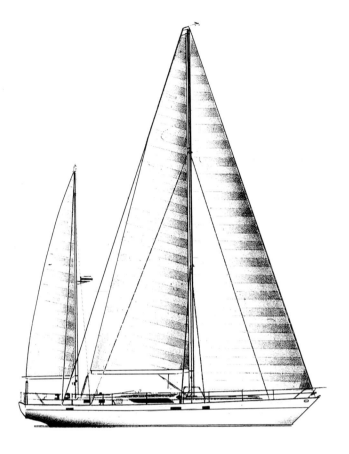

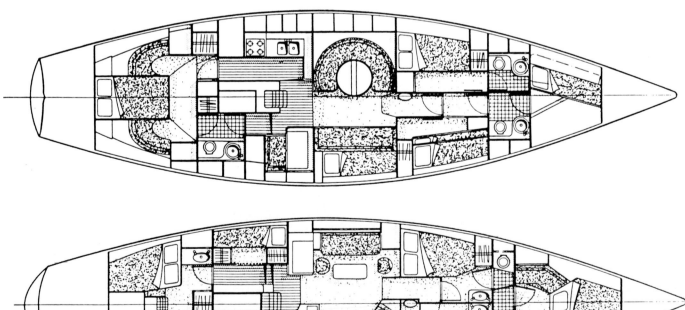

CHERUBINI 44

LOA: 50'
LWL: 40'
Beam: 12'
Draft: 4'10"
Displacement: 28,000 lbs.
Sail Area: 1,133 sq.ft.
S.A./Disp: 19.67
Disp./LWL: 195.3
Rig: Ketch, cutter, schooner-rod
Ballast: 12,000 lbs.-internal
Fuel: 100 gals.
Water: 145 gals.
Power: 72 hp diesel "Nannidiesel"
Hull Construction: Solid
Type of Roving: Biaxial & unidirectional
Bulkheads: Bonded to hull and deck
Designer: John Cherubini
Builder: Cherubini Boat Co.
222 Wood Street
Burlington, NJ 08016

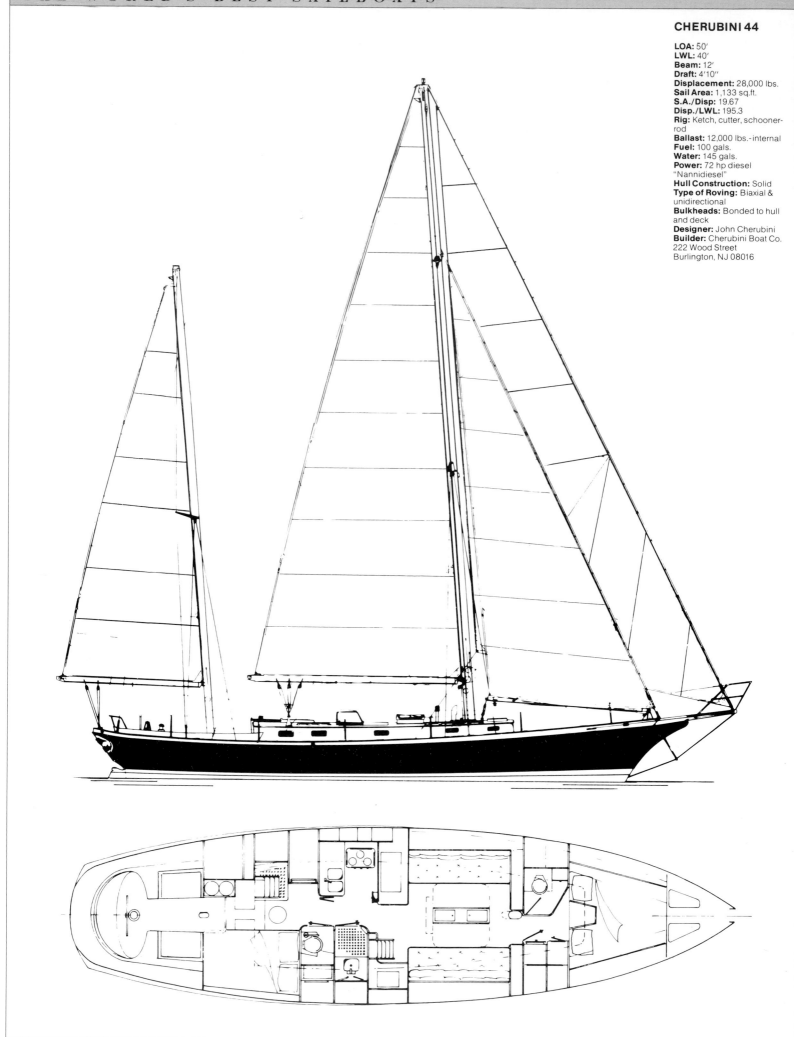

CHERUBINI 48

LOA: 56'8"
LWL: 44'
Beam: 13'
Draft: 5'
Displacement: 37,000 lbs.
Sail Area: 1,218 sq.ft.
S.A./Disp.: 17.2
Disp./LWL: 196.5
Rig: Ketch, schooner-rod
Ballast: 16,900 lbs.- internal
Fuel: 140 gals.
Water: 185 gals.
Power: 88 hp diesel
"Nannidiesel"
Hull Construction: Solid
Type of Roving: Biaxial,
unidirectional
Bulkheads: Bonded to hull
and deck
Designer: John Cherubini
Builder: Cherubini Boat Co.

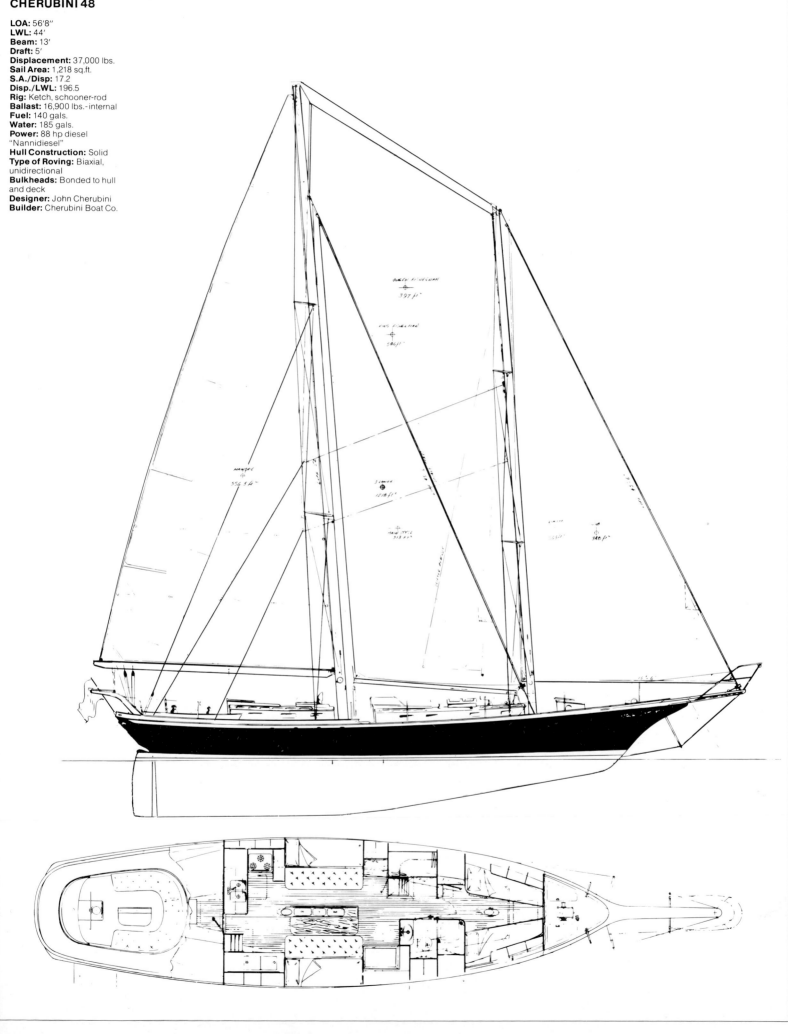

CAMBRIA 40

LOA: 41'5"
LWL: 32'6"
Beam: 12'3"
Draft: 4'11" (board up)
7'3" (keel)
Displacement: 22,200 lbs.
Sail Area: 801 sq.ft.
S.A./Disp: 16.23
Disp./LWL: 289
Rig: Cutter, sloop-rod
Ballast: 7,500 lbs.-external
Fuel: 60 gals.
Water: 140 gals.
Power: 46 Westerbeke (127 cubic inches)
Hull Construction: Core-Airex
Type of Roving: Unidirectional, biaxial
Bulkheads: Bonded to hull and deck
Designer: David Walters
Builder: David Walters Yachts, Ltd.
31 Lagoon Rd.
Portsmouth RI 02871

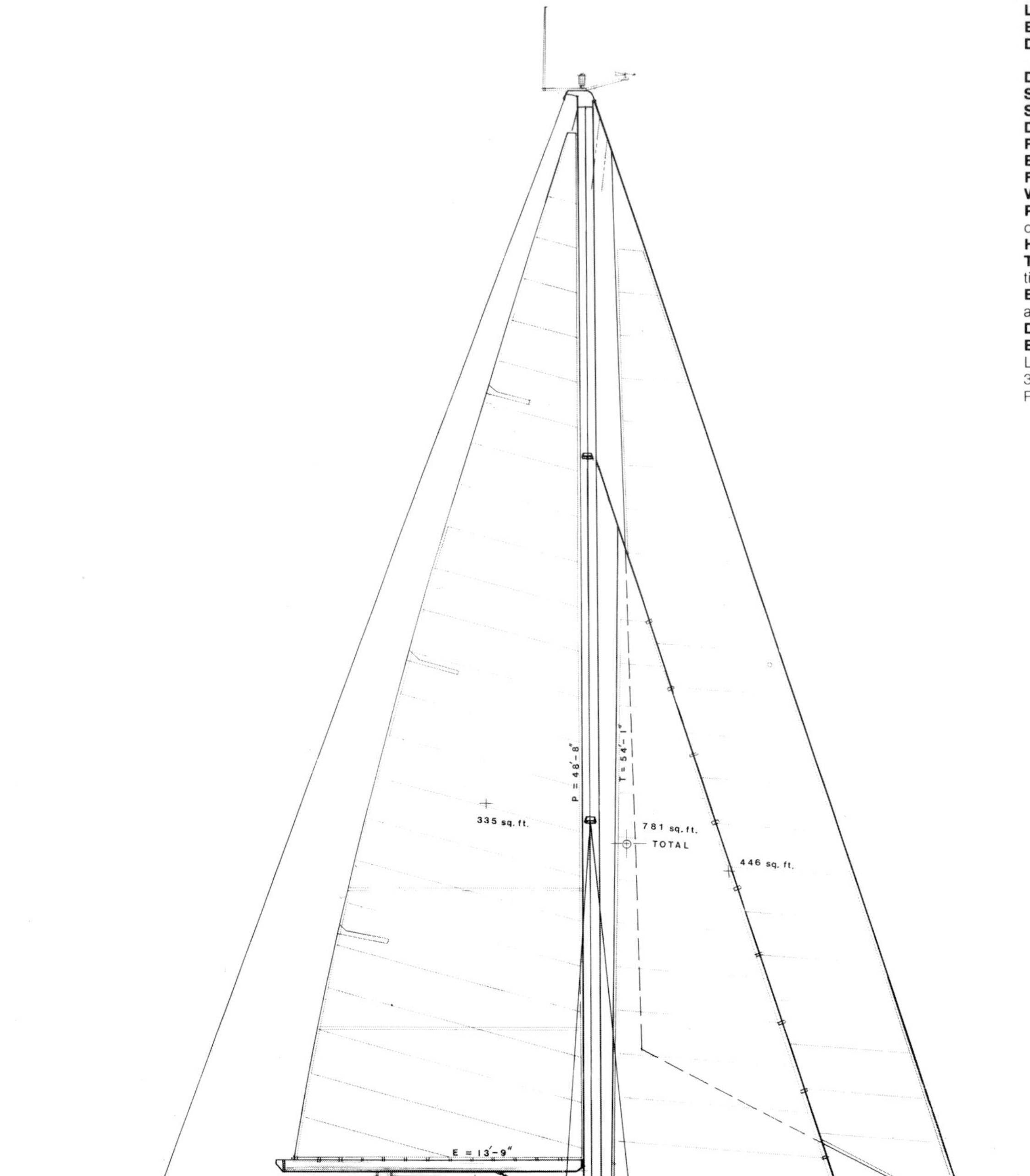

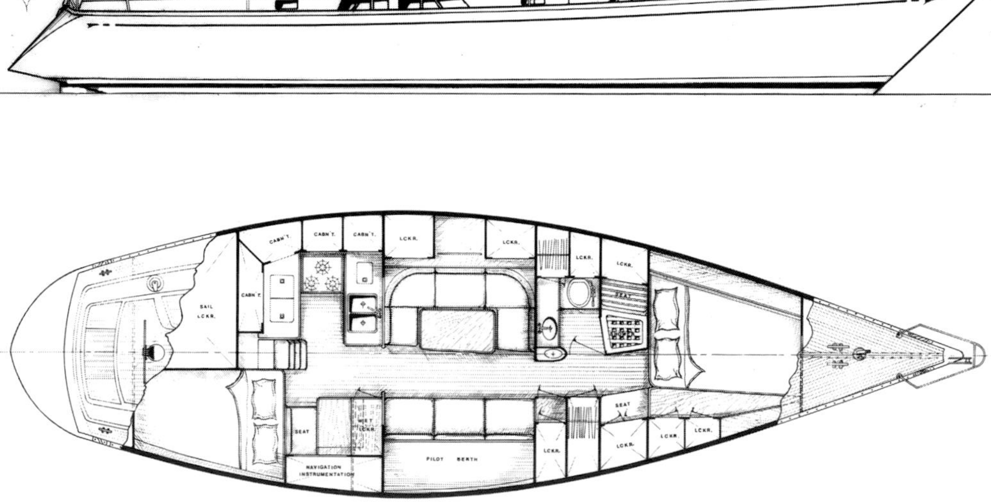

CAMBRIA 44

LOA: 45'10½"
LWL: 36'3"
Beam: 13'5½"
Draft: 5'
Displacement: 28,600 lbs.
Sail Area: 943 sq.ft.
S.A./Disp: 249
Disp./LWL: 16.97
Rig: Cutter, sloop-rod
Ballast: 11,500 lbs.-external
Fuel: 80 gals.
Water: 175 gals.
Power: 58 Westerbeke (154 cubic inches); Perkins 62 (154 cubic inches)
Hull Construction: Core-Airex
Type of Roving: Unidirectional, biaxial
Bulkheads: Bonded to hull and deck
Designer: David Walters
Builder: David Walters Yachts, Ltd.

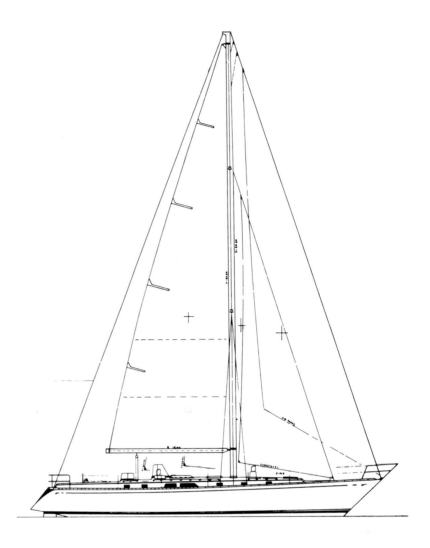
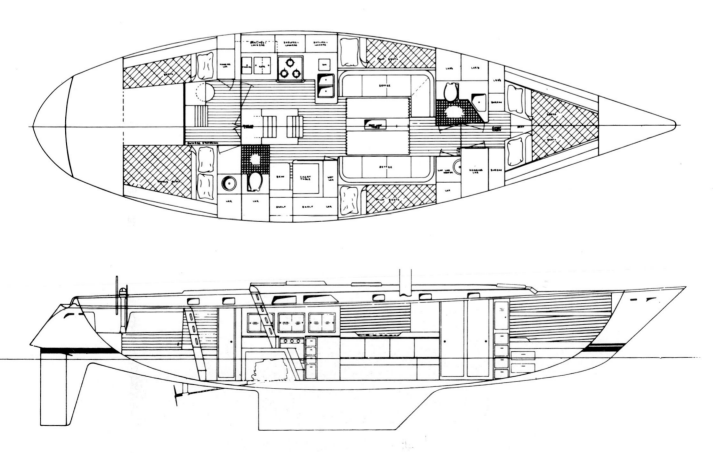

DICKERSON 37

LOA: 37′
LWL: 28′10″
Beam: 11′6″
Draft: 4′6″
Displacement: 15,950 lbs.
Sail Area: 675 sq.ft.
S.A./Disp: 17.1
Disp./LWL: 297
Rig: Ketch, cutter, sloop-wire
Ballast: 6,000 lbs.-external
Fuel: 48 gals.
Water: 90 gals.
Power: 4 cyc. diesel
Hull Construction: Core-balsa
Type of Roving: Biaxial
Bulkheads: Bonded to hull and deck
Designer: George Hazen
Builder: Dickerson Boat Builders Inc.
RD2 Box 92
Trappe, MD 21673

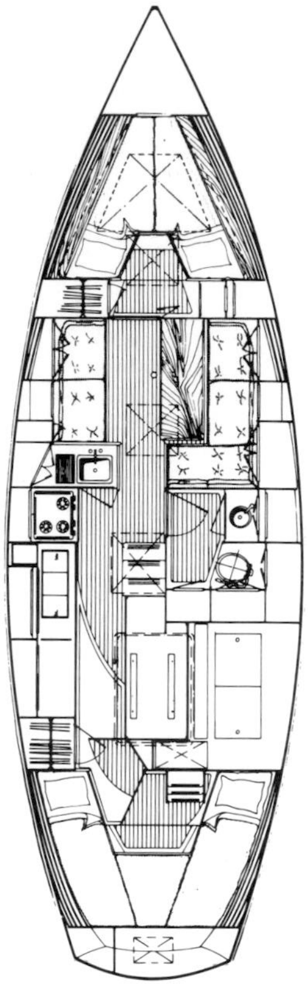

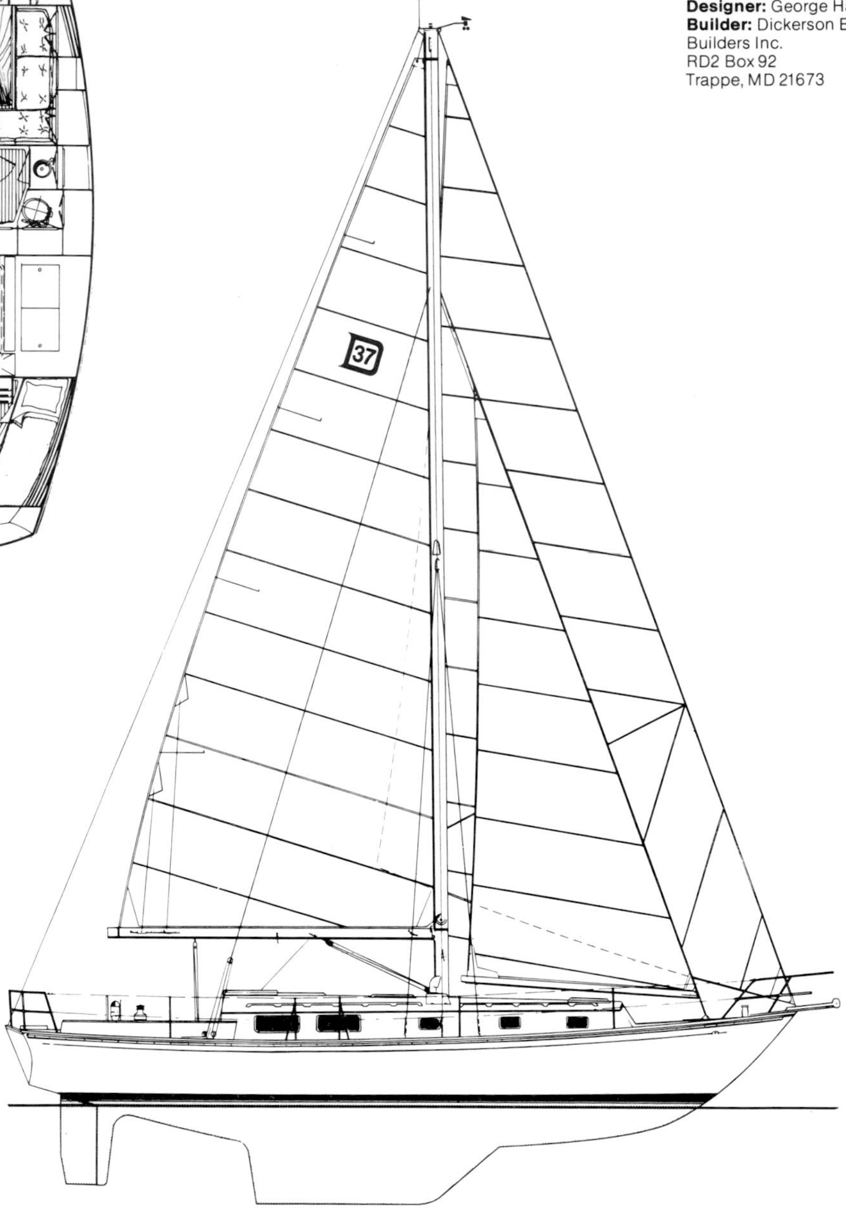

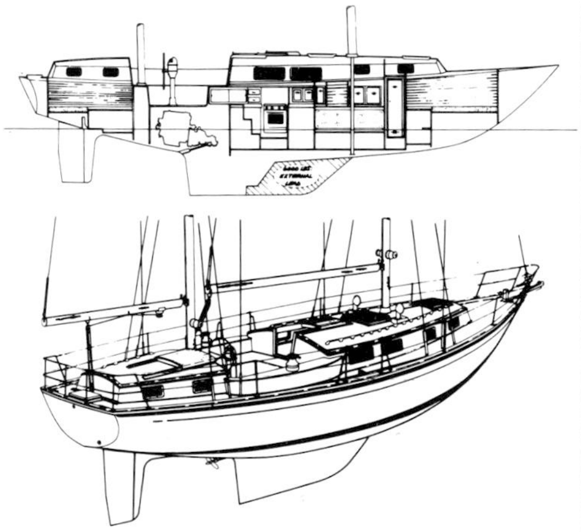

Profile and three-quarter view of center cockpit.

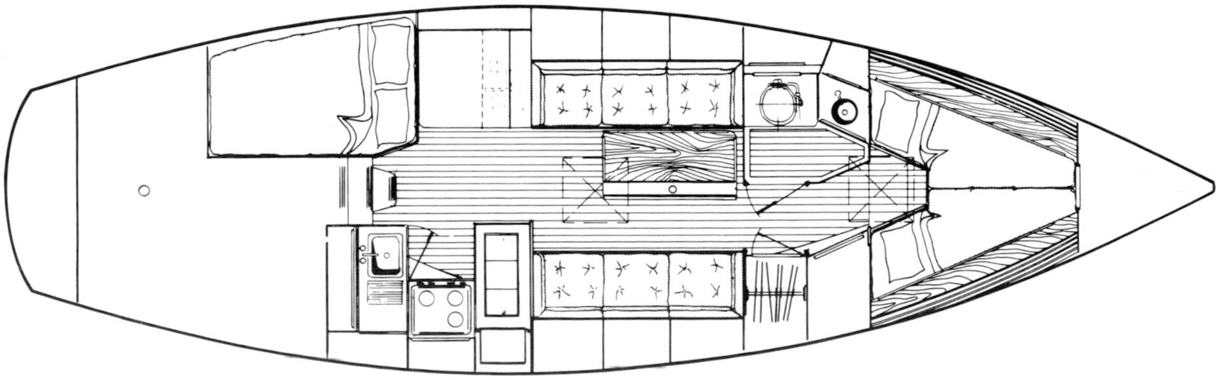

DICKERSON 50

LOA: 50′
LWL: 38′9″
Beam: 13′8″
Draft: 6′6″
Displacement: 33,900 lbs.
Sail Area: 1,162 sq.ft.
S.A./Disp: 17.75
Disp./LWL: 260
Rig: Ketch, cutter, sloop-wire
Ballast: 14,000 lbs.
Fuel: 135 gals.
Water: 200 gals.
Power: 62 hp diesel
Hull Construction: Core-balsa
Type of Roving: Biaxial
Bulkheads: Bonded to hull and deck
Designer: Kaufman and Associates
Builder: Dickerson Boat Builders Inc.
Base Price in USA, April 1986: N/A
Also Available: Farr 37′ racer

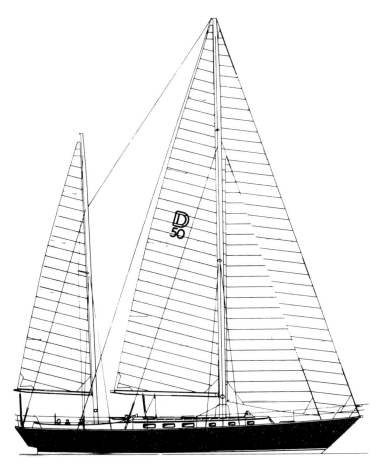

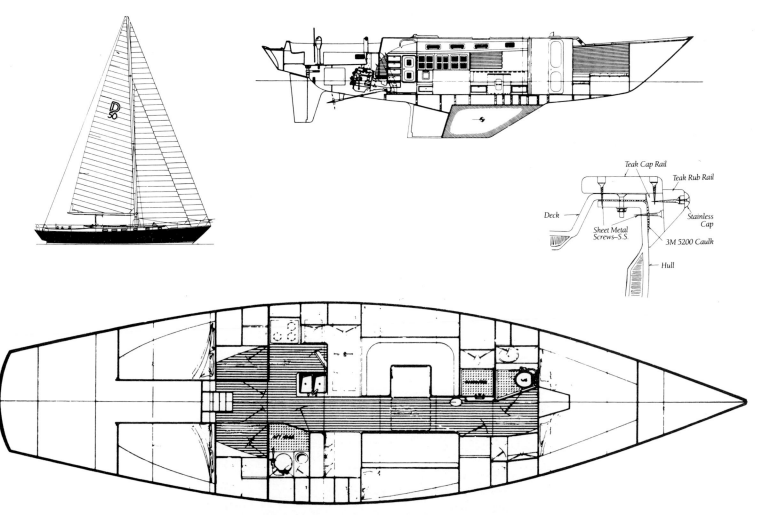

Teak Cap Rail
Teak Rub Rail
Deck
Stainless Cap
Sheet Metal Screws—S.S.
3M 5200 Caulk
Hull

FREEDOM 30

LOA: 29'11½"
LWL: 25'5"
Beam: 10'9"
Draft: 4'6"
Displacement: 7,660 lbs.
Sail Area: 485 sq.ft.
Rig: Sloop
Ballast: 3,150 lbs.-external
Fuel: 20 gals.
Water: 50 gals.
Power: 18 hp diesel
Hull Construction: Core-balsa
Type of Roving: Unidirectional, woven, biaxial
Bulkheads: Bonded to hull and deck
Designer: Gary Mull
Builder: Freedom Yachts
Alexander Road
Melville-Newport, RI 02840

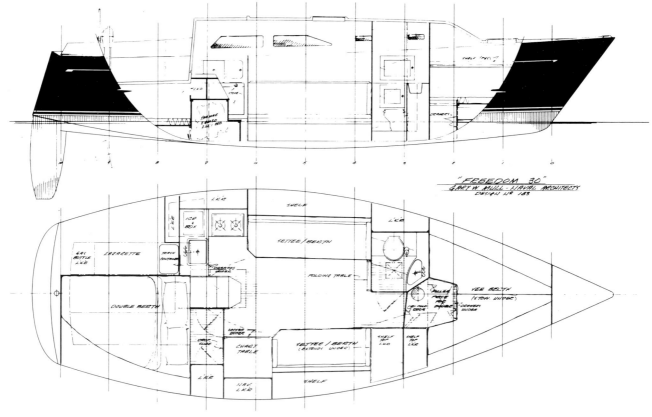

FREEDOM 36

LOA: 36'5"
LWL: 30'8"
Beam: 12'6"
Draft: 4'6" (board up)
        6' (board down)
Displacement: 13,400 lbs.
Sail Area: 685 sq.ft.
Rig: Ketch, sloop
Ballast: 5,530 lbs.
Fuel: 35 gals.
Water: 64 gals.
Power: 27 hp diesel
Hull Construction: Core-balsa
Type of Roving: Unidirectional, biaxial
Bulkheads: Bonded to hull and deck
Designer: Gary Mull
Builder: Freedom Yachts

Also Available: 39', 44'

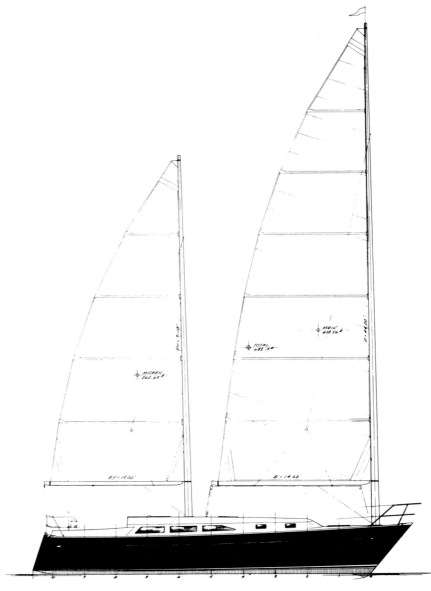

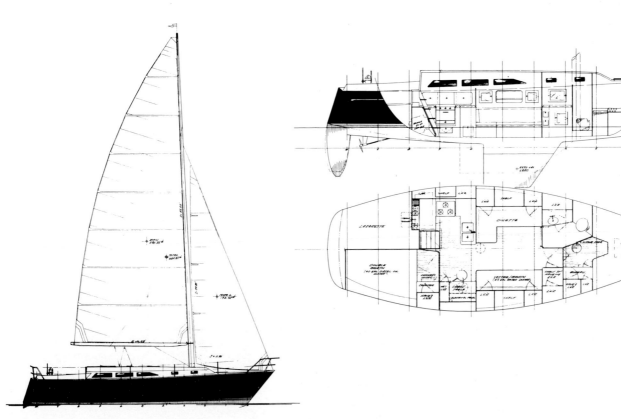

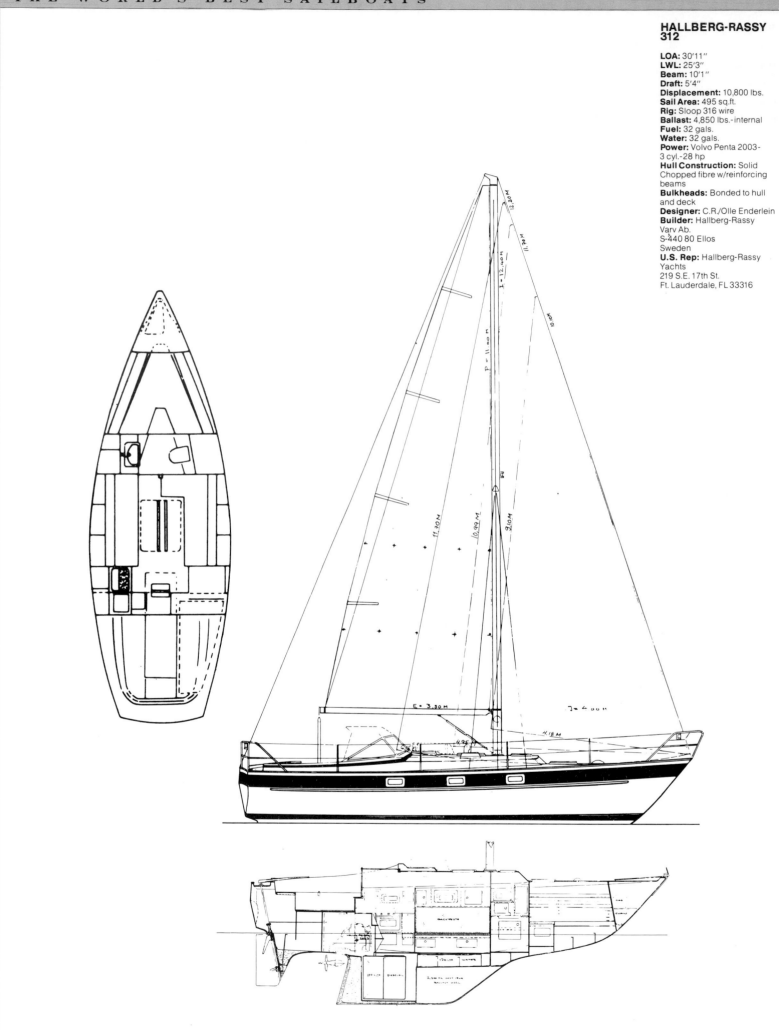

HALLBERG-RASSY 312

LOA: 30'11"
LWL: 25'3"
Beam: 10'1"
Draft: 5'4"
Displacement: 10,800 lbs.
Sail Area: 495 sq.ft.
Rig: Sloop 316 wire
Ballast: 4,850 lbs.-internal
Fuel: 32 gals.
Water: 32 gals.
Power: Volvo Penta 2003-3 cyl.-28 hp
Hull Construction: Solid Chopped fibre w/reinforcing beams
Bulkheads: Bonded to hull and deck
Designer: C.R./Olle Enderlein
Builder: Hallberg-Rassy Varv Ab.
S-440 80 Ellos
Sweden
U.S. Rep: Hallberg-Rassy Yachts
219 S.E. 17th St.
Ft. Lauderdale, FL 33316

HALLBERG·RASSY
42

LOA: 42′
LWL: 34′5″
Beam: 12′5″
Draft: 6′9″ (iron)
5′8″ (lead)
Displacement: 25,368 lbs.
Sail Area: 824 sq.ft.
Rig: Wire
Ballast: 10,365 lbs.
Fuel: 117 gals.
Water: 190 gals.
Power: Volvo Penta MD30
65 hp
Hull Construction: Solid, hand lay up
Type of Roving: Woven
Bulkheads: Bonded to hull and deck
Designer: Rassy/Enderlein
Builder: Hallberg-Rassy Varv Ab

Also Available: 29′, 35′, 38′, 49′

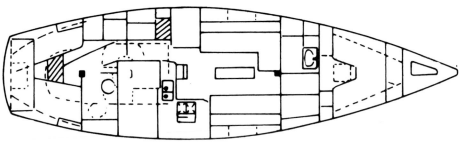

BERMUDA 40

LOA: 40'9"
LWL: 28'10"
Beam: 11'9"
Draft: 4'9" (board up)
    8'9" (board down)
Displacement: 20,000 lbs.
Sail Area: 727 sq.ft. (sloop)
    776 sq.ft. (yawl)
Rig: Sloop, yawl-rod or wire
Ballast: 7,000 lbs.-external
Fuel: 48 gals.
Water: 110 gals.
Power: Westerbeke 40 hp diesel
Hull Construction: Solid hand lay-up F.G.
Type of Roving: Unidirectional, biaxial
Bulkheads: Bonded to hull and deck
Designer: William H. Tripp, Jr.
Builder: Henry R. Hinckley & Co.
Southwest Harbor, ME 04679

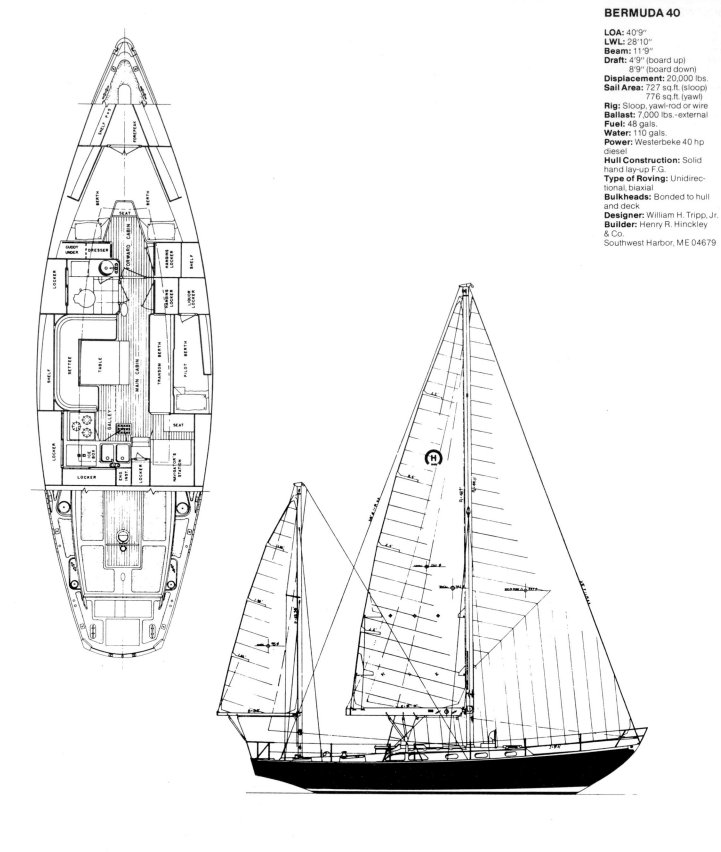

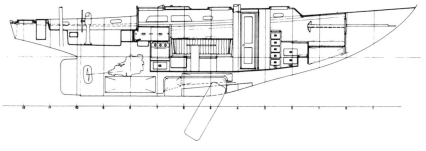

SOU'WESTER 42

LOA: 42'9"
LWL: 31'3"
Beam: 12'6"
Draft: 5' (board up)
  9'2" (board down)
  7" (fixed keel)
Displacement: 24,000 lbs.
Sail Area: 818 sq.ft.
S.A./Disp: 15.73
Disp./LWL: 298
Rig: Cutter, sloop, yawl-rod or wire
Ballast: 8,500 lbs.-external
Fuel: 60 gals.
Water: 150 gals.
Power: 46 hp diesel
Hull Construction: Core-PVC Foam
Type of Roving: Unidirectional, biaxial
Bulkheads: Bonded to Hull and deck
Designer: McCurdy & Rhodes
Builder: Henry R. Hinckley & Co.

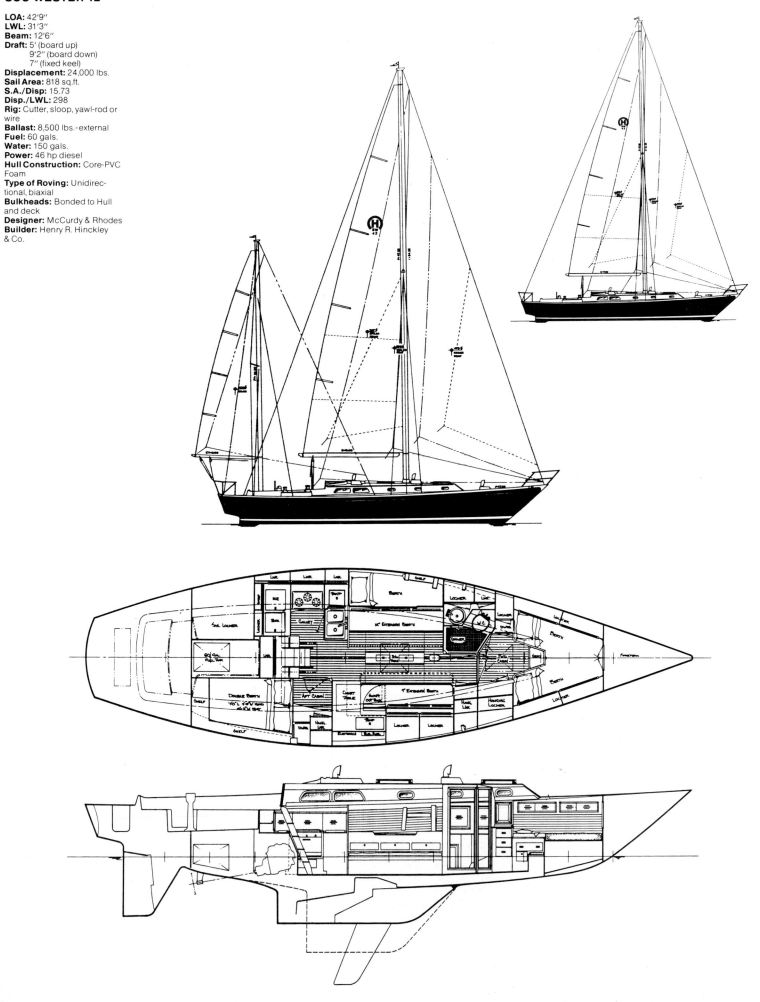

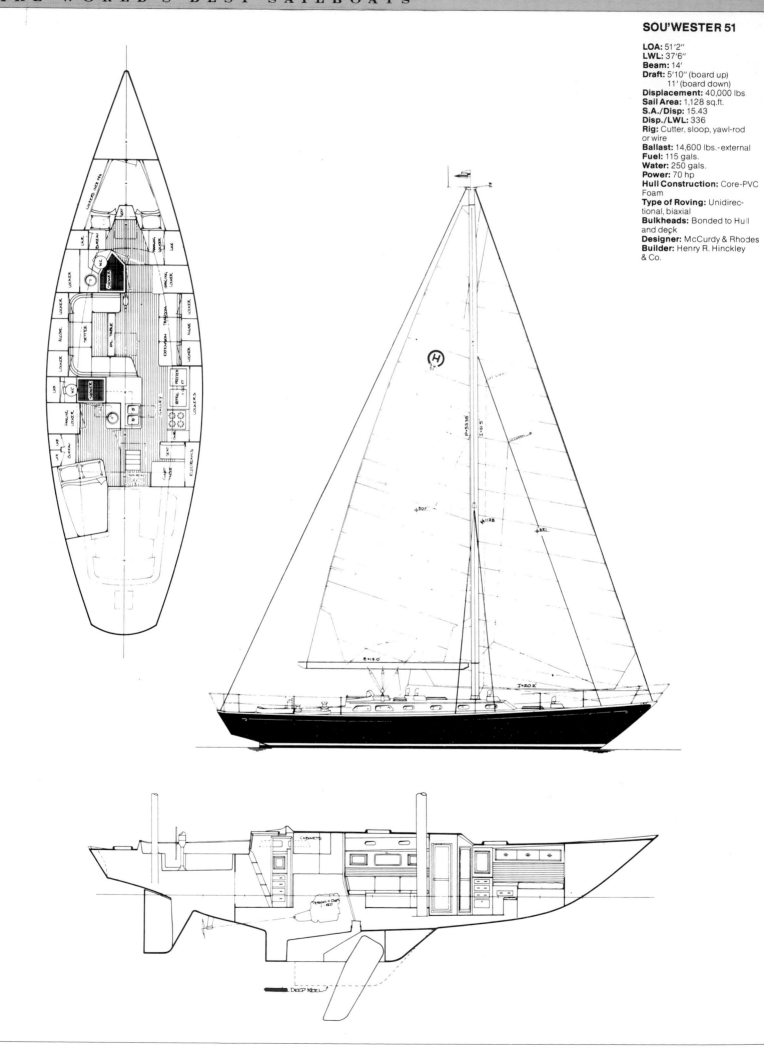

SOU'WESTER 51

LOA: 51'2"
LWL: 37'6"
Beam: 14'
Draft: 5'10" (board up)
   11' (board down)
Displacement: 40,000 lbs.
Sail Area: 1,128 sq.ft.
S.A./Disp: 15.43
Disp./LWL: 336
Rig: Cutter, sloop, yawl-rod or wire
Ballast: 14,600 lbs.-external
Fuel: 115 gals.
Water: 250 gals.
Power: 70 hp
Hull Construction: Core-PVC Foam
Type of Roving: Unidirectional, biaxial
Bulkheads: Bonded to Hull and deck
Designer: McCurdy & Rhodes
Builder: Henry R. Hinckley & Co.

SOU'WESTER 59

LOA: 59'3"
LWL: 44'2"
Beam: 15'6"
Draft: 6'6" (board up)
    12'6" (board down)
Displacement: 69,000 lbs.
Sail Area: 1,548 sq.ft.
S.A./Disp: 14.65
Disp./LWL: 296
Rig: Ketch, cutter, sloop-rod
& wire
Ballast: 23,250 lbs.-external
Fuel: 300 gals.
Water: 450 gals.
Power: 135 hp
Hull Construction: Core-PVC
Foam
Type of Roving: Unidirectional
Bulkheads: Bonded to Hull
and deck
Designer: McCurdy & Rhodes
Builder: Henry R. Hinckley
& Co.

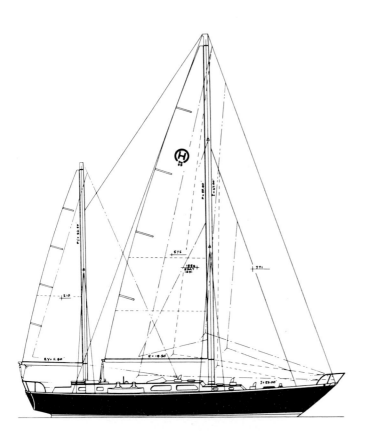

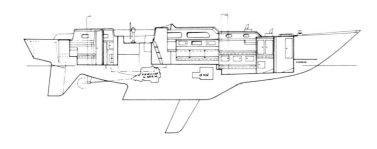

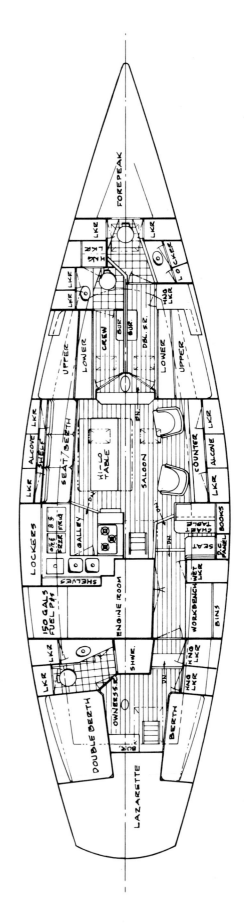

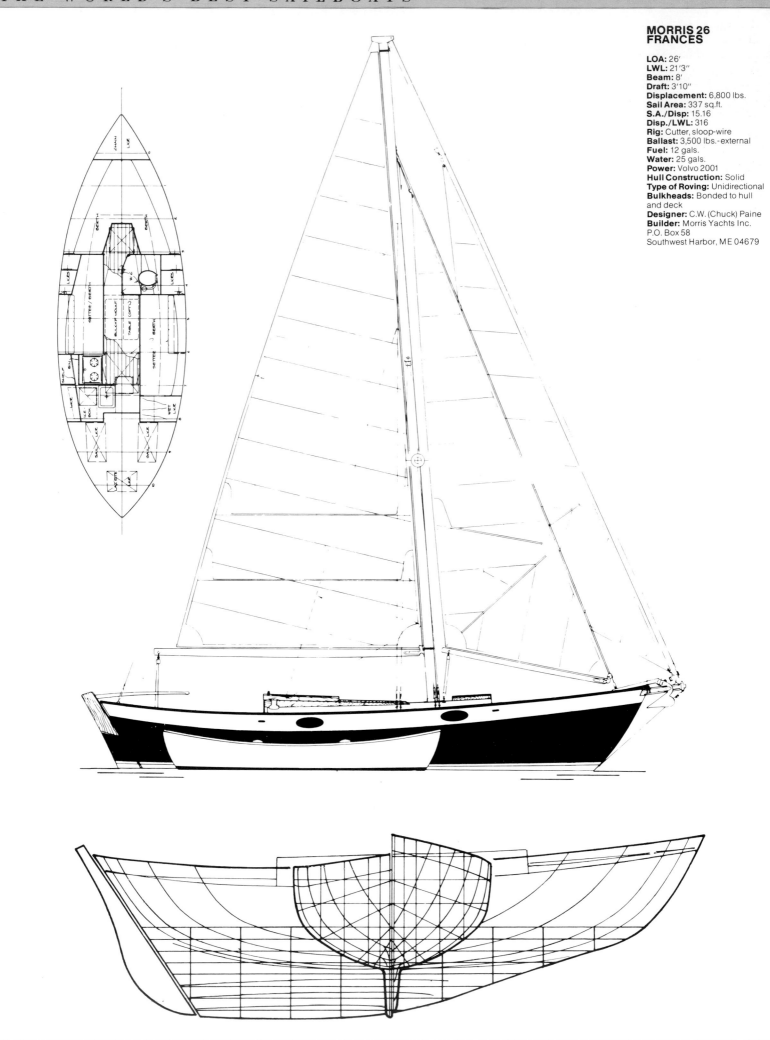

**MORRIS 26
FRANCES**

LOA: 26'
LWL: 21'3"
Beam: 8'
Draft: 3'10"
Displacement: 6,800 lbs.
Sail Area: 337 sq.ft.
S.A./Disp: 15.16
Disp./LWL: 316
Rig: Cutter, sloop-wire
Ballast: 3,500 lbs.-external
Fuel: 12 gals.
Water: 25 gals.
Power: Volvo 2001
Hull Construction: Solid
Type of Roving: Unidirectional
Bulkheads: Bonded to hull and deck
Designer: C.W. (Chuck) Paine
Builder: Morris Yachts Inc.
P.O. Box 58
Southwest Harbor, ME 04679

MORRIS 28
LINDA

LOA: 28'1"
LWL: 23'1½"
Beam: 9'2"
Draft: 4'4"
Displacement: 8,300 lbs.
Sail Area: 410 sq.ft.
S.A./Disp: 16
Disp./LWL: 316
Rig: Cutter, sloop-wire
Ballast: 3,700 lbs.-external
Fuel: 15 gals.
Water: 30 gals.
Power: Volvo Diesel
Hull Construction: Solid
Type of Roving: Unidirectional
Bulkheads: Bonded to hull
and deck
Designer: C.W. (Chuck) Paine
Builder: Morris Yachts Inc.

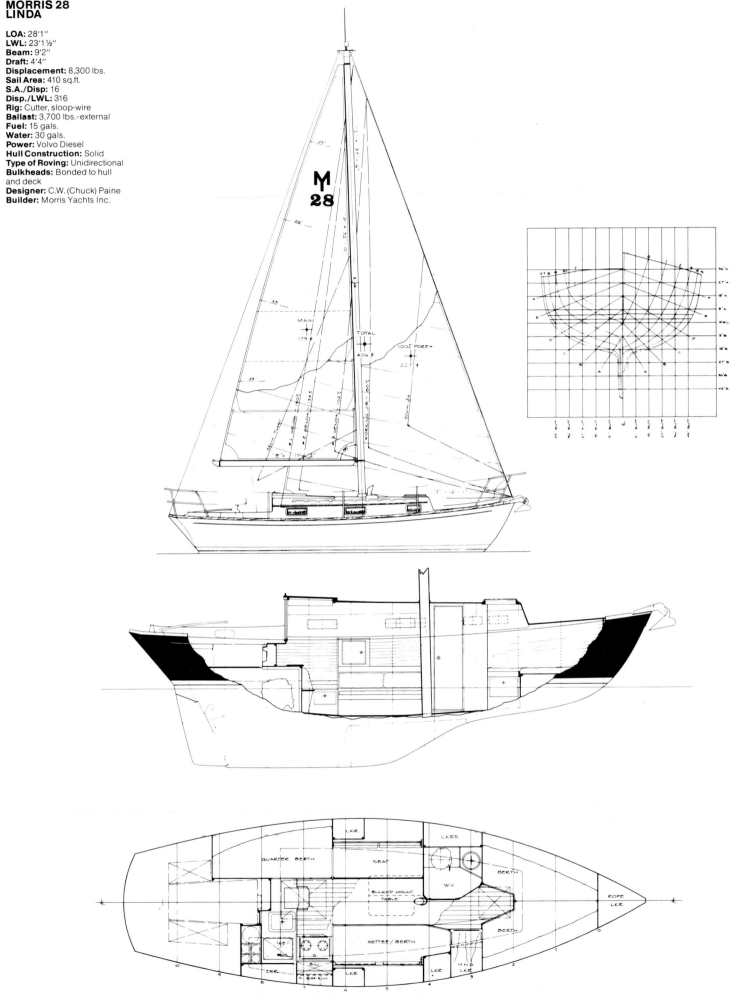

**MORRIS 30
LEIGH**

LOA: 29'8"
LWL: 23'4"
Beam: 9'7"
Draft: 4'7"
Displacement: 9,100 lbs.
Sail Area: 420 sq.ft.
S.A./Disp: 15.52
Disp./LWL: 316
Rig: Cutter, sloop-wire
Ballast: 4,400 lbs.-external
Fuel: 16 gals.
Water: 37 gals.
Power: Volvo 2002
Hull Construction: Solid
Type of Roving: Unidirectional
Bulkheads: Bonded to hull
and deck
Designer: C.W. (Chuck) Paine
Builder: Morris Yachts Inc.

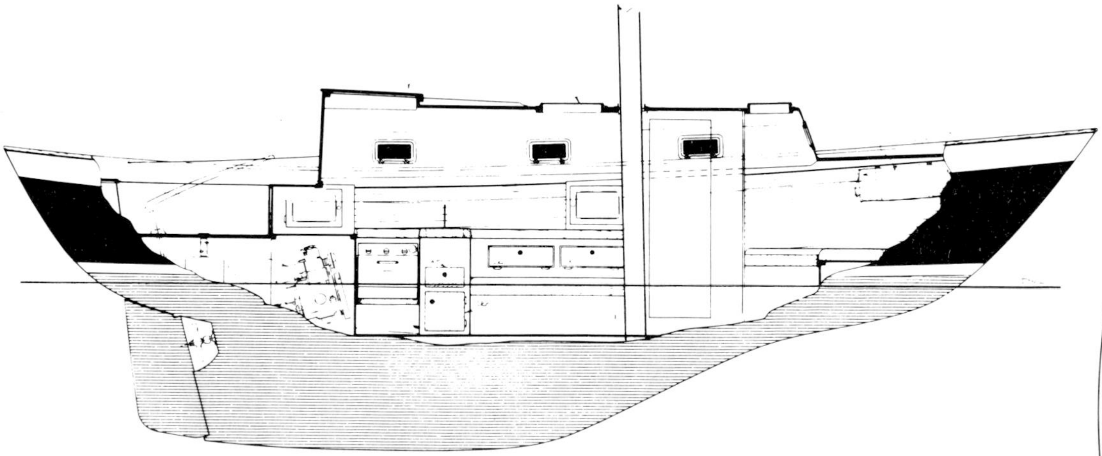

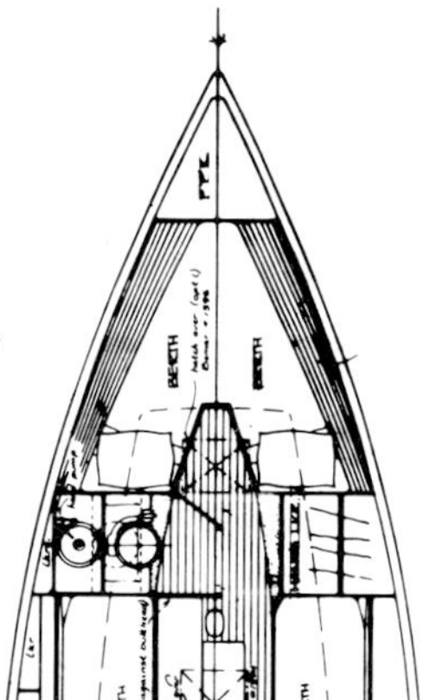

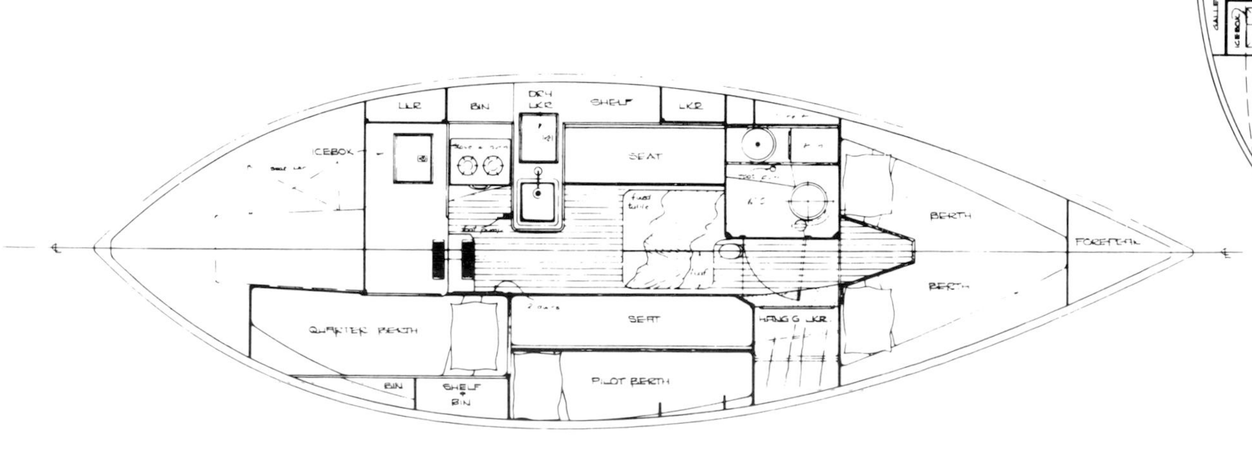

MORRIS 36
JUSTINE

LOA: 36'3"
LWL: 29'6"
Beam: 11'6¾"
Draft: 4'6" (board up)
         5'6" (board down)
Displacement: 15,602 lbs.
Sail Area: 627 sq.ft.
S.A./Disp: 16.07
Disp./LWL: 271
Rig: Cutter, sloop-wire
Ballast: 6,000 lbs.-external
Fuel: 37 gals.
Water: 100 gals.
Power: Volvo 2003T
Hull Construction: Solid
Type of Roving: Unidirectional
Bulkheads: Bonded to hull
and deck
Designer: C.W. (Chuck) Paine
Builder: Morris Yachts Inc.

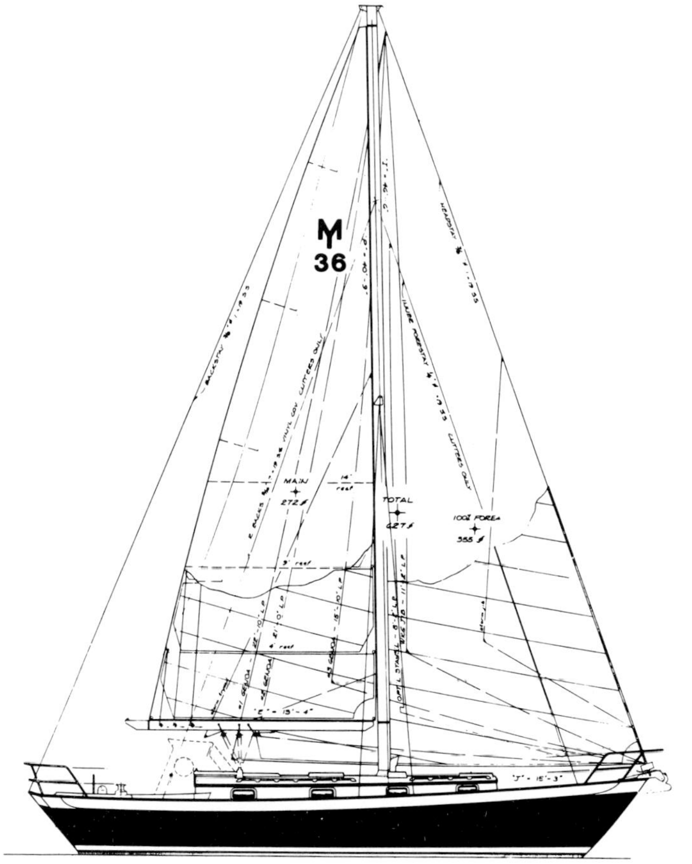

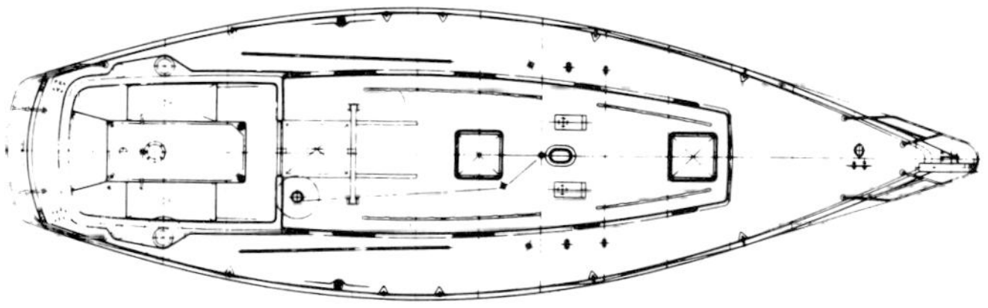

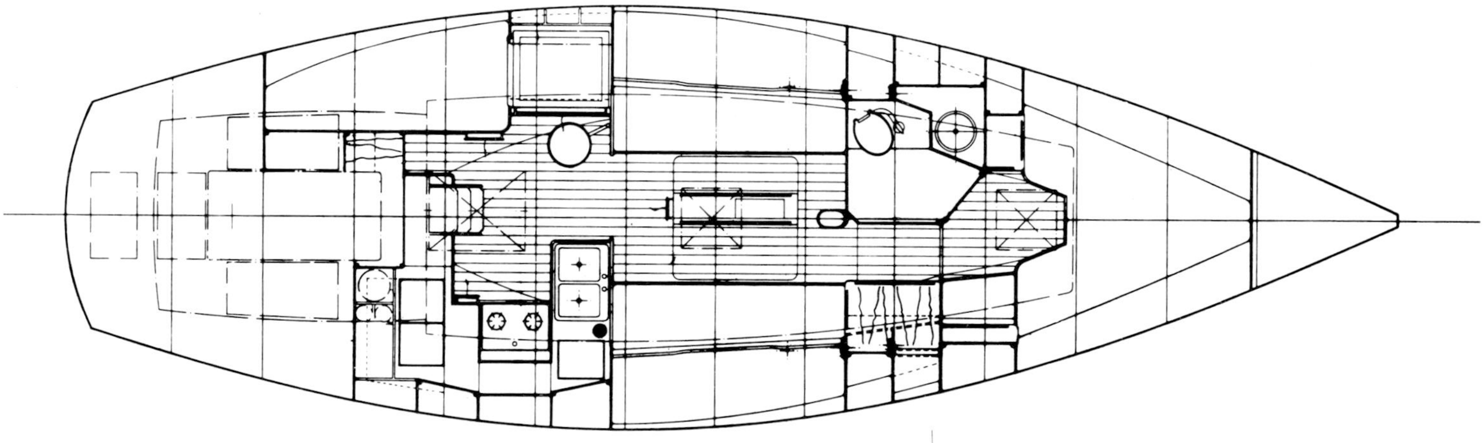

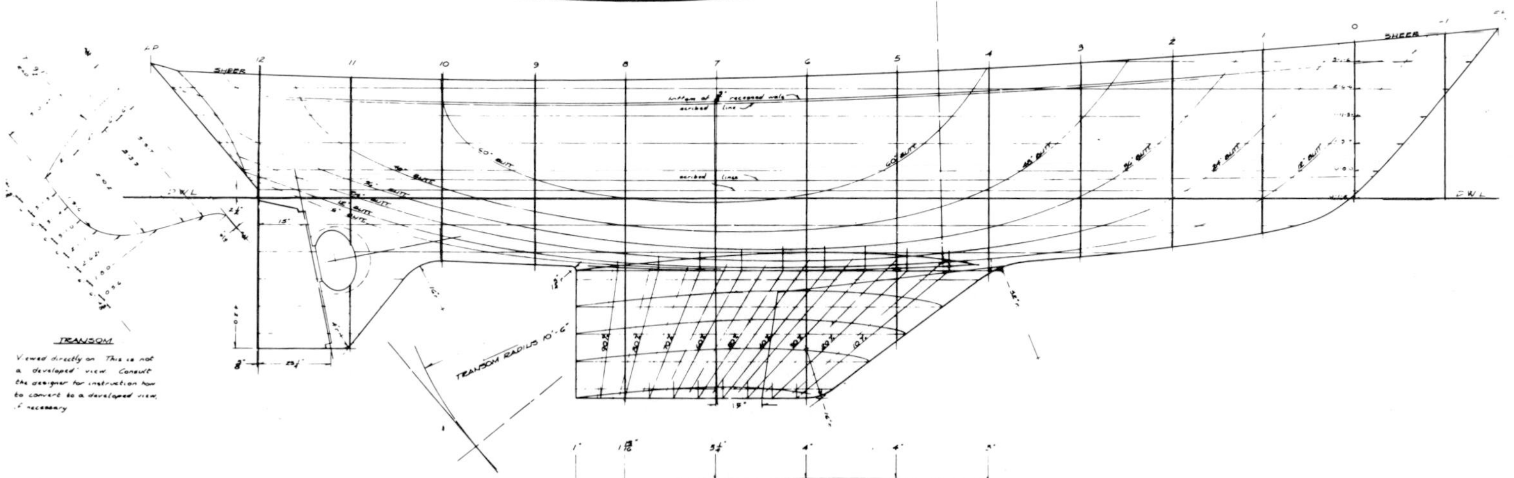

SWAN 391

LOA: 40'
LWL: 31'1"
Beam: 12'6"
Draft: 7'2"/ or 5'8" (scheel)
Displacement: 18,900 lbs.
Rig: Cutter, sloop-rod
Ballast: 6,800
Fuel: 40 gals.
Water: 77 gals.
Power: Perkins 40 hp
Hull Construction: Solid
Type of Roving: Unidirectional, woven
Bulkheads: Bonded to hull and deck
Designer: Ron Holland
Builder: Nautor/Oy Wilh. Schauman Ab.
Pietarsaari
Finland

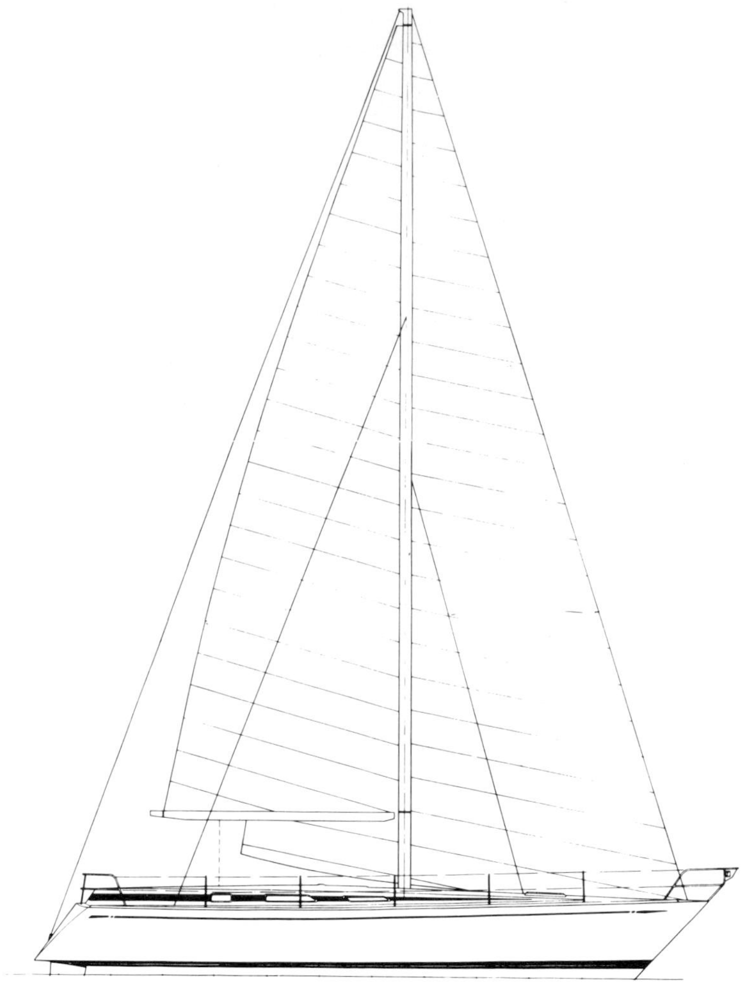

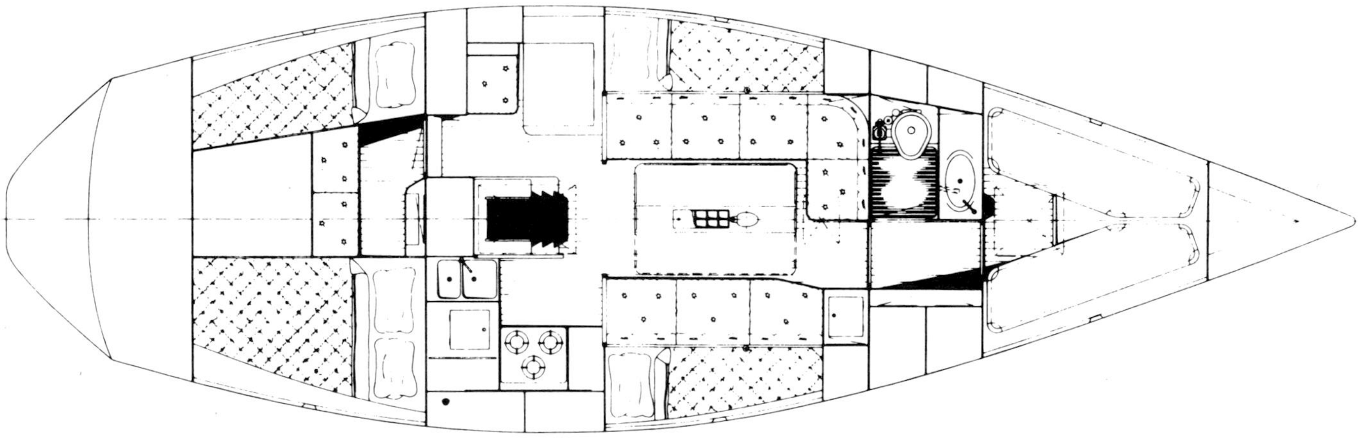

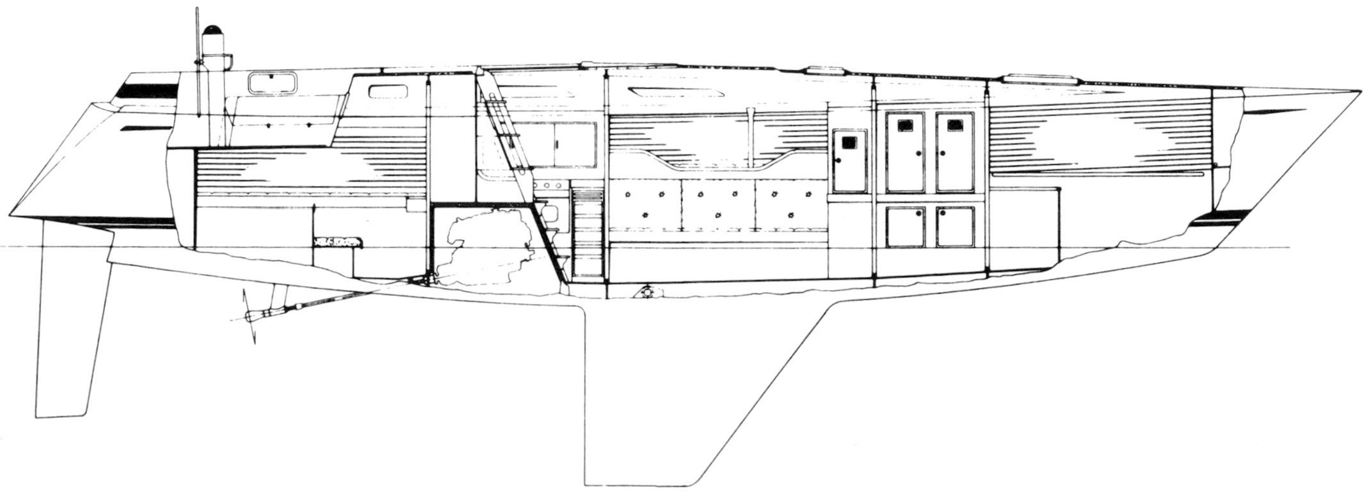

SWAN 651

LOA: 65'7"
LWL: 55'1"
Beam: 17'5"
Draft: 11'6"
Displacement: 79,300 lbs.
Sail Area: 2,669 sq.ft.
S.A./Disp: 24.5
Disp./LWL: 194
Rig: Cutter, sloop, ketch-rod
Ballast: 31,700 lbs.-external
Fuel: 290 gals.
Water: 388 gals.
Power: Perkins 115 hp
Hull Construction: Solid
Type of Roving: Unidirectional, woven
Bulkheads: Bonded to hull and deck
Designer: German Frers
Builder: Nautor

Also Available: 51', 53', 59', 61'

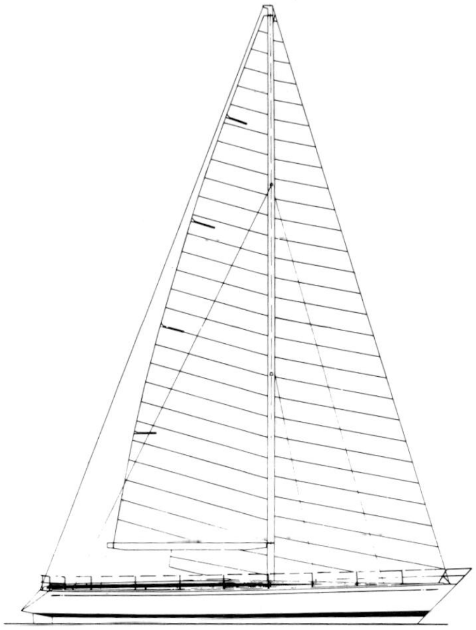

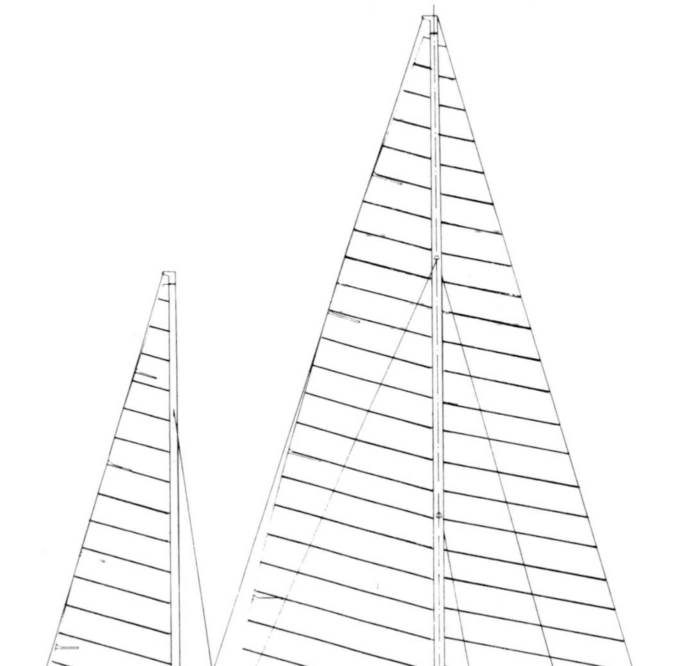

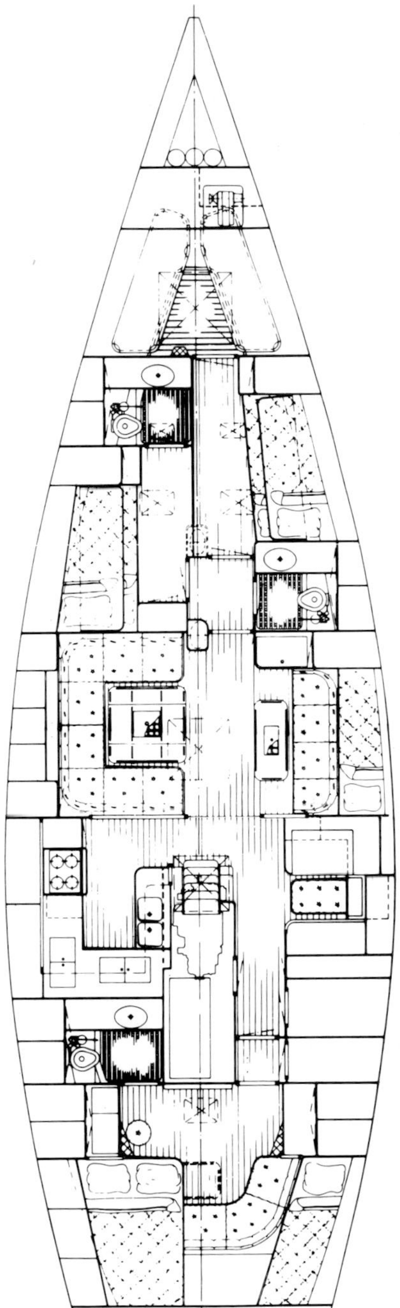

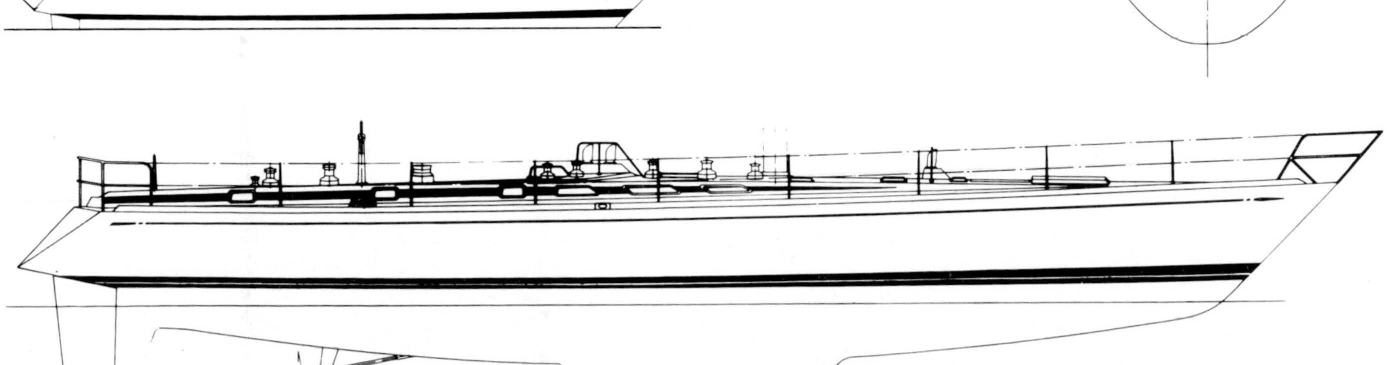

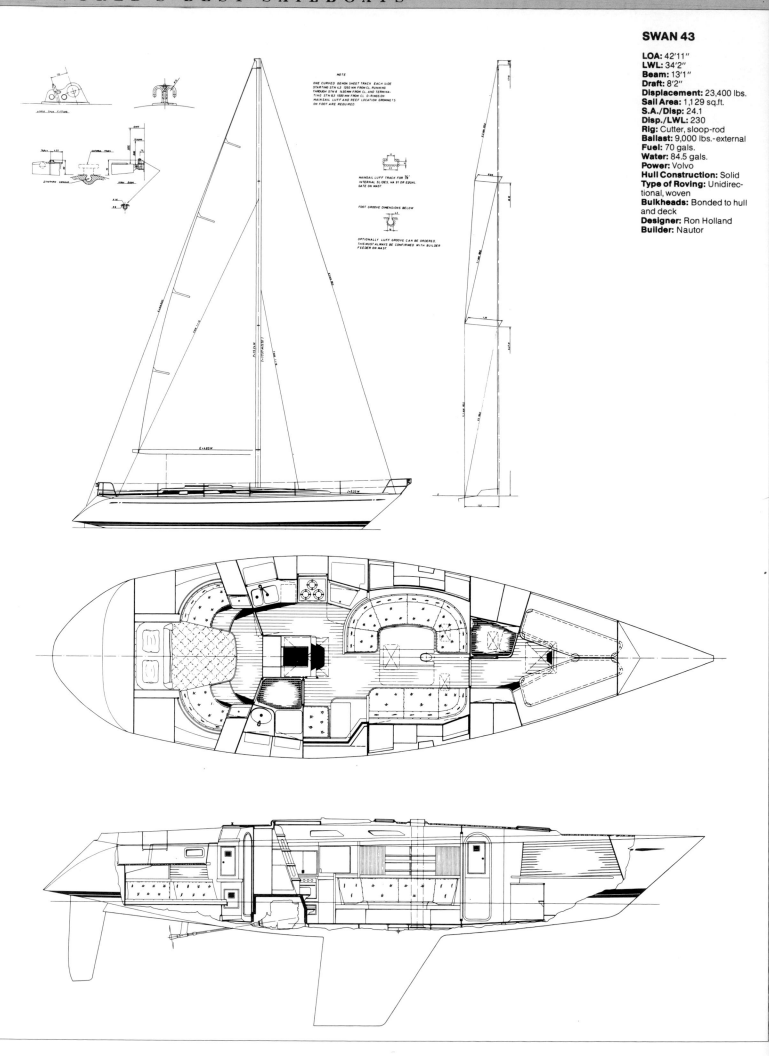

SWAN 43

LOA: 42'11"
LWL: 34'2"
Beam: 13'1"
Draft: 8'2"
Displacement: 23,400 lbs.
Sail Area: 1,129 sq.ft.
S.A./Disp: 24.1
Disp./LWL: 230
Rig: Cutter, sloop-rod
Ballast: 9,000 lbs.-external
Fuel: 70 gals.
Water: 84.5 gals.
Power: Volvo
Hull Construction: Solid
Type of Roving: Unidirectional, woven
Bulkheads: Bonded to hull and deck
Designer: Ron Holland
Builder: Nautor

SWAN 46

LOA: 47'1"
LWL: 37'11"
Beam: 14'6"
Draft: 8'2"
Displacement: 31,300 lbs.
Sail Area: 1,250 sq.ft.
S.A./Disp: 22.7
Disp./LWL: 226
Rig: Cutter, sloop-rod
Ballast: 11,400 lbs.-external
Fuel: 99 gals.
Water: 126 gals.
Power: 58 hp
Hull Construction: Solid
Type of Roving: Unidirectional, woven
Bulkheads: Bonded to hull and deck
Designer: Ron Holland
Builder: Nautor

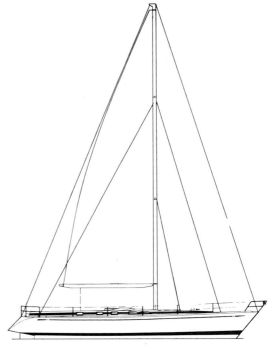

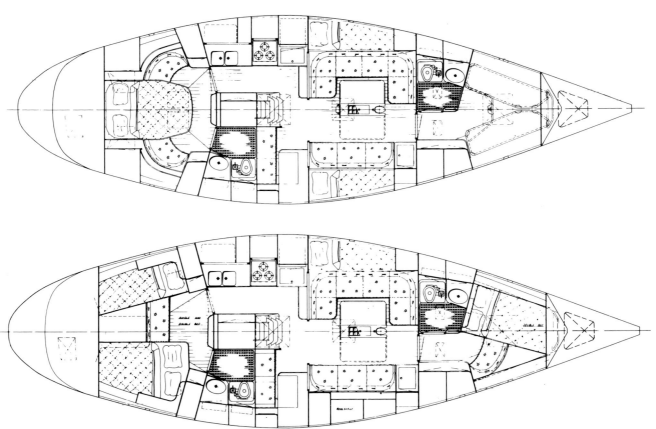

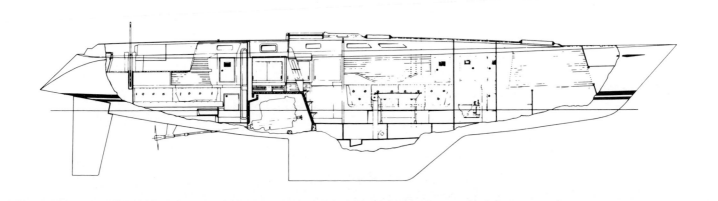

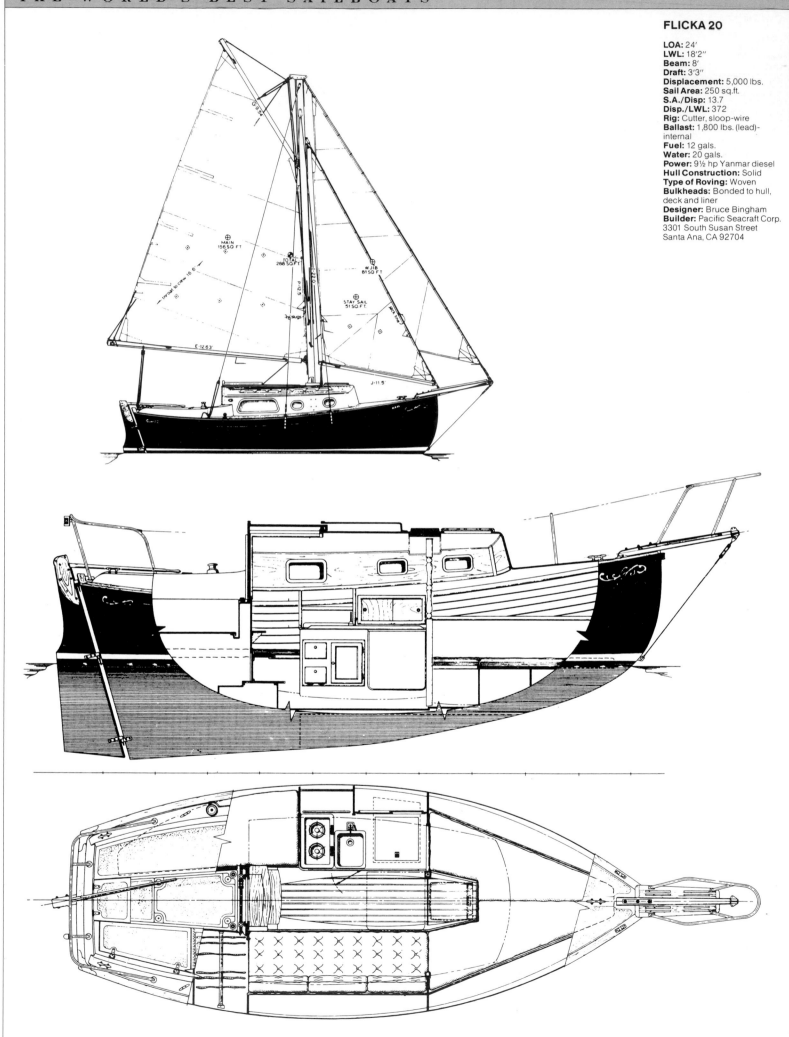

FLICKA 20

LOA: 24'
LWL: 18'2"
Beam: 8'
Draft: 3'3"
Displacement: 5,000 lbs.
Sail Area: 250 sq.ft.
S.A./Disp: 13.7
Disp./LWL: 372
Rig: Cutter, sloop-wire
Ballast: 1,800 lbs. (lead)-internal
Fuel: 12 gals.
Water: 20 gals.
Power: 9½ hp Yanmar diesel
Hull Construction: Solid
Type of Roving: Woven
Bulkheads: Bonded to hull, deck and liner
Designer: Bruce Bingham
Builder: Pacific Seacraft Corp.
3301 South Susan Street
Santa Ana, CA 92704

ORION 27 MKII

LOA: 30'11"
LWL: 22'2"
Beam: 9'3"
Draft: 4'
Displacement: 10,000 lbs.
Sail Area: 428 sq.ft.
S.A./Disp: 14.8
Disp./LWL: 409
Rig: Cutter, sloop-wire
Ballast: 3,800 lbs. (lead)-internal
Fuel: 30 gals.
Water: 80 gals.
Power: 18 hp Yanmar diesel (std.); 27 hp Yanmar (opt)
Hull Construction: Solid
Type of Roving: Woven
Bulkheads: Bonded to hull, deck and liner
Designer: Henry Mohrschladt
Builder: Pacific Seacraft Corp.

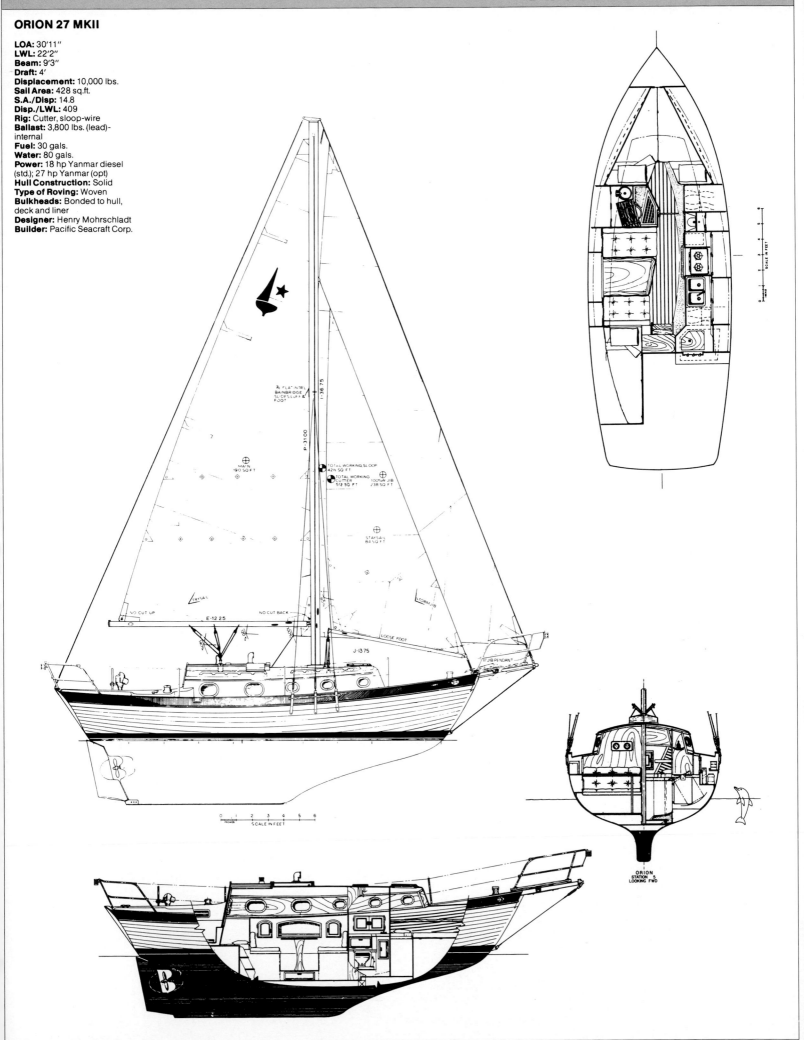

261

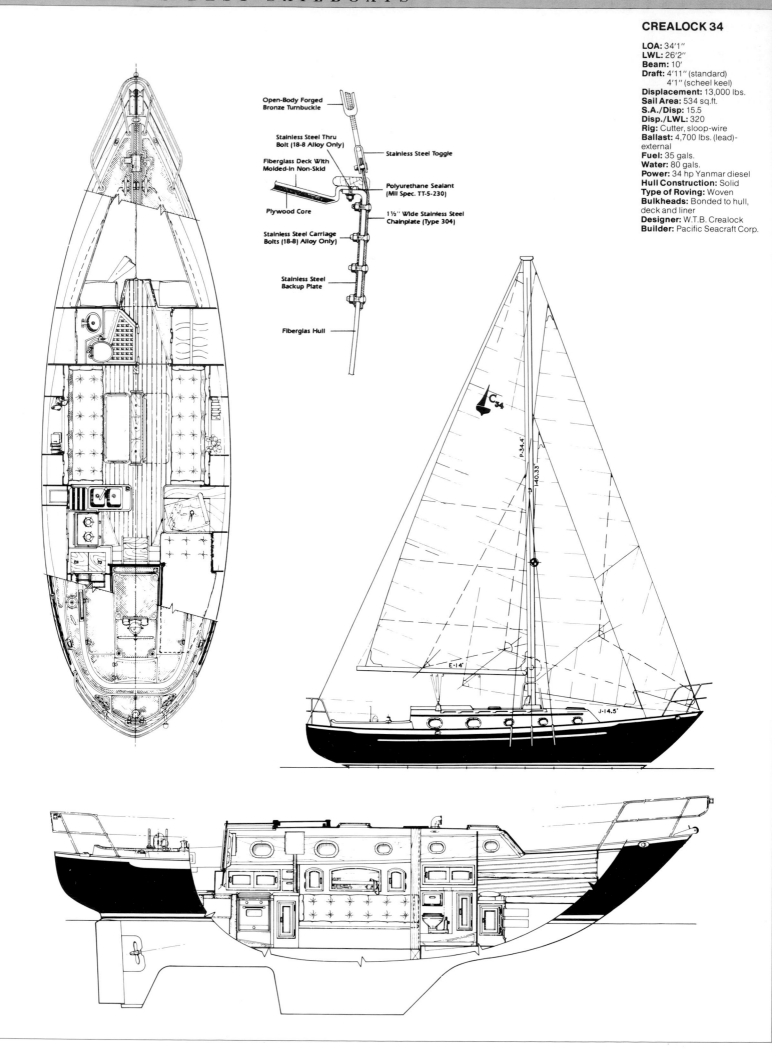

CREALOCK 34

LOA: 34'1"
LWL: 26'2"
Beam: 10'
Draft: 4'11" (standard)
4'1" (scheel keel)
Displacement: 13,000 lbs.
Sail Area: 534 sq.ft.
S.A./Disp: 15.5
Disp./LWL: 320
Rig: Cutter, sloop-wire
Ballast: 4,700 lbs. (lead)- external
Fuel: 35 gals.
Water: 80 gals.
Power: 34 hp Yanmar diesel
Hull Construction: Solid
Type of Roving: Woven
Bulkheads: Bonded to hull, deck and liner
Designer: W.T.B. Crealock
Builder: Pacific Seacraft Corp.

Open-Body Forged Bronze Turnbuckle

Stainless Steel Thru Bolt (18-8 Alloy Only)

Stainless Steel Toggle

Fiberglass Deck With Molded-In Non-Skid

Polyurethane Sealant (Mil Spec. TT-5-230)

Plywood Core

1½" Wide Stainless Steel Chainplate (Type 304)

Stainless Steel Carriage Bolts (18-8) Alloy Only)

Stainless Steel Backup Plate

Fiberglas Hull

CREALOCK 37

LOA: 36'11"
LWL: 27'9"
Beam: 10'10"
Draft: 5'6" (standard)
4'5" (scheel keel)
Displacement: 16,000 lbs.
Sail Area: 573 sq.ft.
S.A./Disp: 14.4
Disp./LWL: 334
Rig: Cutter, sloop, yawl-wire
Ballast: 6,200 lbs. (lead)-external
Fuel: 40 gals.
Water: 90 gals.
Power: 44 hp Yanmar diesel
Hull Construction: Solid
Type of Roving: Woven
Bulkheads: Bonded to hull, deck and liner
Designer: W.T.B. Crealock
Builder: Pacific Seacraft Corp.

Also Available: Dana 24, new Crealock 30

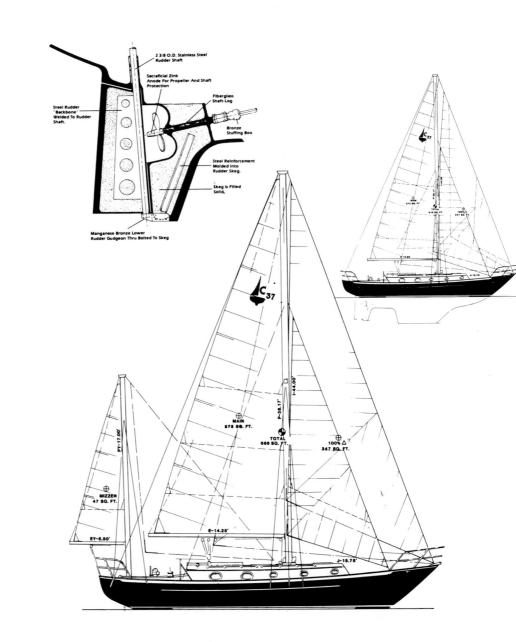

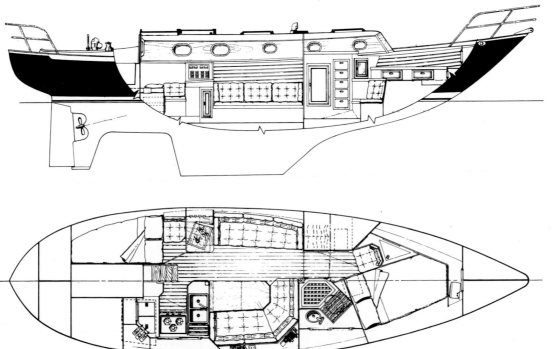

FALMOUTH CUTTER

LOA: 22'
LWL: 20'10"
Beam: 8'
Draft: 3'6"
Displacement: 7,400 lbs.
Sail Area: 357 sq.ft.
S.A./Disp: 15.04
Disp./LWL: 365
Rig: Cutter-wire
Ballast: 2,500 lbs.-internal
Fuel: 23 gals.
Water: 33 gals.
Power: 7 hp Yanmar diesel
Hull Construction: Solid
Type of Roving: Woven
Bulkheads: Bonded to hull and deck
Designer: Lyle C. Hess
Builder: Sam L. Morse Co. 1626 Placentia Avenue Costa Mesa, CA 92627

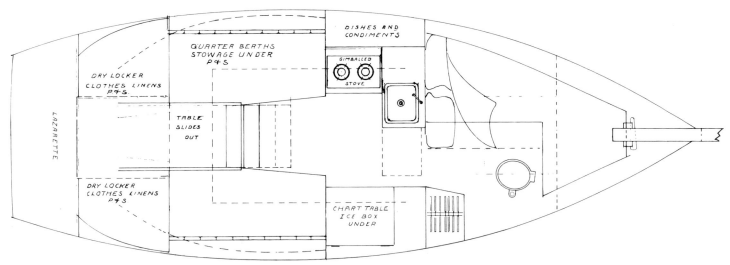

BRISTOL CHANNEL CUTTER

LOA: 28'1"
LWL: 26'3"
Beam: 10'1"
Draft: 4'10"
Displacement: 14,000 lbs.
Sail Area: 576 sq.ft.
S.A./Disp: 16.02
Disp./LWL: 345
Rig: Cutter-wire
Ballast: 4,600 lbs.-internal
Fuel: 26 gals.
Water: 76 gals.
Power: 18 hp Volvo diesel
Hull Construction: Solid
Type of Roving: Woven
Bulkheads: Bonded to hull
and deck
Designer: Lyle C. Hess
Builder: Sam L. Morse Co.

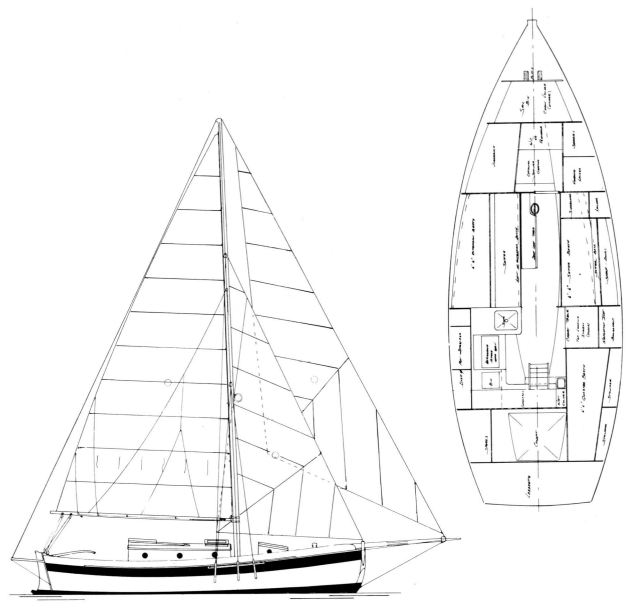

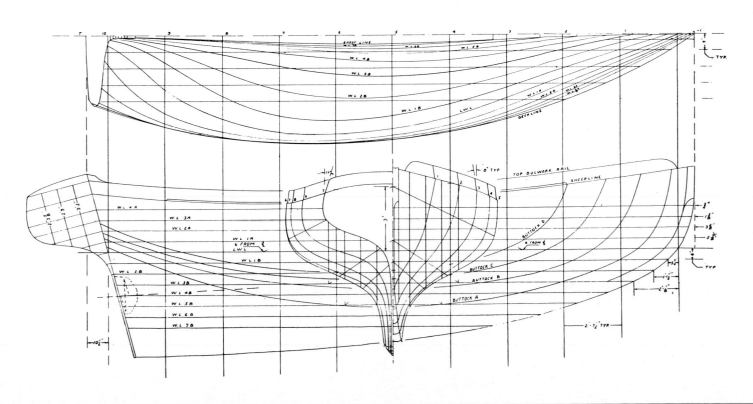

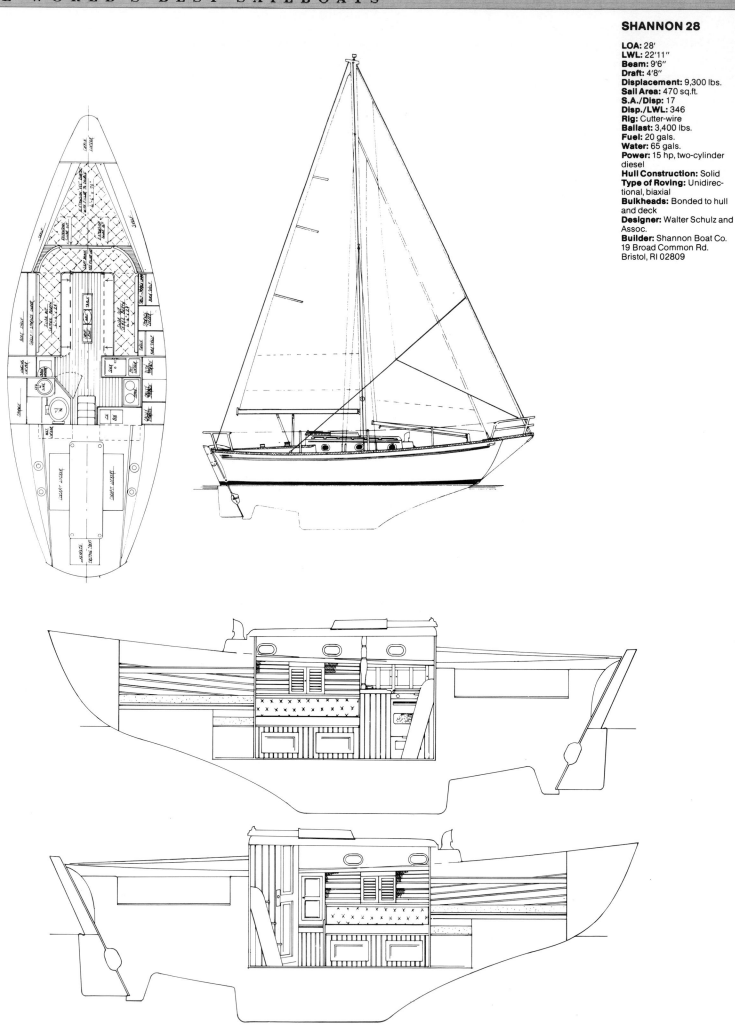

SHANNON 28

LOA: 28'
LWL: 22'11"
Beam: 9'6"
Draft: 4'8"
Displacement: 9,300 lbs.
Sail Area: 470 sq.ft.
S.A./Disp: 17
Disp./LWL: 346
Rig: Cutter-wire
Ballast: 3,400 lbs.
Fuel: 20 gals.
Water: 65 gals.
Power: 15 hp, two-cylinder diesel
Hull Construction: Solid
Type of Roving: Unidirectional, biaxial
Bulkheads: Bonded to hull and deck
Designer: Walter Schulz and Assoc.
Builder: Shannon Boat Co. 19 Broad Common Rd. Bristol, RI 02809

SHANNON 38

LOA: 37'9"
LWL: 30'10"
Beam: 11'6"
Draft: 5'
Displacement: 18,500 lbs.
Sail Area: 703 sq.ft. (cutter)
    751 sq.ft. (ketch)
S.A./Disp: 16 (cutter)
    17 (ketch)
Disp./LWL: 283
Rig: Cutter, ketch-rod
Ballast: 6,800 lbs.
Fuel: 70 gals.
Water: 125 gals.
Power: Perkins 4.108 40 hp diesel
Hull Construction: Core on 37 CB, solid on 38
Type of Roving: Unidirectional, biaxial
Bulkheads: Bonded to hull and deck
Designer: Stadel, Schulz & Assoc.
Builder: Shannon Boat Co.

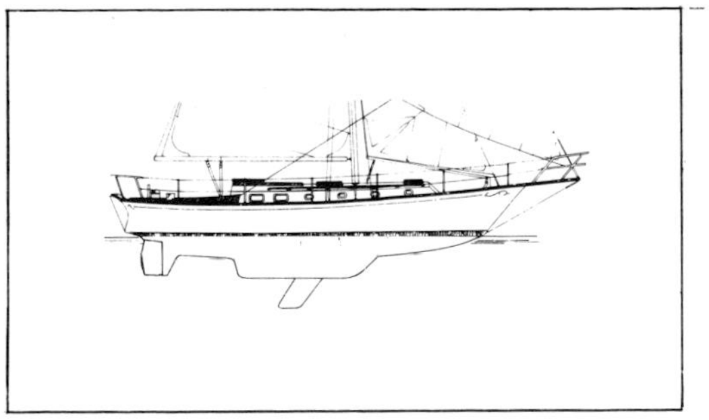

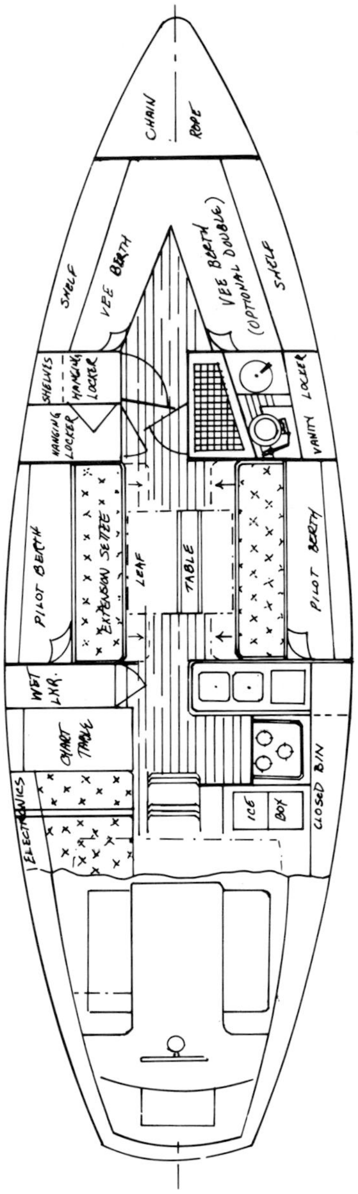

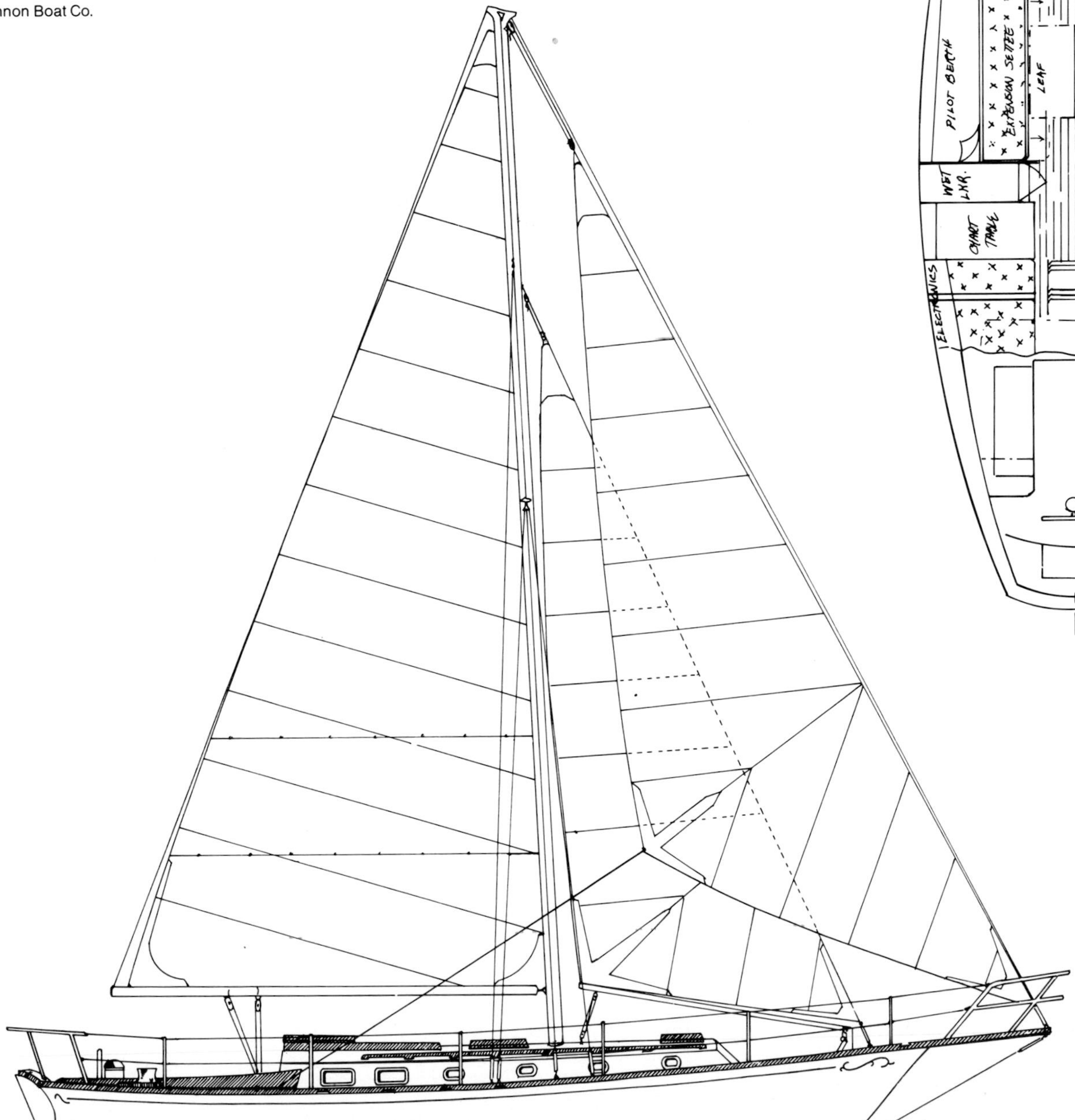

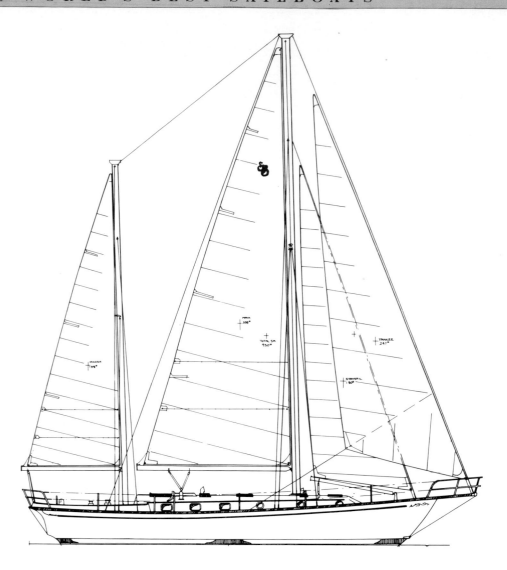

SHANNON 43

LOA: 43'10"
LWL: 36'7"
Beam: 13'
Draft: 6'6" (keel)
4'9"/8'7" (c.b.)
Displacement: 27,000 lbs.
Sail Area: 950 sq.ft. (ketch)
S.A./Disp: 17 (cutter)
18 (ketch)
Disp./LWL: 250
Rig: Cutter, ketch-rod
Ballast: 10,700 lbs.
Fuel: 100 gals.
Water: 200 gals.
Power: 60 hp diesel
Hull Construction: Core-Airex
Type of Roving: Unidirectional, biaxial
Bulkheads: Bonded to hull and deck
Designer: Walter Schulz & Assoc.
Builder: Shannon Boat Co.

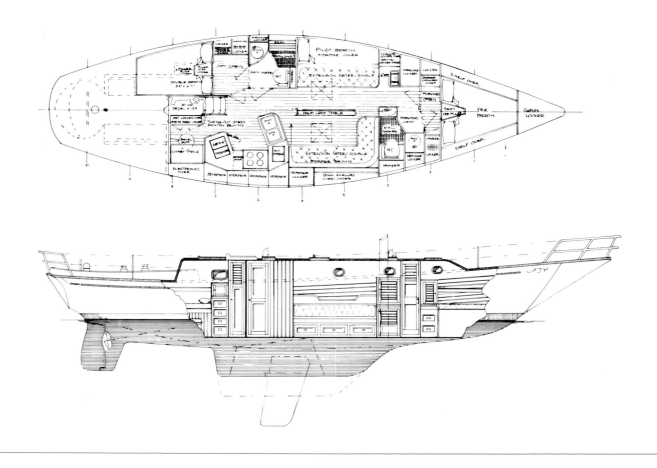

SHANNON 50

LOA: 50'11"
LWL: 42'9"
Beam: 14'3"
Draft: 7' (keel)
5'8"/9'9" (c.b.)
Displacement: 39,000 lbs.
Sail Area: 1,227 sq. ft. (cutter)
1,317 sq.ft. (ketch)
1,326 sq.ft. (staysail schooner)
S.A./Disp: 17 (ketch)
Disp./LWL: 222
Rig: Ketch-rod
Ballast: 15,500 lbs.
Fuel: 150 gals.
Water: 300 gals.
Power: Perkins 85 hp diesel
Hull Construction: Core-Airex
Type of Roving: Unidirectional, biaxial
Bulkheads: Bonded to hull and deck
Designer: Walter Schulz & Assoc.
Builder: Shannon Boat Co.

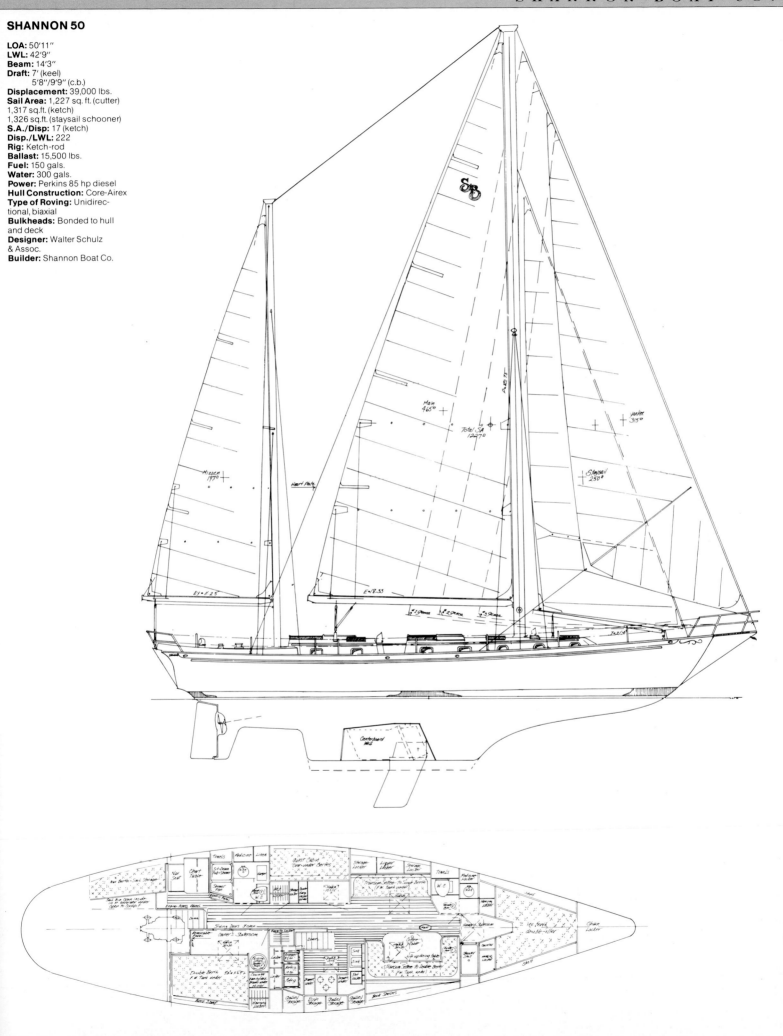

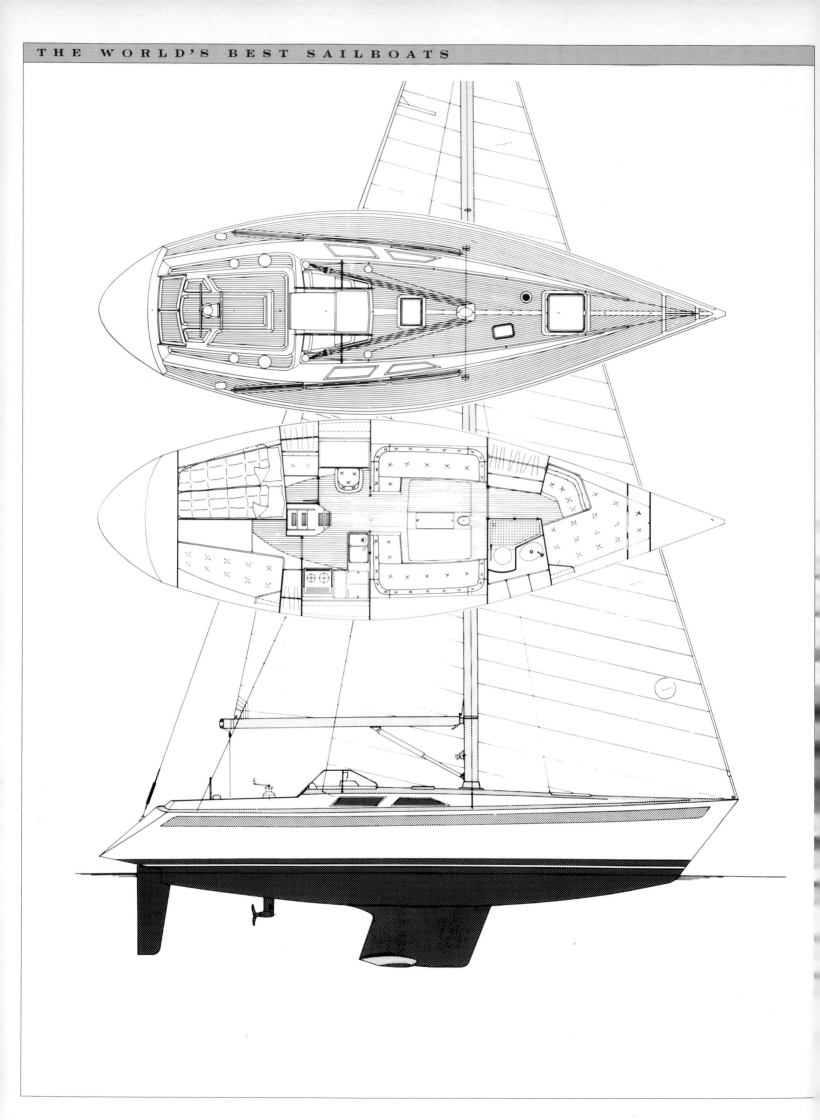

SWEDEN YACHTS 38

LOA: 38'8"
LWL: 31'2"
Beam: 12'7"
Draft: 7'4"
    5'8" (wing keel)
Displacement: 16,300 lbs.
Sail Area: 761 sq.ft.
S.A./Disp: 18.5
Disp./LWL: 240
Rig: Sloop-wire
Ballast: 6,950 lbs.
Fuel: 32 gals.
Water: 86 gals.
Power: Volvo Penta 28 hp
diesel
Hull Construction: Core-balsa
Type of Roving: Woven
Bulkheads: Bonded to hull
and deck
Designer: Peter Norlin/
Jens Ostmann
Builder: Sweden Yachts

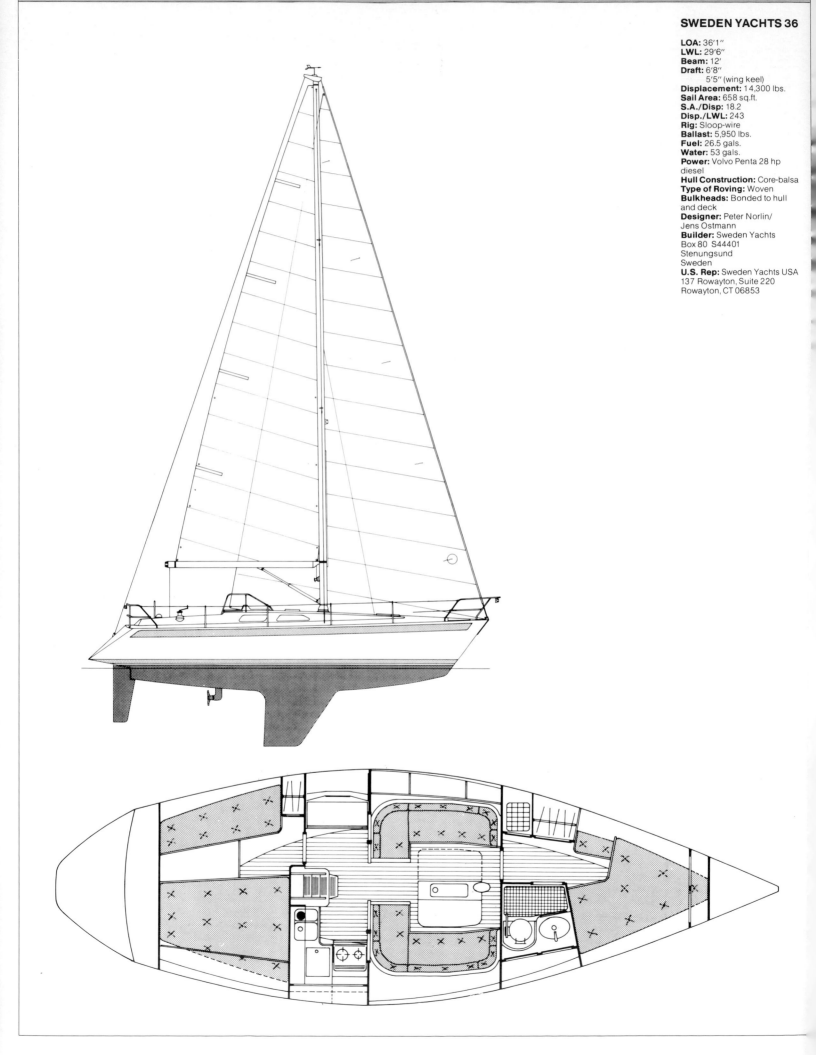

SWEDEN YACHTS 36

LOA: 36'1"
LWL: 29'6"
Beam: 12'
Draft: 6'8"
    5'5" (wing keel)
Displacement: 14,300 lbs.
Sail Area: 658 sq.ft.
S.A./Disp: 18.2
Disp./LWL: 243
Rig: Sloop-wire
Ballast: 5,950 lbs.
Fuel: 26.5 gals.
Water: 53 gals.
Power: Volvo Penta 28 hp diesel
Hull Construction: Core-balsa
Type of Roving: Woven
Bulkheads: Bonded to hull and deck
Designer: Peter Norlin/ Jens Ostmann
Builder: Sweden Yachts Box 80 S44401 Stenungsund Sweden
U.S. Rep: Sweden Yachts USA 137 Rowayton, Suite 220 Rowayton, CT 06853

SWEDEN YACHTS 41

LOA: 41'
LWL: 32'9"
Beam: 12'11"
Draft: 7'4", 6' (wing keel)
Displacement: 18,700 lbs.
Sail Area: 834 sq.ft.
S.A./Disp: 18.9
Disp./LWL: 236
Rig: Sloop-wire
Ballast: 8,150 lbs.
Fuel: 41 gals.
Water: 86 gals.
Power: Volvo Penta 43 hp diesel
Hull Construction: Core-balsa
Type of Roving: Woven
Bulkheads: Bonded to hull and deck
Designer: Peter Norlin/ Jens Ostmann
Builder: Sweden Yachts

Also Available: New Sweden Yachts 340

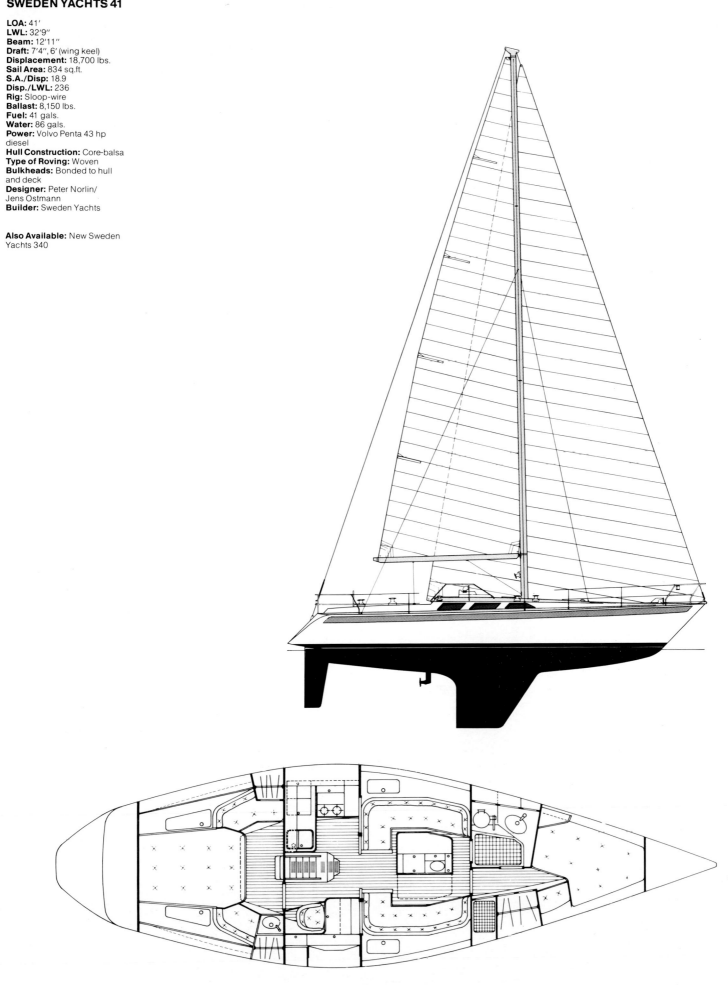

LITTLE HARBOR 44

LOA: 44'3"
LWL: 36'6"
Beam: 13'8"
Draft: 5' (board up)
  10'2" (board down)
Displacement: 32,500 lbs.
Sail Area: 966 sq.ft.
S.A./Disp: 15.5
Disp./LWL: 281.8
Rig: Sloop-rod
Ballast: 13,800 lbs.
Fuel: 100 gals.
Water: 200 gals.
Power: Westerbeke 58 hp
Hull Construction: Core-Airex foam
Type of Roving: Woven & biaxial
Bulkheads: Bonded to hull and deck
Designer: Ted Hood
Builder: Little Harbor Custom Yachts
Little Harbor Landing
Portsmouth, RI 02871

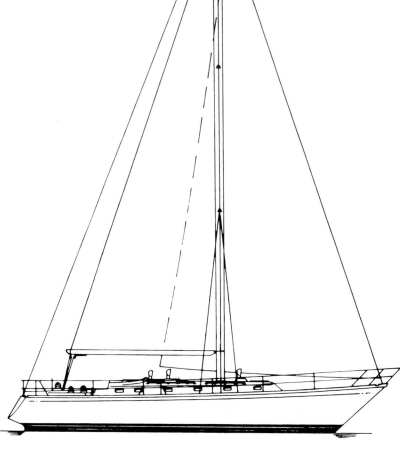

Aft Cockpit

Center Cockpit

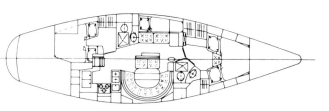

Plan A

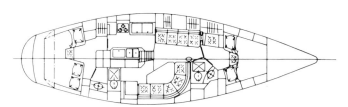

Plan A

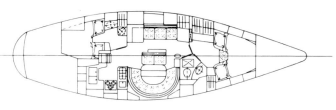

Plan B

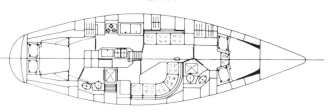

Plan B

LITTLE HARBOR 46

LOA: 45'8"
LWL: 36'6"
Beam: 13'8"
Draft: 5' (board up)
  10'2" (board down)
Displacement: 32,500 lbs.
Sail Area: 1,036 sq.ft.
S.A./Disp: 15.48
Disp./LWL: 281
Rig: Ketch, sloop-rod
Ballast: 13,800 lbs.
Fuel: 100 gals.
Water: 200 gals.
Power: Westerbeke 70 hp
Hull Construction: Core-Airex foam
Type of Roving: Biaxial
Bulkheads: Bonded to hull and deck
Designer: Ted Hood
Builder: Little Harbor Custom Yachts

Aft Cockpit

Center Cockpit

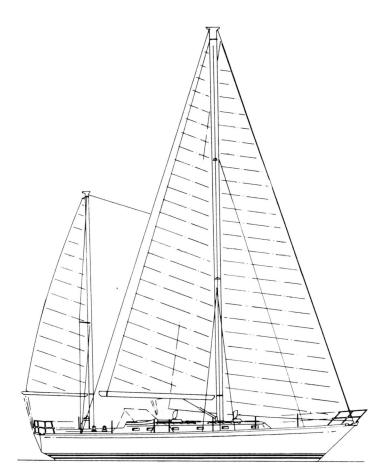

Plan A

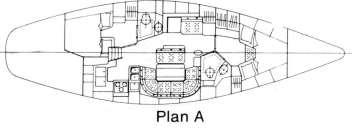

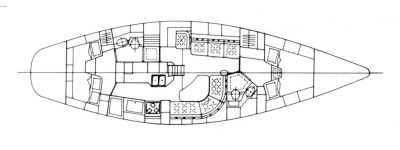

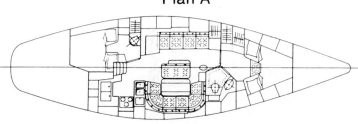

Plan B

LITTLE HARBOR 50

LOA: 50'9"
LWL: 42'2"
Beam: 15'1"
Draft: 5'6" (board up)
11'6" (board down)
Displacement: 43,200 lbs.
Sail Area: 1,249 sq.ft.
S.A./Disp: 15.2
Disp./LWL: 256.6
Rig: Sloop-rod
Ballast: 18,000 lbs.
Fuel: 175 gals.
Water: 330 gals.
Power: Westerbeke 100 hp
Hull Construction: Core-Airex foam
Type of Roving: Biaxial
Bulkheads: Bonded to hull and deck
Designer: Ted Hood
Builder: Little Harbor Custom Yachts

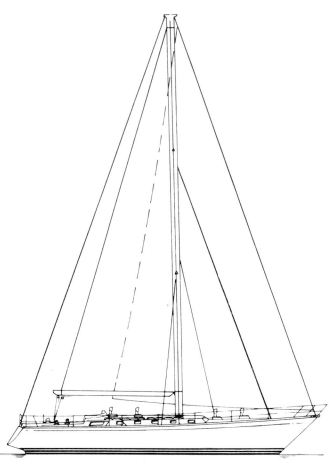

Aft Cockpit

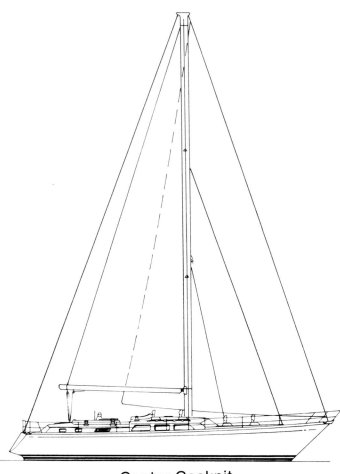

Center Cockpit

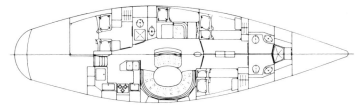

Plan A

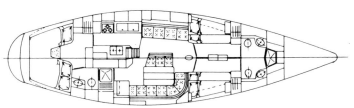

Plan A

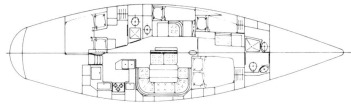

Plan B

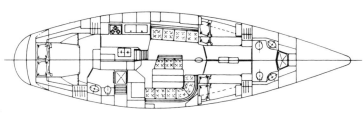

Plan B

LITTLE HARBOR 53

LOA: 52'8"
LWL: 42'2"
Beam: 15'1"
Draft: 5'6" (board up)
     11'4" (board down)
Displacement: 43,200 lbs.
Sail Area: 1,278 sq.ft.
S.A./Disp: 15.22
Disp./LWL: 256
Rig: Ketch, sloop-rod
Ballast: 18,000 lbs.
Fuel: 175 gals.
Water: 310 gals.
Power: Westerbeke 100 hp
Hull Construction: Core-Airex foam
Type of Roving: Biaxial
Bulkheads: Bonded to hull and deck
Designer: Ted Hood
Builder: Little Harbor Custom Yachts

Also Available: 42'

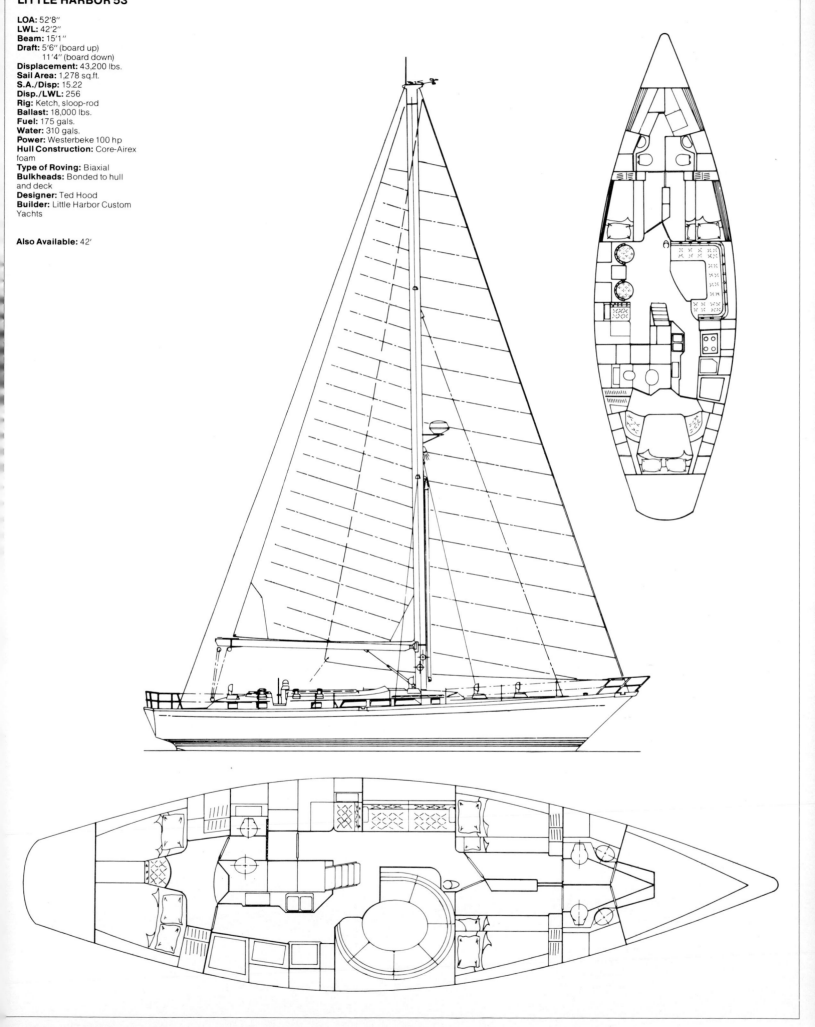

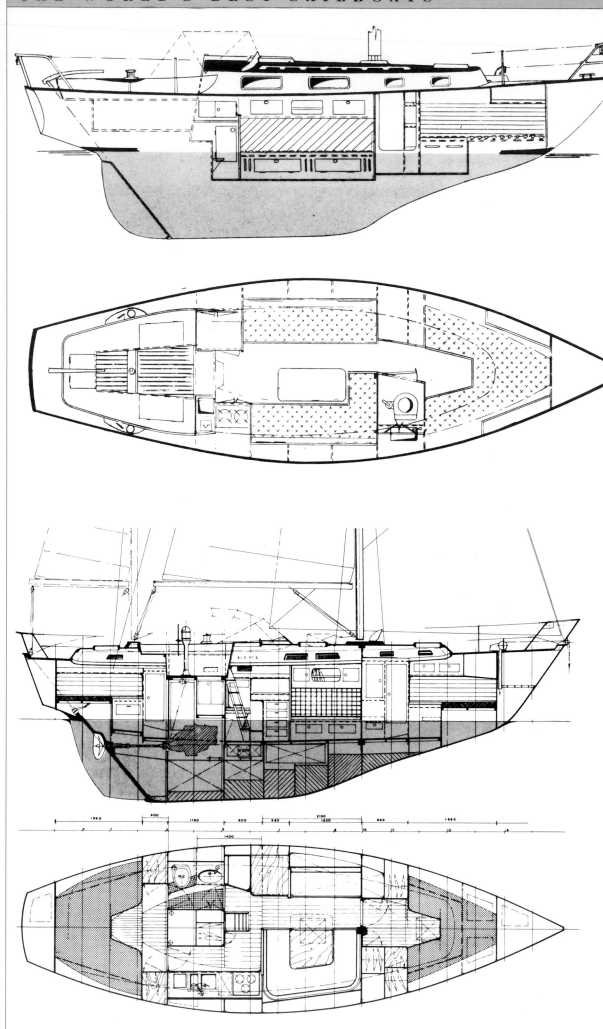

VINDO 32

LOA: 29'
LWL: 23'
Beam: 9'
Draft: 4'3"
Displacement: 8,269 lbs.
Sail Area: 344 sq.ft.
Rig: Sloop-wire
Ballast: 3,858 lbs. (lead)-internal
Fuel: 16 gals.
Water: 30 gals.
Power: 18 hp
Hull Construction: Core
Type of Roving: Hand layup, woven roving optional
Bulkheads: Bonded to hull only
Designer: Carl Andersson
Builder: Vindo Sweden Ab.
Box 74
440 90 Henan, Sweden
U.S. Rep: Vindo North American Inc.
Main Street, P.O. Box 1383
New London, NH 03257

VINDO 65

LOA: 39'
LWL: 31'
Beam: 12'
Draft: 6'
Displacement: 24,000 lbs.
Sail Area: 700 sq.ft.
Rig: Ketch, sloop-wire
Ballast: 9,922 lbs. (lead)-internal
Fuel: 66 gals.
Water: 66 gals.
Power: 62 hp
Hull Construction: Core
Type of Roving: Hand layup, woven roving optional
Bulkheads: Bonded to hull only
Designer: John Lindblom and Carl Andersson
Builder: Vindo Sweden Ab.

VINDO 45

LOA: 34'
LWL: 27'
Beam: 10.92'
Draft: 5'3"
Displacement: 13,230 lbs.
Sail Area: 484 sq.ft.
Rig: Sloop-wire
Ballast: 5,510 lbs. (lead)-internal
Fuel: 20 gals.
Water: 40 gals.
Power: 28 hp
Hull Construction: Core-Divynicell
Type of Roving: Hand layup, woven roving optional
Bulkheads: Bonded to hull only
Designer: John Lindblom
Builder: Vindo Sweden Ab.

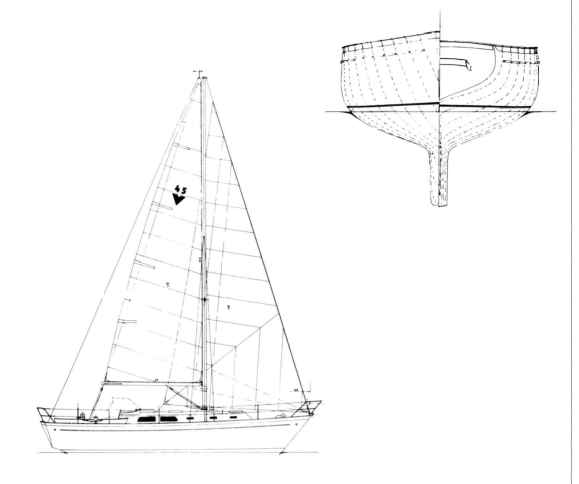

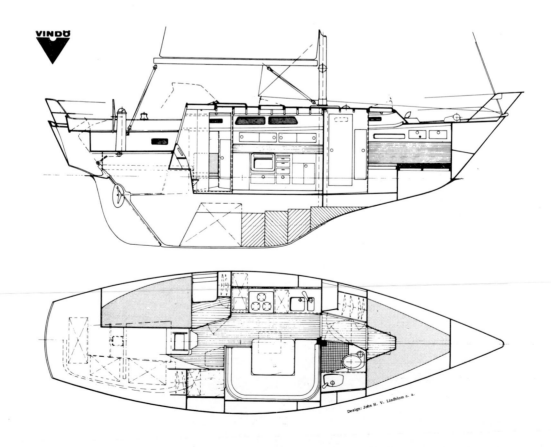

PHOTO CREDITS

Able Marine: Pages 9–15
Alden Yachts: 23–28
Allain, Frederick: 48–51, 52B, 53B
Barlow, Peter: 208
Beck Studios: 29
Brown, Jim: 36, 37, 41T, 180T
Bild-Cale: 113T, 114T, 115T
Bottini, Margherita: 125BR
Camper & Nicholsons: 58–61
Cunningham, Christopher: 201, 202–203, 204–205, 206UR, 207
David Walters Yachts: 80–81
Dickerson Boatbuilders: 90–93
Foley, Robert: 178BL, 179BL, 182B
Freedom Yachts: 103–105, 108
Gadd, Owe: 190B, 191, 192–193
Green-Armeytage, S: 124B, 127T, 128BL
Hall, George: 177
Jan Mark Marinefoto: 109, 112, 113B, 116–117
King, Brian: 124BL
Lindgren, Mats: 189, 190T, 196
Litchfield, Story: 126
Maté, Candace: 209
Maté, Ferenc: 16–18, 31, 40–41, 52T, 53T, 54, 55, 62–65, 80TR, 81CR, 84–86, 87, 94–95,
    106–107, 124T, 128–129, 131, 134TL, 138–140, 141, 150–152, 168–169, 171T, 173, 178TR, 179T,
    182–183, 185, 194–195, 197, 203RC, 205LL, 206, 207UR, 212TL, 214–215, 216–217, 218
Mendlowitz, Benjamin: 127B
Morris, Tom: 136T, 137T
Morris Yachts: 134–137
Nautor Yachts: 146–147
Nerney, Dan: 119, 156T, 157BR
Olson, Roger: 166, 167B
Pacific Seacraft: 153, 161–162
Paine, Art: 134
Peterson, J.H.: 156B
Poggenpohl, Eric: 72BL, 76
Puranen, Pertti: 38–39, 148–149
Raley, John: 158–159
Rosenfeld, Morris: 19
Sam Morse Co.: 163, 167T, 170, 171BR, 172
Sheppard, Amos: 180BR, 181T
Vindö, A.B.: 212–213
Williams, Paul: 36B
Wootton, Michael: 70–71, 72B, 73
Weitz, Allen: 72T, 74T, 75